D0191796

PRODUCER
TO
PRODUCER
2ND EDITION

MICHAEL WIESE

PRODUCER
TO
PRODUCER
INSIDER TIPS FOR ENTERTAINMENT MEDIA
2ND EDITION

MICHAEL WIESE

Edited by Brian McKernan
Editor, VIDEOGRAPHY

PN
1992.94
.W49
1997

Published by Michael Wiese Productions, 11288 Ventura Blvd., Suite 821, Studio City, California 91604, (818) 379-8799, (818) 986-3408 fax, wiese@earthlink.net

Cover Design by Wade Lageose, Art Hotel, Los Angeles
Proofreading by Robin Quinn
Author Photograph: Geraldine Overton

Printed by Braun-Brumfield, Inc., Ann Arbor, Michigan
Manufactured in the United States of America

Copyright 1997 by Michael Wiese
First Printing, February 1997

All rights reserved. No part of this book may be reproduced in any form or by any means without permission in writing from the author, except for the inclusion of brief quotations in a review.

Note: The information presented in this book is for educational purposes only. The author is not giving business or financial advice. Readers should consult their lawyers and financial advisors on their business plans and procedures. The publisher is not liable for how readers may choose to use this information.

Printed on recycled stock.

First edition previously published as PRODUCER TO PRODUCER: *The Best of Michael Wiese in Videography Magazine*

Library of Congress Cataloging–in–Publication Data

Wiese, Michael, 1947–
   Producer to Producer: Insider Tips for Success in Media
  by Michael Wiese; edited by Brian McKernan
       p.   cm.
   ISBN 0-941188-61-2
   1. Video recordings—Production and direction. 2. Television- Production and direction. I. McKernan, Brian. II. Title.
PN1992.94.W49   1993
791.43'0973—dc20   93-23177

CIP

oclc 35718680

Books by MICHAEL WIESE

On The Edge of a Dream
Producer to Produce-2nd Edition
Film & Video Financing
Film & Video Marketing
Home Video: Producing for the Home Market
Film & Video Budgets-2nd Edition Wiese and Deke Simon
The Independent Film & Videomakers Guide

Audiotapes by MICHAEL WIESE

The American Film Institute Seminar:
Financing & Marketing Video

Books from MICHAEL WIESE PRODUCTIONS

Film Directing: Shot by Shot by Steven D. Katz
Film Directing: Cinematic Motion by Steven D. Katz
Fade In: The Screenwriting Process, 2nd Edition by Robert A. Berman
The Writer's Journey by Christopher Vogler
Persistence of Vision by John Gaspard and Dale Newton
Film & Video on the Internet by Dan Harries & Bert Deivert
Directing Actors by Judith Weston
The Director's Journey by Mark W. Travis

For

B. B. Wiese, my father, a man of integrity,
Geraldine Overton-Wiese, my loving wife and photographer,
Julia Bronwyn, our daughter, already an explorer and world traveler

TABLE OF CONTENTS

ACKNOWLEDGEMENTS
2nd Edition

A lot of people can make one person look really good.

I am very grateful to Brian McKernan, friend and editor of Videography magazine. When I first mentioned the idea of compiling these articles several years ago, he enthusiastically came to the rescue with his fully-edited floppy disks of the articles. (Unless you've read my raw manuscripts, you don't have any idea how valuable an editor's input is!) Videography publisher Paul Gallo also supported the project from the get-go. I can't tell you how delightful it is to "get it done" when you are supported by people as terrific as the folks at Videography.

Graphic designer Wade Lageose has created a fabulous new cover for this second edition that creates expectations for what is to be found instead.

My thanks go to Robin Quinn who brought her meticulousness to proofread and correct the final pages. (How does anybody have that much patience?)

I am grateful to MWP's Vice President Ken Lee who managed the book production process by overseeing all the elements, making sure they got to the right place at the right time, and for reading, then re-reading everything herein even though he hears it on a daily basis. What fortitude! What stamina! What dedication!

My wife Geraldine Overton is the smart one in our family. She was the one who first suggested I compile all these articles into a book. She probably came up with the idea after remembering the early morning/late night writing that went into the *Film and Video Financing* book, and thought this would be a quick and easy book. (It wasn't.)

1

And lastly, my thanks go to the readers of Videography Magazine and those who've attended my seminars over the last 18 years and who have written and called, asked their questions, participated in consulting sessions, and contributed their own knowledge and experience to my memory banks.

Without all of you, there would be no books, and no one with whom to share this information. I hope you find it useful.

Michael Wiese
Studio City, CA
January, 1997

FOREWORD
by Brian McKernan

I first met Michael Wiese in 1990 at a UCLA Extension seminar on the then-new topic of "desktop video." Michael had organized the event, which turned out to be one of the most useful I'd ever attended. Lecturers included people I've come to regard as visionaries on the uses and impacts of media's digital future: Eric Martin, Dean of the California Institute of the Arts; Michael Nesmith, President of Pacific Arts and creator of the first "music video"; and Scott Billups, producer/director extraordinaire and one of America's leading media integrators.

By the end of the day, the opportunities of the new visual media were foremost on everyone's mind. Martin likened technology's quickening evolution to a giant vortex. Nesmith observed that virtual reality was a window into a new world that requires us to expand our communication abilities. And Billups showed a tape of his desktop facility that prompted executives from video and computer companies to sequester him in a back room for an ad hoc mind meld.

Michael had organized and moderated a knockout seminar, but–interestingly enough–in my subsequent conversations with him he emphasized the enduring importance of the business side of production. If you can't sell what you've produced, he argued, you're not producing. The new economies of media technology are opening wide the gates of production opportunity; an entire new universe of video professionals needs to learn the basics of how to find the capital to fund their dreams. This was a subject Michael knew intimately, having launched more than 300 programs that cumulatively grossed over $80 million at companies such as Vestron Video.

Continuing our dialogue, Michael and I came to the mutual agreement that he be designated a Videography magazine Contributing Editor with his own column, *Producer to Producer*. Videography became the monthly magazine of professional video technology, production and applications in 1976, when portable cameras and VTRs ushered in a new era of visual communication. Fourteen years later, with the emergence of Video Toasters, CD ROM and digital studios, Videography continued its leadership as the information resource for video professionals at all levels. Michael's column, meanwhile, would ensure that readers would be exposed to innovative business ideas as part of our editorial package.

This book is a collection of Michael's Producer to Producer columns, which I've had the honor to edit at Videography. They await your attention, so–as Michael would say–now go get 'em!

Brian McKernan
Editor, Videography
New York

INTRODUCTION

Writing the *Producer to Producer* columns for Videography magazine has been very rewarding. It's given me a timely outlet for up-to-the-minute knowledge recently harvested from my own fields of endeavor from location shooting to infomercials, from money-raising to marketing, from videos to feature films.

My process has always been to work hard, learn a lot, and then share the most relevant information with colleagues and fellow film and videomakers. I am very passionate and committed to this sharing aspect. It is part of my contribution. It's painfully clear how important and valuable the right information is; without it, we would all have perished at the hands of clients, distributors or co-production partners. Learning first-hand is time-consuming and expensive. Learning from others speeds up your time on the learning curve and saves money.

In rereading the articles, I was pleased to see that they evenly covered the entire creative spectrum from program development, financing, production, through marketing and distribution. The information is as timely and valuable as when I first wrote it. At the beginning of most articles, I've added a little nugget to bring a reflective spirit or new perspective to the article. (And now, with this second edition I've added another twenty chapters.)

There's nothing we can't accomplish. We just need the right information at the right time. I hope that the ideas in this book will bring you success in your own projects.

THE APPROACH

INDEPENDENT PRODUCING

This article first appeared in the premiere issue of "New Screenwriter & Director" magazine published in London. I like the article because it bursts some of the self-limiting concepts that we may, at one time or another, believe about ourselves and our abilities.

Making films is a tough business. Fail the first time out and you rarely get a second chance. It's a shame there is so little information available that you can read that will give you the information you need to be successful. Other producers don't want to share it. They must think the less competition the better.

I don't feel that way. That's why I've been writing and publishing professional film and video books and giving seminars in the US for the last 11 years. The publishers of this magazine don't feel that way either. The more practical information you have during your career the better. We want to see you succeed. We are sure you have many important and valuable films to make and we'd like to help you accomplish your dreams.

Welcome to the first issue of *New Screenwriter & Director*. The publishers called on me because they read my books and because I've been producing, directing and writing for the last 24 years. I've made films, television programs, books, games, audios and most recently infomercials. I love the art <u>and</u> the business of producing. Start with an abstract idea–and then 6 months, or 12 months, or 24 months later that idea is projected for millions of people. *It is creating something from nothing.*

Between the idea and the finished product are hundreds, even thousands, of steps that must be completed. Those steps and insights into getting them done are what this column will cover. Each issue you'll find hard-core, practical, how-to-get-it-done information that I've gathered about this business including script and product development, packaging, negotiating, budgeting, financing, producing, directing, post-production, distribution and marketing. The whole arc of creating media. Some of what I'll write about will make distributors, financiers and banks quite mad because I'll be sharing things they do not want you to know. How can you negotiate contracts which favor you? What do things really cost? How can you leverage deals? I'll share very specific information that will help you on your way.

Hopefully reading this column will lift you higher on the learning curve so that you can realize your projects. And you won't just hear about movies. You'll learn about many related products (TV programs, infomercials, CD-ROMs, books, audios) that you can create simultaneously (or prior) to your feature film idea.

A few years ago I was invited to the Sundance Institute (which was founded for independent filmmakers by Robert Redford) to speak to a group of minority women producers at the request of PBS (public television). These women were powerful, committed film- and videomakers. They were Hispanic, Japanese, Chinese, Korean, Navajo, Hopi, Vietnamese, Philippino and Black. I was the only white male in the room. Renowned poet and writer Alice Walker spoke immediately before me. She read from a diary she had written during the making of *The Color Purple*. She told of her struggles with Steven Spielberg and the difficulties of bringing her book to the screen. As I looked across the audience, I could see that these women were dreaming that someday too their small and personal story could be a major motion picture.

Then it was my turn to speak. I knew this was not going to be easy but that I had to tell them my version of the truth. I encouraged them to hold onto their dreams of making a feature film from their personal stories. But I also warned that *The Color Purple* got made because one of the most powerful filmmakers was interested in the book and that without his involvement it may never have happened. Given that white males dominate the decision-making process in Hollywood and prefer comedies, erotic thrillers and action/adventure films, I just couldn't see a whole lot more *Color Purples* being made. However I suggested that rather than getting bitter, angry and frustrated by the system, these creative, highly talented and expressive women might consider resources more immediately accessible to them and create other "communication pieces." How about a video, a one-act play, a radio show, an interactive disk, a cable television program, or a music album? These require significantly less resources than a multi-million dollar theatrical film. I can't say I was received very warmly after bursting so many bubbles however over the next few days every woman came up to me and said something like: *"I didn't like what you said, but after I thought about it, you did give me many, many ideas of what else I could do."*

In this column I also hope to inspire you to create products that open up your self-expression, generate revenues, and find a greater audience for your work.

Like everyone else in Hollywood, I have a few features that I'd like to make. But while I am developing these projects, I've gained experience from other work that will benefit me later. I've spent millions of dollars (of other people's money) and made tens of million dollars (for other people!) through 29 independent shorts and documentaries, 90 political television commercials, 60 radio spots, 1200 cable television segments, and several dozen television programs. I have produced and/or acquired and/or marketed over 300 home video programs. If I would have waited until Hollywood sent over a limousine to take me to the studio to start my first feature, I'd still be waiting. Worse yet, none of these other projects would have been made nor found their audiences.

And a word about *"directing."* Even though this magazine is for writers and directors, I came to a realization that has served me well. When I started out, I wanted to direct. (Sound familiar?) No matter what the project, whether it was my idea or someone else's, <u>I wanted to direct</u>! Now this is a very limiting concept. Unless I directed, I wouldn't work on a project. This kept me low on the learning curve. If you're not working at your craft, you're not learning your craft. (You're in your head.)

Today there are a great many things that I am able to do that generate a lot of income and allow my self-expression. What happened is that I stopped thinking of myself as a "feature film maker" or a "director" and started thinking of myself as a *"communicator."* If you're a communicator then you don't get stuck in producing a single format product (like a feature film) but can work in many media formats. I may *direct* one or two television programs a year. Or I may *produce* half a dozen shows. Or I may *executive produce* a dozen projects. Or I may *consult* with producers on dozens of projects. Actually my year is a mixture of directing, producing, executive producing and consulting but the point is that because I stopped narrow-casting myself as a director, I am able to contribute to a great many projects in a great many roles. And I'm therefore always learning, always expanding. When a project appears on my desk (or in my head), I can cast myself for the role where I am most suited and valuable to the project. I try to see how the project can best be served by my abilities. Not the other way around. And often, even when I could, I don't direct. Maybe I feel the idea isn't compelling enough to absorb me for the year or more that it will take to make it. Once I changed my mindset about the oh-so sacred word *"directing,"* I found there were a great many more opportunities waiting for me.

In the months to come, I will draw upon my experience (and the experiences of others) to share empowering ideas that will help you realize your dreams, earn a livelihood at something you love to do, and help you market that vision to greater and greater audiences.

Until then, if you can dream it, you can do it. Now go get 'em!

THE LEARNING CURVE

This article was originally written for "New Screenwriter & Director" magazine of London.

MISSION STATEMENT

When I started out, I didn't have a strategy. I wish I would have. My career has been a series of opportunities too good to pass up. My learning curve crosses many different moving image careers–but not by conscious design. (But you can plan your career–I'll get to that in a moment.

Even before film school, I wanted to be a filmmaker. Inspired by the art films of the '60s, I decided *I would be a director.* I apprenticed on documentaries. I learned how to operate a camera. My film school teachers were experimental filmmakers.

During the 10 years after film school, I held many non-film jobs to finance my own films which I worked on at night. They won awards. They found distribution. I toured with my films. I raised money through limited partnerships. I had many creative partners. Together we co-produced and co-directed many small films. But the life of the independent was very up and down, both emotionally and financially. It was very tough and I was getting older (30!).

As an independent, the best I could hope for was to produce one short or documentary film a year. Budgets never exceeded $160,000, usually much less. I simply could not learn all I needed to learn with a few projects and limited dollars. It was time to get on the learning curve. It was time to get a job.

Over the next ten years, I held many jobs. I produced variety television shows, political campaign commercials, cable television segments, and hundreds of home video programs. I spent tens of millions of dollars of someone else's money. I got on the learning curve.

Had I stayed on the course of the independent filmmaker, I doubt I would have been able to learn so much. The films I produced had very limited distribution and learning was slow and difficult. I only came into contact with other independent filmmakers.

I didn't have a mission statement. (But you can!) When one job ended, I looked for the next. To those starting out or to those midway like myself, I suggest that there is tremendous power in knowing what it is you want to do, defining it, writing it down, and articulating it every chance you get. By defining what you are, you attract what you need. Everything else is a distraction and is dismissible. You focus. You get very good at your niche. You become known for that one thing. You differentiate yourself from the pack.

YOUR ASSIGNMENT

Hopefully you will avoid a career that "just sort of happens" by planning now. Spend some serious quiet time writing and rewriting one sentence: your mission statement. It's very important, so feel free to rework the statement for weeks or months until every word feels right. My company's mission statement is:

> *"Our mission is to empower and improve*
> *the quality of human life by creating*
> *worthwhile and educational communication tools."*

(Notice that I am not specific. I didn't say television shows, films or videos [although we do a lot of these]. We say *communication tools* because we are aware that we can produce a variety of products. This increases our ability to communicate and generates additional streams of revenues. Our current projects include a television show, three books, six audios and two videos.

Fill in the following: My mission is to _____

What a mission statement allows you to do is sort out all your choices. In evaluating new ideas and opportunities, you can say, "Yes, that fits our mission statement," or "No, that doesn't fit." Because you've designed your mission statement from a very deep and insightful place, it will be very powerful. It will come from your passion and probably be applicable your entire life. With clarity you can call in what you want to do with your skills. You can develop a strategy. You begin your ascent on the learning curve knowing what you will need to learn and where to go to get it. You will be able to develop and nurture life-long relationships with people that will help you accomplish your mission.

PASSION

Without passion, there is no drive. Passion is your body's fuel to get you through a project. An idea today may sound great but fizzle in six months because you lost passion for it. Why do you lose passion? Because there isn't enough depth and learning in the original idea to keep you going. That's why: (1) you need a mission statement, and (2) you need to make sure whatever you choose to do, you do it with passion.

Doing something for money alone is a mistake. At almost any trendy Hollywood restaurant you will overhear get-rich-quick movie ideas. The roar is deafening. If you pick this route alone then passion will probably not sustain you. At some point you'll wonder why you are doing it. I am not suggesting that you can't or shouldn't make money from your passion, just be sure that when you say "yes" passion is saying "yes" and not your wallet.

If your mission statement clearly defines what you are here to do, you will be supported. (A metaphysical statement I admit, but why not?) The reward is in the process of creating. The pot of gold at the end of the rainbow is an illusion. So choose something you will enjoy moment to moment.

If you pick projects that satisfy your soul then you can be assured that however it turns out you'll be fine. You will have grown. You will ascend on the learning curve.

When I follow my own advice and my own mission statement, <u>and</u> have a good time producing the project, it is usually also financially rewarding. There's a principle working here. I get my cake and eat it too. This also means I say "no" to a lot of projects (that *look* like they will make money) because they don't fit my mission statement. I trust my own instincts and do what I have to do. (Now that's the passion talking.)

"Where do I begin to look for work to get on the learning curve?" you ask. The wonderful thing about a career in moving images is that there are a great many avenues to pursue to expand your abilities.

THE PLAYING FIELD

Here are only some of the playing fields where I've had some experience. All are doorways into the business–onto the learning curve. Each has its own eccentricities. What follows are thumbnail sketches on each area.

Theatrical

The toughest. The most lucrative. Highly creative. Entertainment based. Everyone wants to see their work on the big screen. Theatrical success translates into additional success in home video and on television. Breaking into the majors is accomplished rarely and only by a few yet it has turned Hollywood into a Mecca for writers, producers, directors and actors.

The best route in is to write your own script. Having a proprietary property gives you a position of strength from which to negotiate. If you are a producer or director, you must acquire a powerful script to create leverage.

Going the independent route–financing your film without studio support–and hoping for a studio or independent distributor to do a "negative pickup" deal is also tough. Independent film budgets are low and screen space is limited. Only a few select films break through each year. If you are looking to support a family on the whims of this market year in and year out, beware. Only a few have done it. You must be very, very passionate and persevering. Access to financing and good scripts is very important.

In the theatrical world, a writer, director or producer can spend most of his or her life pitching and developing projects and never get anything made.

I have little patience with the theatrical market even though I too have a theatrical film I hope to make. (And I have a strategy for making it.) But in the meantime, there are so many other areas where you can actually get something made, and if you are just starting out, learn a great deal.

The Non-Theatrical Market

Non-theatrical is a kind of generic term meaning "everything but features." A lot of moving image media falls into this one category.

Non-Theatrical (Educational)

I started out making short films for the non-theatrical educational market. These are 10-22 minute, 16mm films (now primarily videos) that are rented or sold to the school, library, prison and institutional markets. Today a 10-15 minute tape sells for $19-$99. A one-hour training tape sells for $250 to $500. This marketplace has its own festivals and publications.

Producers create materials that fulfill the needs of a classroom curriculum or corporate agenda (e.g., teach kids geography, train secretaries how to use a word processor). Producers are relatively free to create their own programs which are marketed by non-theatrical educational distributors. Royalties are generally around 25 percent of wholesale revenues. Sometimes distributors will advance some or all of the production budgets which range from $10,000 to $50,000. Corporate training films have much higher budgets: $25,000 to $200,000 or more.

Industrials

Industrials or corporate communication pieces are also non-theatrical products and are often distributed free. No royalties are paid to the producers since these productions are not sold. The films and videos are generally promotional pieces commissioned by corporations for sales and marketing. They range in length from a few minutes to 30 minutes or more. Budgets can be very high or very low. Producers are given a wide creative range as long as the corporate objectives are met. Industries that are economically viable are the best clients. When an industry is in trouble, one of the areas that's cut is corporate communications. Some corporations have their own in-house production facilities. Some hire on a freelance basis.

Non-Theatrical (Home Video)

The video stores are filled with movies on videocassette. However there is growing interest and sales of non-theatrical programs. Exercise, sports and children's videos are all burgeoning genres. These videos are also sold through direct response, print, television and magazine ads. Prices range from $9.95 to $39.95. These tapes are designed for and sold to consumers. A producer may receive a 10-20 percent royalty on wholesale revenues (which may be shared with celebrity talent, if any).

Video producers of non-theatrical programming are more akin to book publishers. In fact, the signage on bookstore shelves may suggest video genres as well.

There are numerous forms of home-video tape distribution and many opportunities for producers. If you can identify and reach a target audience with your video program, many producers have found that they can produce, market and distribute their own tapes. A producer I know is grossing hundreds of thousands of dollars from a video about sexual harassment in the workplace which he sells through direct mail to corporations.

I am very optimistic about this market because with budgets ranging from $10,000 to $300,000 producers can develop, produce and see their works in distribution in less than a year. In the first four years of the US video boom, I was fortunate to have developed, produced and/or distributed over 300 video programs. The amount of learning was enormous. Once you've been through the process, <u>you can refine it and get better at it</u>. (That can be your goal as well.)

Television (Network)

From a producer's point of view, at least in the states, it's very difficult to work for the networks (ABC, CBS, NBC) unless you've worked with them earlier. How do you break out of this catch-22? You partner with someone that the networks trust. You go in to pitch your project with a partner.

There are numerous entry level jobs with the networks where you can learn and observe. That's another way in.

Television (Cable)

In the US, there are numerous pay- and non-pay cable networks which give producers many opportunities. Some, like HBO, are hard to crack. But others are more willing to work with independent producers if for no other reason than they have a lot of airtime to fill.

A strategy a producer might employ is to match their own mission statement with the programming the prospective network produces. If you are into environmental programming then you might solicit The Discovery Channel; if you're into art, then A&E; education, it's The Learning Channel; sports, ESPN; and so on.

The next level down are the local public-access cable stations found in every major US city. Here producers (who work for free) are invited to use the facilities free. In exchange, the station broadcasts the programs. Many people get their production experience firsthand by creating shows that are seen by more limited audiences. As their skills improve, they have the resumes (and programs) to prove their abilities at one of the basic or pay television networks. Or they may seek employment at a network affiliated television station.

Commercials

While commercials leave no room for a producer to make a statement of their own, producers are able to employ all the latest production technology and equipment and are paid top dollar for doing so. The goal of the commercial is to sell products and services. If you are good at it, you will be paid well. Budgets ranging from $50,000 into the millions give you the resources to hire the best production talent and facilities. And you learn to tell a story very, very quickly.

Another form of commercials are political campaign spots. I worked in New York City for a year producing 75 campaign television spots for 18 different political candidates. It was a very intense job. The spots had to be created and produced quickly and put on the air. Rather than sell products, these commercials elicited votes at the ballot box. (We lost only one campaign.) The learning curve was steep. I had a crash course in New York City's production facilities, crews and talent pool. I spent several million dollars just like that.

Another form of commercials are PSAs (public service announcements) which are short 30-second or one-minute spots that television stations have the option to run between programs. The stations run them for free because they are for non-profit charities, environmental or health organizations, or promote a cause (just say "no" to drugs). Rarely are the budgets very high but producers who want to support an issue have a great deal of creative freedom, especially when they donate their time and services.

Music Videos

Only a few have been able to make a real business out of producing music videos. Budgets range from $10,000 to hundreds of thousands of dollars (if you are dealing with the largest music acts). Budgets are often an extension of the star's ego. Music videos give producers an opportunity to be very creative. Just when it seems there are no more new production techniques to be employed someone comes up with something truly wonderful.

Since music videos are primarily promotional pieces, few producers share in any revenues should the videos be compiled and sold as home videos. Any income producers see are from their fees. Music videos are frequently shot very quickly which means 20-hour days. It's a great gig if you're young and have lots of energy. Many producers end up spending their fees on the production in order to have a portfolio piece to show.

New Media–CD ROMs

CD ROMs make me a little nervous right now. I am not sure they are a stand-alone business yet. Only a few titles have sold well. Those who are producing already have a database of visual, sound and text material. Budgets are in the $400,000 range and higher. It's expensive. If you are a producer with a database of materials, then it makes sense to look for a CD ROM publisher who will format and distribute a CD ROM based on your visual database. It may provide additional income. However I am wary of creating anything solely for this emerging market. Do we really know that people want interactive materials (beyond games)?

Summary

If you're just starting out–good! It's a great time to think about where you want to be in 5, 10, 20 or 30 years. Start planning now. The best place to begin is to write your mission statement. Pick projects or subject areas you are passionate about. Then select one of the many theatrical or non-theatrical areas of the moving image. Most important, get yourself on the learning curve. I hope this article has given you some great ideas. I wish you all the best success.

Now go get 'em.

GETTING THERE FROM HERE

I love "The Four Quadrants" planning exercise. Give it a try. It cleared a lot of things up for me.

I'm one of those producers who loves planning and goal-setting.

About twice a year–around New Year's Eve and again in mid-July–I sit down and review my personal and professional goals, assess what I've accomplished in the past six months, and–to use an archery metaphor–re-aim my arrows and draw back my bow.

In between these two periods, I don't much look at the plans I've written down. My unconscious stores the information, and then goes about achieving the goals I've set for myself. Human beings are already goal-seeking creatures, so if you don't put anything into your brain, nothing much comes out. You get what you ask for.

What Worked, What Didn't

The first thing our production company does is review last year's goals. These goals could include anything from setting up a new computer system, to producing videos, TV shows, scripts, books or events. These goals can also include finding new suppliers, vendors or customers, or starting new businesses. We review last year's list and applaud ourselves for what worked. We also look at what didn't work and analyze why. This sets the context for planning. We build on our strengths and try to cut out practices that weren't "successful."

Everyone has a different definition of success. It's not only profitability; for me success is personal satisfaction, growth and whether or not my work made a contribution to society. There are a lot of ways to measure your success. Last year my first novel was published. It was tremendously satisfying after years of writing. Will it pay for the time I put in? No. But that's okay. For me, getting it done has already made it a success.

The Top 10

The next thing we do in our process is to list the top 10 goals that we want to accomplish in the next year. Here's our 1996 list:

Quadrant*

(*explained later in article)

1.	Improve marketing of publications	(1, 2)
2.	Market new video series	(1, 3)
3.	Find new investors	(1, 2)
4.	Revise and reprint several books	(1)
5.	Present European seminars	(3, 4)
6.	Produce more videos in our series	(1)
7.	Frequently update our home page	(1)
8.	Executive-produce a health special	(4)
9.	Finish feature film script	(4)
10.	Develop our children's TV program	(4)

The next thing I do is meet with my staff and give them a sense of what the priorities are. Some of these things are clearly new projects or projects in development, and some are ongoing business. The staff then takes these items and maps out how they will spend their time achieving these goals. (By the way, everyone is on profit sharing, so there are rewards for getting the job done.)

I review their action plan and make any adjustments. After that, it's "Go get 'em" time.

The Dangers of Being an Entrepreneur

Part of why I go through this process is to keep my company and myself on track. One of the downsides of being an entrepreneur is that you are easily distracted by the next "great idea" that comes along. We instantly want to steer our whole operation in new directions. (That's why we ended up with 12 items on our "top 10" list.)

I recently was shown a simple process that you can do to evaluate your own strategic planning. I'm on the board of the Publishers Marketing Association (PMA), which has about 2500 members. The board recently performed this process to plan for the next couple of years, and I found it extremely useful.

"The Four Quadrants" exercise: Determine which activities are in which quadrant. Take a look at the grid reproduced below. It breaks down customers and products into two categories–existing and new. By using this grid to analyze your activities, you can see how your business is doing and how you should spend your resources.

THE FOUR QUADRANTS

When you review your action plan this year, analyze it using this grid, and you will notice a few things.

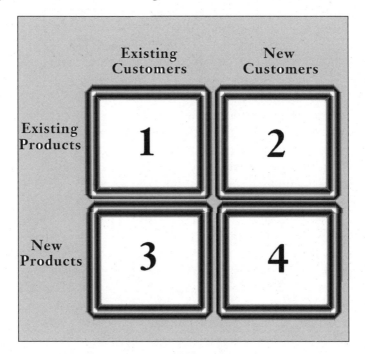

In Quadrant 1, you are not expanding your business. You are doing something you already know how to do. You are selling existing products to current customers—the status quo. You are not putting anything new on your plate, but rather refining what you currently do well. For example, my company publishes a successful line of professional video and film books. One of our goals is to revise several books. This clearly belongs in Quadrant 1.

In Quadrant 2, things begin to get more interesting. Here you look for new customers for your existing products. You are developing new markets for your existing products. That's something we can do in many ways.

In Quadrant 3, the fun (and risk) really begins. Here you are creating new products for your existing customers. You know these loyal customers, now you hope to interest them in new products. For example, when we published our Film and Video Budgets book, it was for our existing customers (Quadrant 1). But when we offered a diskette of those budget formats, we created a new product (Quadrant 3) which we marketed to our existing customers. It worked. But we had no idea at the outset whether they would welcome a computer product from us, since we hadn't marketed one before.

Ah, Quadrant 4, my favorite! Only an entrepreneur could love Quadrant 4, which offers the most risk, the most creativity, but also has the potential for disaster. Here you are not only creating a new product, but you are selling it to a new audience. You are starting a new business! You are doing something you haven't done before. You only have that gut sense that it's going to work. You're making it all up and sailing into the wind.

Now on my list there are a lot of things in Quadrant 4 because this is where the learning and expansion are for me. I expect to be able to support these risky Quadrant 4 activities by my ongoing businesses. For example, over the last two years, I have given seminars in Sydney, London, Dublin, Helsinki and Paris. Our books are known there, so the seminars are a new product for both existing customers (3) and new customers (4). But it's really a Quadrant 4 project.

I haven't made a feature in years (Quadrant 4), nor have I ever produced a syndicated children's series (Quadrant 4 again).

Summary

This process lets you and your staff see, on paper, what your goals are and whether you have the resources to accomplish them. Everyone is different. You might have a business that operates very well in Quadrant 1. Or the quadrant analysis will give you the idea that–yes–you could and should expand your production services or your customer base. For me, I've found that I have to balance my creative impulses against ongoing safer businesses that can buffer the fall, should my entrepreneurial ideas fail. But hey–nothing ventured, nothing gained. See you in Quadrant 4.

Now, go get 'em.

IF I'D ONLY KNOWN . . .

What do you have to say to film- and videomakers just starting out? Knowing what you know now, what would you do differently? These are questions I am asked a lot and they will be the focus of this article.

In no particular order, here are some things I wish I had learned or contemplated earlier.

The Learning Curve

I started making films in the mid-sixties: shorts, documentaries, experimental films. My student film was invited to the Cannes Film Festival, and a few years later, *Hardware Wars*, a parody of *Star Wars*, had a greater profit margin between its cost and its gross than almost any Hollywood movie. I thought filmmaking was easy. Instead, these early successes clouded my vision.

And then there was the problem that–if I was lucky–I would only make one short film or documentary a year. The scale of the films was so small that I just wasn't learning much. It was time to get on the learning curve. It was time to get a "real job."

I'd been independent for 13 years. Over the next eight years, I worked on staff in many traditional industry jobs: producing political campaign television spots, producing on-air segments for Showtime/The Movie Channel, developing and producing home videos for Vestron Video, and consulting with many video suppliers, broadcasters, publishers and producers.

The upside was that I learned a lot. I probably spent over $30 million dollars of someone else's money learning. I produced dozens of live television segments, hundreds of television spots, over 1200 pay cable segments, and some 300 videos. That's a lot of stuff! And a lot of learning! On the production side I learned the NYC talent pool of actors, voices, DPs, producers and directors. I negotiated with facilities, stages, film and tape houses, and the unions. I also picked up knowledge about financing, marketing and distribution.

I had to momentarily (eight years) put down the projects I wanted to make while I learned the aspects of our business that film school never touched on. Skills that were necessary for not only survival but for getting a film or video out into the world.

Am I proud of what I produced during that period? Not especially. It certainly won't save the world. But I learned an enormous amount.

The point: Get on the learning curve and hold onto your vision, your own particular and unique perspective that is truly your own.

Worthy Projects

The responsibility is to now put that knowledge to good use.

For me, media, be it television or video or film or new media, is very powerful. It has the power to literally capture people's minds and emotions and tremendously influence behavior. Therefore we should be extremely careful about what we do with these technological tools.

This is not however the goal of any of the commercial entities for whom I produced programs. Their objectives, respectively, were to: (1) get ratings, (2) get elected, (3) keep subscribers, and (4) sell videos.

In short, they wanted to make money. There are few film- or video-makers who care about saving the world <u>and</u> who can actually get something made, distributed and shown.

Now I've returned to the world of the independent and have tried to carve out my niche as a "quality" producer, meaning that we will only do worthy projects. I am trying to take the experience that I garnered in the commercial world and apply it to making meaningful, worthy and life-enhancing media. No small feat. Once in a while I am successful. A few years ago I produced *Diet for a New America* (based on John Robbins's Pulitzer-nominated book) for PBS. Making it was difficult enough but then when it was finished many special interest groups tried to block its airing by every means possible. Nevertheless some 65 stations were bold enough to show it. The video has sold over 45,000 copies. Recently Robbins got a grant to distribute another 8500 videos free to schools.

The point: Do something worthy with your skills. Leave something behind. Try to ignore the seduction of *"I'll just make a lot of money doing* _____ (fill in the blank: commercials, sitcoms, horror films) *and I'll make enough money to do what I really want to do."* No, what really happens is that you'll get really good at _____ (fill in the blank) and be ill-equipped to do anything else.

Writing/Literature

I've always enjoyed books. In high school I enjoyed writing reports and term papers (no, really!). But I didn't like nor pay attention in English class, and I never did really learn good grammar. Regardless of all that, I find myself earning a lot of income from writing! I have written eight books and have ongoing columns in *Videography* and other magazines. Remarkable. I never planned to be a writer. In fact, I still don't consider myself one.

I'm sorry I didn't apply myself more when I had the chance. I should have read classic and English literature, understood grammar, and learned other languages. (I did learn to type like a fiend however so even if I don't know how to say it well I can type it really fast!)

The point: Read! Write! Writing is the one basic skill that you'll need for everything from creating proposals, speeches and scripts to letters, dialogue and ad copy. If you are planning to write screenplays, it is absolutely essential that you understand structure. It took me decades to realize this. Without a well-structured screenplay, you literally do not have a chance. (*The Writer's Journey: Mythic Structure for Screenwriters and Storytellers* by Chris Vogler is the best book out there. We published it.)

A Marketable Image

Film school taught me the crafts. I have a master's degree in cinematography but haven't shot any film in nearly 15 years. I learned editing and post-production and then as the projects got larger, I would hire camera operators and editors. I would produce and/or direct.

By the time I was working at Vestron, I had too many titles to produce so I acted as Executive Producer. It was not uncommon to have 12 videos in production and another 50 in development in any given month. I've had all the jobs from development through marketing and became a generalist and oversaw the entire process. As you get higher and higher on the totem pole, there are fewer and fewer jobs where executive producer skills are required. Once you do identify those positions (there are many in network television, for example) then you have to ask yourself do you really want to produce what is required?

I've been too eclectic perhaps. Too interested in all the jobs to focus on one. I write books. I produce videos, films, audios, books and television. I just wrote my first novel, finished a screenplay based on the novel, and am rehearsing it in a directing workshop. (The most fun I've had in years.) I just signed a deal to do a CD-ROM based on the *Goin' Hollywood* board game which I co-created a few years ago. My publishing company started a health line last year. I can't sit still. New projects and forms are very seductive. Two months ago I put up my home page on the Internet. (http://websites.earthlink.net/~mwp)

Now that's great for me but my publicist says, "You've got a real image problem." People like pigeonholes. It makes hiring easy. He's a cameraman. She's a script doctor. He's great with digital special effects. She's a publicist. Not Wiese. What is he? A writer? A publisher? A producer? A consultant? Very confusing.

The point: Find an aspect of the film or video business that you really like and stick with it. Be the best. Build your reputation. Don't flit from position to position. (Most all of my fellow vice-presidents from my Vestron days now hold senior positions with the studios or large home video companies.) Your career strategy will affect your emotional and financial life. It will also affect your spiritual life and bring up questions such as: "Am I doing what I should be doing with my life?"

Summary

Our childhoods greatly influence what we do as adults. Can you remember playing as a child? What did you really, really enjoy doing? This was the unique you expressing yourself. If you can find a job or career that is an extension of that time not only will you enjoy what you do, you'll also make a very special contribution and feel like you are living a purposeful life.

In high school I was given an aptitude test that would answer the big question of what Michael should do in this world. I got stuck at the third question. It asked a question and demanded that I "check one": *Would I rather: (1) design a chair, (2) make a chair, (3) sit in a chair, (4) sell a chair?*

I thought it would be great to design a chair, but it would also be great to take cherrywood and bend it into a rocking chair, and then, of course, you'd have to sit in it and rub your hands along the smooth sides, and if you really loved it, you'd want to sell it so other people could enjoy it. By the time I finished thinking about this question, the test was over. The answer for me was really all these things. That's what I am doing today and loving it.

DEVELOPMENT

NETWORK SPECIAL

It's amazing how this town works. Just when you think you've got a deal...

Imagine that you had a real shot at producing a network show on your dream project. My adventure over this last year has been riding this roller coaster called network television. What are the lessons that I've learned?

He was the head of the television network. The meeting was set up by one of his friends. We didn't expect more than five minutes of his time. And sure enough, five minutes later my producing partner and I were out the door. Except that he said "yes."

"He did say yes?" "Yes, he said yes." "He said yes?" "He said yes he'd buy our show." "Wait. Let's sit down." "Right. Catch our breath." "Yes, he said yes!"

The game had begun. We had the feeling that we were entering a video game–one that we hadn't played before....

It was February when my producing partner and I had our first pitch meeting at the major network. We knew it was a long shot. We were pitching a hard-hitting documentary about the state of children's health in this country and what parents could do to improve it. We felt we didn't stand a snowball's chance but, what the heck, maybe the network head would like us, remember us, and give us a shot at something in the future. After all, you don't get to meet the head of a TV network every day.

It was like a filmmaker's ultimate dream. When I was 18 (and even then a filmmaker), I had this dream. Yeah, that's it. I'll walk into the head of a network's office, I'll pitch a hard-hitting documentary, yeah, and, and, he'll agree to pay for it and air it in prime time. Yeah, and my film will help save the world. Yeah, that's it!

Well that's exactly what happened. We were so surprised by the enthusiasm we received that we had to catch our breath for 20 minutes in the lobby before we were fit to drive.

Maybe it was fate or the position of the stars. Maybe things just line up like this once a lifetime. Heck, should we quickly go to the other networks and pitch some more shows? Why waste a good shave?

We had carefully worked out our presentation. I would give a passionate overview of the project, hitting the key points. I'd reference a few things we had done. Then my partner would go into detail about the content of the show.

Before I had finished my key points pitch, the network head said, "Yes, yes, fine. I like it. Yeah, 50 ways to improve your child's health. We'll do it." (Fortunately for me, I didn't keep pitching because our show wasn't 50 ways but more of a PBS-type show. Somehow it was presold on his own tag line before we even walked in.)

Then he called in his lieutenant, a production executive who also liked the show. When asked how much the show would cost, we foolishly quoted a PBS-level budget of $250,000 to $350,000. No problem. They said they would pay for the show, that they didn't need sponsors. And could we finish by June of 1994? We said yes, that would give us about 16 months to do the show. I cautioned that we needed to be careful about sponsors; I didn't want some junk food company sponsoring our show about how to safeguard our children's health. I didn't want it to look like a sponsor cared about children's health if in fact they actually made high-fat, high-sugar, highly processed food products. Everyone understood. We were told to call in a few weeks for another meeting to get things rolling. Our original PBS-oriented proposal sat on the coffee table.

We didn't know the rules. We had somehow passed by the threshold guardian and entered the castle door. It was very mysterious. We didn't know what the next move would reveal....

We called a few weeks later. Then a few weeks after that. Then a few weeks after that. Finally we were told to come by in late June, about three months after our first meeting. We had reworked our original material into a show titled *Healthy Kids: 50 Ways* that was closer to the show we had discussed with the network head.

The June meeting was with the production executive. (After talking with people who had worked with him, we learned that his nickname was "Dr. No." Terrific!)

We learned that he wanted this show to be an "important" television event. We discussed the content of the show segment by segment. We wanted to report on American-style eating habits in three segments: (1) the dangerous junk food diets, (2) what most children eat (The Standard American Diet that includes some junk food), and (3) a healthy, low-fat diet headed in the direction of vegetarianism that is being recommended by more and more experts.

Oh, oh, a scowl! The executive didn't like the third act that was vegetarian-oriented. To no avail, we explained that meat consumption had been falling off since the '70s. The executive had no problem with us reporting on the junk food side (despite the fact that many manufacturers advertise on the network) but reporting on trends toward vegetarianism was too extreme. We finally agreed that we would go no further than what the American government recommends–a diet that consists of no more than 30 percent fat. We rationalized, "At least we can get people moving in the right direction." (In all fairness, we didn't really know what his objections were. Based on his own diet? (He is a meat eater.) Journalistic balance? We'll never really know.

When I asked him who would prepare our contract, a second issue arose. The executive intimated that first we'd write a treatment. I said, "No, that's a development deal. We understood that you agreed to buy the show. We are not interested in writing a treatment. We're interested in producing the show we discussed. We'll work with you and come up with a show we agree upon." He said, "We don't normally do it that way, but okay."

Then a third issue arose. "You haven't produced anything for us, have you?" the executive said. That was true. We had both produced numerous specials for PBS and various cable networks. My television programs had aired on 33 foreign television networks and "You're right, nothing on your network." This fact bothered him. First he *recommended* that we team up with some other executive producers who had produced for his network but by the end of the meeting he *insisted*. I said that the budget would have to be increased to accommodate the new co-producers. He said, "Fine, no problem," and said since he was requesting it, he would pay for the comfort it would give him. He said to call him for some names. (We congratulated ourselves on the fact that Dr. No did not say "no.")

We found ourselves inside a giant courtyard. There were large wooden doors on each side. We couldn't read the mysterious inscriptions on the doors....

A few days later we obtained the names of "approved" producers. After a month we had interviewed three "approved" teams of producers. They were all interested in working with us and amazed that the network had bought our show.

At first I was insulted that the production executive wanted other producers involved. But after my ego recovered, it was clear that these co-producers "knew how to play the network game." We sure didn't. An alliance could be beneficial.

We chose a team of producers on the East Coast (we're on the West Coast) that we felt we could work with well. They had a strong track record with the network and great sensibilities. They were basically good guys.

On the advice of our new partners, and because they worked with higher production values, we prepared a new budget. We expanded the number of shooting days, the number of locations, and added some scientific medical photography and other expenses that the network had approved in their previous budgets. The budget came to $700,000 not including their producing fees which would be negotiated separately (probably another $100,000 or more).

In addition, we inherited their agent (a good friend of the production executive) who would receive a "packaging fee" of 3 percent of the budget ($21,000+) even though we packaged the show and sold it. The agent agreed to negotiate the budget and terms with the network. We messengered the agent our budget and asked him to begin negotiations with the network's business affairs department. Nothing happened. We called the network. They had not received our budget. We called the agent. He hadn't sent the budget. Pressure from our co-producers got him to send the budget.

After many weeks of waiting, there was still no response from the network. What's going on? The agent said he was not getting "good vibes" on the project. I asked how he could get any vibes since he hadn't talked to the network. He said I should talk to the production executive.

I finally got the executive on the phone who said the budget's too high and they won't do it for that. I reminded him that it was his idea to add the co-producers, that the show has been redesigned to meet the production values the network was accustomed to receiving. He said that he didn't care, the budget was too high. He reminded me of my $350,000 budget quote in the meeting. I said "that was before we knew what kind of show you wanted." He said if we wanted him to reconsider the show we'd have to submit a lower budget.

We regrouped with our co-producers. We cut everywhere we could in the budget while still keeping the funds needed to deliver a quality show. Our partners warned us about cutting too much. "If the network doesn't like something, even if they've approved your script, they'll make you reshoot it at your expense. You have to be fiscally responsible. If the show goes over budget, you pay for it." (One of our partner's first network deals required that he put his house up for collateral!) Cautiously we reduced the budget. We left out the host's fee assuming that the network would make the decision of who they wanted in the show and what they were willing to pay for him or her. We resubmitted the budget along with an outline to remind them of the show that had been discussed. Still no answer. Months passed.

We opened the large wooden door and walked in. There were more and more corridors leading in every direction. There wasn't much oxygen. Our torch began to flicker and dim....

We were beginning to feel that the network was looking for a way to say "no" without saying "no." I was in Europe when my partner finally got the network executive on the phone. (He had to work fast. None of us ever had a conversation with him that lasted longer than one minute. He could probably return 100 phone calls a day–short ones–a measurement of how powerful you are in Hollywood.) The executive said that their ad sales man in New York was having trouble finding a sponsor.

The call was over before my partner could remind the executive that the network had agreed to "buy" the show, and "even pay for it ourselves if we have to." Admittedly, we were inexperienced in the art of the nine-second phone call.

My partner called back a few days later. The production executive said it was "always a sponsored show." We are very clear that the network head had earlier said, "We don't need a sponsor. We can pay for it." And that the ad guy was called in just in case a sponsor might be found. Now everything was resting on whether or not the show would have a sponsor. Somewhere there was a slip between the cup and the lip.

On the advice of our partners, we did not call up the network head. Apparently it's common knowledge that all concept shows are sponsor-driven. You cannot get a show on the air without a sponsor. (In fact, many producers come in with sponsors already attached to their shows.) It's still a mystery why the network head said he'd pay for the show without a sponsor.

Weeks passed. My partner called the network ad sales guy in New York. No one was willing to sponsor the show.

Suddenly the earth under our feet shifted. It turned into sand. We were sinking....

The ad sales guy said, "If you still want to move forward, <u>you</u> will have to find a sponsor who will pay $550,000 for the commercials and $450,000 for the production budget." And we had to find a sponsor by December 31 (it was now October) in order for them to hold a June 1994 airdate. (To include our co-producers, our budget was greater than $450,000. Were we being asked to deficit finance the show?) The ad sales guy gave my partner the name of one broker and said, "If you need more names, call."

We regrouped with our co-producers. They said, "Listen, it's your baby. We'll be glad to help however we can. We'll take a lesser position or consult so that you can bring it in on a low budget. It's an important show." Their agent was no longer helping to sell the show. (Had he ever? We speculated: (1) maybe he was embarrassed by the show and didn't want to try to sell it to his friend, (2) from his point of view, it wouldn't help his client's career.)

I told the agent that we would try to get sponsors and said that he could continue to help sell the show to the network but we needed him to really devote some attention to it. He took the opportunity to back out but not before reminding us that he still expected to get his "packaging fee." I said, "No, you didn't package it, we did, and we chose your clients. You can take your fee from their producer's fees." The agent went ballistic and said he'd pull his clients from the show. After talking with the co-producers, they were confident that they could "work out something with their agent that would be fair."

We struggled to get free from the quicksand. We pulled ourselves out and climbed to the top of a stone wall....

My partner followed up with the broker who liked the show, said he was busy now but would be able to begin pitching advertisers in February 1994. We explained that we needed to find a sponsor before that in order to keep the airdate. He said he was sorry but he couldn't work on it now. His fee would be 15 percent and an advertising agency (which he would work with) would also require 15 percent. This added over $300,000 to our budget. The new budget was $1,333,000 higher than our highest budget to the network which they rejected.

My partner called the network back for more broker names. The ad sales guy said, "Did I say I had more names? No, I guess I only had the one name. Good luck, I hope you find someone."

It was dark. We couldn't see through the dense fog. A rock gave way and we fell headlong into the cold water of a moat. A huge alligator opened its jaws. End of game....

We had a hot project that the head of the network loved, a timely subject, a hot agent, a perfectly competent team of producers, but no sponsors. We wound up in the moat again. This was the first skirmish, the first flirtation with network television. What happened? What did we learn from this year-long experience? Here's what I can suggest to other producers knocking on the same doors.

The Lessons

•   Beware if it's too good from the start.

•   The network has shareholders and the bottom line is that they are running a business. Despite their public relations, the networks are not crusaders. They pick their projects very carefully. A producer should answer the question: What's in it for the network? If he doesn't know or can't answer that question, the project probably doesn't belong there in the first place.

•   Concept documentaries are difficult. You don't want to offend anyone who might pay for airtime.

•   Editorially you may not be able to go as far as you thought you could. Networks primarily entertain. Entertainment does not concern itself with the truth.

•   You cannot get a show on the air without a sponsor.

•   Think about what it means to have a sponsored show. How does that shape the content? It doesn't take a genius to figure out what that means. (By the way, this is also a very real concern at PBS who has to deal with this all the time.)

•   You have a better shot pitching a sequel to *Battle of the Network Teenage Stars* than a save-the-world documentary. Advertisers will love it!

•   We're all in the communication business but sometimes we don't know what we are saying to each other and what it means.

•   Every industry has their shorthand. Make sure you are speaking the same language and understand what is being said.

•   Don't expect to walk in having never produced for the network before. You'll need an ally.

•   Partner with someone who's been through the ropes before. Who understands "netspeak," what behavior is appropriate between producer and client, the procedures, deal structures, and budgets. Shortcutting the process will be worth what you have to give up in equity and fees.

•   Even in retrospect you will never really know what happened. You'll never know what went on in the minds of the network executives. You can only guess. And guessing is usually wrong.

•   If you can, find out who is really responsible for making the decisions. The head of the network, the production executive, or the ad sales guy? We don't know.

•   Know that it is possible for a "green-lighted" project to end up on the street.

•   When you don't know what's going on, the tendency is to make something up to fill the void in the mind. The way out of this is to ask and clear up what is vague and foggy.

•   If you don't feel you are getting straight answers–ask. If you have a question, don't worry about appearing naive. Write it down and repeat it. Document your meetings in a courteous letter. ("Let me understand this. What you're saying is that you will buy the show?") Or later it may come back to haunt you.

• The networks are a club. Why should the big guys work with you if you haven't done it before? You could waste their money, make a bad show, require a lot of maintenance. The way they are doing it works just fine. There are no villains here. This is just how the television world works. We were walking the corridors of the castle but couldn't get to the throne.

• Anytime something seems too good to be true, it probably is.

We opened our eyes. The alligator was gone. We dried ourselves off and put another quarter in the machine....

Now you go get 'em.

CONSULTING SESSION I

Consultants have an edge. They aren't "in the soup" and are able to see things clearly. To jar your own sensibilities and to help return your own clarity, listen without judgment to people outside your projects for every "whack-a-doo" idea. You'll be surprised what you might learn.

I'm a producer. I'm also a distributor/marketer. This gives me an edge, and so I have lots of consulting clients.

After leaving Vestron, I started a consulting business which parallels my production and publishing businesses. It all fits together and makes sense, although to outsiders it doesn't always look that way. Producers buy my books, and if they want further information they can call me. Some become consulting clients. Although most have some pieces of the video marketing puzzle figured out, they look to me to help direct them to the other pieces–design production, budgets, and distribution strategies that will get their programs made and distributed.

Sometimes I will produce their programs. Although my three businesses appear very different, they do fit together. I've been able to cross-market my services as a publisher, consultant, producer and marketer.

My consulting clients have problems. And most of them have the same problems. Since they are video producers, I assume that many of you have these problems as well. So save some bucks, and read on.

Consultants have the ability to look at a client's problems, see them afresh, and offer solutions in what looks like breakthroughs. Part of the reason for this is that a consultant's special knowledge can speed up the process for his client in reaching a goal. The client has been in a thick "pea soup" for so long, struggling with the problem, that he or she can no longer think clearly about it. Enter the consultant.

What follows are common problems of many producers. See anyone you know?

1.   You Don't Have an Audience in Mind.

Producers rarely think about the audience who will watch or buy their program. They are too concerned with budgets, schedules, casting and political maneuvers to pay attention to one of the most important aspects of production on which the very real success of their program hinges.

Solution: Ask yourself specifically who makes up your market. Write it down. Where do they live? What is their income? Look at their level of education, sex and other psycho-demographics. What does your program have to offer your audience? Make sure it delivers to your audience. And how are you going to let them know about your program?

2.   You Don't Know Whether or Not Distribution Channels Exist.

Even if they can identify their audience, a producer may not be sure of this.

Solution: Do your homework and research these issues before you roll any tape. Is there a television series that may acquire your single show? Does your program meet the criteria of that series? Is there a home video or non-theatrical or industrial distributor that can (and will want to) distribute your program? Is your program the correct length?

3.   You Don't Know Where to Look for Markets.

Producers are very adept at solving production problems, but down-right lazy when it comes to finding distribution information.
Solution: There are numerous books (including my own) and refer-

ence works that list film and video distributors. But that's not enough. You must start calling around and find those that specialize in your kind of product. If you ask the right questions, by the third phone call you should be hot on the trail of the handful of distributors appropriate for your product.

4.   You Over-Produced for the Marketplace.

Producers like to produce. And they'll spend whatever money they can get their hands on, even if it's not appropriate. I know of a producer who spent $500,000 on a sports video and was only able to recoup a $30,000 advance from the distributor. But he didn't care. He worked with two big sports stars, shot for days, ran up a hefty expense account, bought expensive music, and has a great "portfolio piece." Most of these things were inappropriate to the level of sales that the video would most likely have. He should have spent about $75,000. Pity the investors.

Solution: Have realistic expectations about what your video or television program can actually earn once it's in distribution. Most producers like to fool themselves (and their investors) and think more about producing the world's greatest video. Sometimes the market doesn't need the world's greatest video.

5.   You Under-Produced for the Market.

The converse of the above is also true. I recently saw a program that was produced for less than $30,000. It was intended for the business market. The producer was expecting to sell his one-hour tape for $500. The tape was underproduced for the market. The business and industry market is very sophisticated. They want valuable information. They are accustomed to commercial television standards.

Solution: The producer should have studied the market (he didn't) to check the quality, production and information levels of the programs being offered at $500 each. He would have spent 5-10 times his actual budget to increase the production value of his program and quadrupled the information he was presenting. He also could have produced

45

a printed workbook or reference book, and put it all in an exquisite package.

6.   You Have Special Knowledge, But Don't Know How to Apply It to the Product.

This is probably part of being too deep in the "pea soup." A producer does not see his or her own expertise. Often a producer or creator of a program idea has special knowledge of the subject area as well as the marketplace and doesn't know it.

Solution: Perhaps you need a consultant to bring out those characteristics and help package it successfully. It's hard to see your own aces sometimes.

7.   You Refuse To Co-Venture.

Producers are control freaks. By gosh, they are going to do their own thing by themselves no matter what. I guess that's all right, but it takes longer and expends all their resources. If the program goes belly up in the marketplace (or never reaches the marketplace), they have only themselves to blame.

Solution: The world is full of support. Money, ideas, resources, sweat equity. You just have to ask. Sometimes the research it takes to find the co-venture partners is well spent. You may have to look in other walks of life and to people with entirely different life experiences than your own. They will have contacts and resources that you cannot access on your own. Spread the risks; share the wealth.

8.   You Have Produced a Great Program, But Don't Know What to do With It.

This is perhaps the most heartbreaking thing to see. People come to me with their half-baked, poorly executed programs that they've spent five years producing. It is immediately clear that their program doesn't have a snowball's chance.... It's not enough to tell them that their photography looks good or you really liked the way they did their titles. Sometimes the truth hurts, but it can keep them from making the same bad mistakes over the next five years.

Solution: None. Why? Because usually they did not have an audience in mind. Therefore their program has no marketing elements that will entice a distributor, let alone an audience, in their program. That's usually the case. (At Vestron, my original program division received 3000 unsolicited submissions: scripts, footage and finished programs. We bought three! And these, we twisted and turned and added in other elements before they were completed. The people who submitted ideas and furnished videos (quite a few were accomplished producers) didn't know the market. Period.

These are just some of the problems my clients bring me. I've seen them before, and I'll see them again. But not from you, right? Hopefully, this will give you some food for thought. Now until next time, go get 'em.

CONSULTING SESSION II

Last month I wrote about the common problems that many of my video producer clients bring me. Well, here I am again, with the balance of the 13 most common producer problems (and solutions). I hope these examples help you to swim to the top of your own "bowl of pea soup" (the confusing mix of questions and knowledge gaps plaguing producers trying to market their products), and to clearly see what must be done to achieve the success you seek.

9.   You Don't Know How to Find or Match Sponsors to Their Programs.

This is a tough problem. Producers are looking to sponsors to finance and/or market their programs. Every other day some client says to me, "This would be terrific for Pepsi (or Honda, IBM, etc.) to sponsor!" That's really easy to say, but too often the producer is looking at the sponsorship match entirely from his or her own point of view.

Why would a sponsor want to finance or market or cross promote your program? Are the demographics the same for their product? How do you know that? How do you know they aren't working on opening up new demographics that you don't know about? Furthermore, corporations are working on promotions and marketing plans two years out. Sure, once in a while, there's some discretionary funds, and someone just happens to walk in at the right time and whammo! it happens. But that's very unusual.

I've been a part of a dozen or so sponsorship deals, and I can tell you that it's pure serendipity that brings sponsors and programs together. What producers will never know is the sponsor's agenda. There's no way to find out exactly what they want. Not even their ad agencies are sure from one moment to the next what will please the sponsor.

Solution: You can send out dozens, heck, hundreds of proposals. But it's generally a waste of postage and photocopying. Besides, the development departments of the dozen or so producing PBS stations are already going after anyone you'll ever target. And these folks are professionals armed with some of the best packaged ideas from America's top producers. But don't let that stop you.

What might be a better approach is to produce your program, and then send it to potential sponsors who might use it as a "premium." Once it's finished, a sponsor can see it. Be sure not to include a given brand-name product in your program. If that company nixes it, you'll never be able to go to their competition. If they like it, you can sell 50,000 or 100,000 videos to them to use in their promotions, and maybe sell more videos to a non-competing sponsor. Try to pull together your video without a sponsor. If you can leverage a major star, then sponsorship becomes more interesting. There's not enough space here to go into everything you can do, but know that sponsorship is great when it happens, very hard to get, and takes a long time to acquire.

10.   You Don't Understand Distribution Deals.

By the time a producer gets to a distributor's doorstep, he or she is probably broke, very tired, and may even be sick of their own project. They want a vacation, and certainly need a deal to put their project to bed. This is not a good posture for negotiation. But it happens all the time. Every week I meet someone like this. They are ready to just turn their program over to a distributor, as they are so happy to have found anyone. They'd like to turn and walk away from the distribution problem. This is not the time to let your defenses down.

Solution: Producers should study distribution. They should read magazine articles on it (such as my columns in Videography), read books (you know whose), and talk to all their producer friends. If a distributor makes you an offer, get their catalog and call several of the producers whose product is handled by that distributor. Ask them their experience. Go through the details of their deals. There is no such thing as a "standard distribution" agreement. What you get is what you (and your lawyer) are able to negotiate.

11.   You Don't Know How to Design a Marketing Plan.

Producers often don't know what they need. They don't know what marketing is. They want their programs to sell, but don't know that marketing is as important and sometimes more important than the actual content of their programs.

Solution: I'm frequently asked to help producers design their marketing plan and materials. This is a very complex task, but follows a logical course. The notion is to use whatever tools necessary to get to their audience. This could involve the design of a cassette package, a sell sheet, counter displays, advertisements, direct mail pieces, press releases, publicity and promotional tours. The marketing takes the form of a plan–a campaign over time–where different media (television, radio, print) may well be used to sell their videos. Sometimes the sales promotion will coincide with a television broadcast of their program or with the release of a book that has the same name. How do producers know what they need? That's a tough one. Producers could study similar programs or videos and examine the marketing strategies they used.

12.   You Did Things Out of Order, Then Got Stuck.

This is fairly common. Producers do things back-asswards. This takes a myriad of forms, but they forget the key task in producing.

Solution: A producer's job is to amass enough agreement (which is expressed as "someone else's money") to get the project off the ground. Producers should put together elements which will attract the other elements. For example, once you've got your script, money, producer, director and broadcaster then you can go after a star.

13.   You're Thinking of Standalone Programs, Not a Series or Line.

For all the talent that resides in a producer's brain, there are often gaps. I've met many producers who've worked for years to write and develop their one short video or one single hour program. That's fine; it really is. However, they frequently miss a terrific opportunity.

Solution: First, if you or your writers are experts in a subject area, it behooves you to think of a dozen program ideas before settling on one. In doing so, you may discover that you have a television series or a series of television programs in front of you. It is not necessarily any harder to raise the money for a series. And it is certainly easier to find a distributor or syndicator for a series than it is for a "one-off." (If you've ever made a single-hour program and tried to sell it to television you know what I mean.)

Okay, you say. You like the idea, but you want to start with one show and see how it does. Fine. Test out the market with your one video program. If it works, then branch out within the subject area. Remember, it's more expensive to market one video than a series of videos. If you and your distributor open up a market with one program, you should continue to work that market with follow-up programs. Don't think single programs, think lines.

When I published my first book, I made sure that the cover design was such that subsequent books could have a similar design. That's line thinking. The marketplace is now used to seeing the books and looks for more. In consulting with large program producers like National Geographic, Nova, Smithsonian, and PBS as well as smaller program producers of diving, surfing, music, how-to and health videos, I've recommended that they all develop lines of programming. There's no reason why you can't do the same thing. Five years from now you could have a line, a corner on a market, and a developed image of as a video publisher within that marketplace.

Does that answer all your questions? Feel better? Good for you. I'm beat. Now go get 'em!

FREE $1000 CONSULTING SESSION

Everyone falls into ruts in their thinking. I continually try to trick myself into new awareness. The more ways I can sneak up on an idea, the more likely I am to find new value. One thing I like to do is free associate. I take an idea and then brainstorm around it–listing everything that comes to mind. Sometimes combinations of elements lead to a third element that is really fresh.

There's nothing like a good headline to get your attention. Offer to give something away, and the masses will flock to you.

Now that I've piqued your interest, let me ask you a few questions. Do you want to increase revenue flow from your productions? Do you want to increase, and even expand, your audience? Do you want to take all that hard work you've put into developing and producing your video and build a business around it? If so, this column is for you. You'll learn just how important these ideas are when you start applying them as you develop your next projects.

Thinking Big

In our consulting business, the notion of "thinking big" surfaces daily. It doesn't matter if the client is a large broadcaster, home video company, or a small producer. It doesn't matter whether the issue is product development, production, marketing or
distribution. "Thinking big" is usually a matter of solutions. Turning an idea into an operating principle in your own work is worth far more than the $1000 you didn't pay for this consulting session. Hey, you are getting something for free!

What You Already Know

By the time you've completed your production, you've spent weeks, months or even years developing your concept, doing research, writing treatments, scripts, final scripts and narration. You may have created storyboards, original art work, graphics, photographs, videotape, and soundtracks. You've structured your material first on paper and then executed a version on video. The finished piece has then made its way through some distribution process–large or small. There has probably been some audience reaction (through a purchase, an evaluation or review, or television ratings). Every producer has done an enormous amount of concentrated work. And the result is usually only one program.

So what's wrong with that? Perhaps nothing. But maybe you've missed opportunities that would expand your original idea into other products, sending your message far and wide.

Let's back up. Say you're ready to produce a half-hour training video, a home video, or a television program. It could be for in-house corporate distribution or consumer distribution. In either case, what normally happens is in the very first development meeting the die is cast–everyone starts talking about one product based on one idea. Why not, however, look at that one idea and slowly turn it to examine its every facet? Why not see what other communication pieces can be developed and produced?

Take out a piece of paper, and brainstorm. Anything goes. And at this stage, it costs you nothing.

Imagine the Possibilities

Here's a list of some products, or as I like to call them, "communication pieces," because they all present the original concept in different forms. Look them over. Ask yourself the following question, substituting each product listed in the second blank space provided. It's great fun and often productive. Give it a try.

"_____ is my concept. Can it be a _____?"

Product choices: feature film; videocassette; television program; television series; educational video; training video; video series; audio series; CD; CD-I; computer program; board game; text book; paperback book; synopsis; storyboard; illustrated book; book; workbook; planbook; photo book; poster; postcard; comic strip; press release; radio interview; television interview; seminar; appliance; invention; doll; action figure; lunch pail; pajamas; model; clothing line; food; franchise trademark.

Once you start working with this sentence and get the hang of it, you can easily add many more products to this list. One product will suggest several other forms.

Now, I am not suggesting that your every concept will father (or mother) every product listed above as one of its offspring. But this process frees your mind to see beyond the original form you invisioned for your idea.

Look at it this way. You have a concept. Is it worthy of expression in other forms? If so, what are those forms? Even if it is worthy of only a few forms, you've doubled or tripled your ability to communicate and generate awareness and revenues.

With all the upfront research you have to do and with all the writing inherent in most projects, why not think bigger and see if you can develop a line of programs and/or products? If it takes you a year to create your program, why not spend a year or two and create an entire product line around the same theme or concept? It will not cost you one cent more to think this way. If there are other opportunities, then you can work up business and marketing plans that will exploit the products you've created.

Here are some real-life examples.

From Documentary to Franchise

I recently reviewed a project that was initially designed as a series of historical documentaries. The research revealed some remarkable discoveries that have changed society's view of history. To illustrate this new point of view, 3-D computer models would be necessary. At this stage, the concept was so compelling that a major movie star agreed to host the program– making a network series possible. Because the producers started to think about what elements they needed for the documentary, they began to discover that other communication pieces or products could be created. They saw how their vast research generated a series, led to visualizing that research, excited a major star, and made a network series possible. The network series allowed international television and home video to be feasible.

From the vast research done for this project, they could create books for adults as well as children and computer games. They could re-edit the network series into educational and home videos. They realized the computer work could be used in a CD-I as well as on postcards, stationery and other printed materials. The list goes on. It has now become a business, which can be franchised–building on the identity which will result from publicity exposure on network television.

A Hot Title

I was recently a consultant on a feature film project. The title of the feature is absolutely captivating. It's one of those rare combinations of words that can mean lots of things to many people. The title sounds like it's talking to you. A great title like this has the ability to transcend niche markets and to reach out or cross over to many other audiences.

It was obvious, too, that the concept's creator had more in his hands than a feature. The film takes place in a Northwestern town. During location scouting, the town fathers learned about the project. They became so inspired by the film's idea and the fact it was taking place in their town, that they invested in the script development. (I believe they had a vision of a Field of Dreams-type phenomena occurring in their town. They wanted it to also be transformed into a tourist attraction that could draw thousands to visit.) They figured the area might sell millions of dollars in T-shirts, hotel accomodations, and food.

This was just the beginning. The title also readily lends itself to being used on beer bottles, new lines of trucks or cars, or even restaurants.

The title suggested a comic strip and an illustrated book. In fact, it may be that the original idea will first be developed as a comic strip and other merchandised items and later as a feature film. By building various franchises on the value of the name, by creating national awareness through various media (be it beer, books or comics), the producer is really creating an entire business around his original concept. Whatever film they create, they are also aware that there are sequel and spin-off opportunities. If the film is not successful enough to warrant a sequel, there is still a chance for a television series. All these communication pieces work together to create a mystery, an excitement, a desire in an audience to get involved and participate through various media.

You've just read two examples of how products can be generated from an original concept. Here's how the marketing strategy too can expand to support various products. Without a way to distribute and sell your additional products, the circle from concept to market cannot be completed.

The Infomercial

This year I am producing three health-oriented infomercials. The product will be sold through long-form television advertising programs. Although I never thought I'd ever produce an infomercial (because of the negative connotations of this media form), I am finding that infomercials are an excellent marketing (and communication) device.

The program is loaded with information, and whether or not someone buys the offered product, they will walk away with something of value. (In this respect, the infomercial is only slightly different from a documentary or a how-to program. Where it is different is that it must sell product to stay on the air since that is its primary purpose.) A mystique and a desire is built up around the product that is offered for sale. If people care about their own and their family's health, they will want more information that is provided in the form of audiotapes, videos, workbooks and other printed materials.

The marketing sequence for these infomercials goes something like this. The program appears, the product is offered, and some people order. Those that do are told that they may order an additional product–for example, an audio magazine series–that is delivered at the rate of one tape per month. Since the audience for the product has been identified, there is a strong likelihood that the same people will order additional products (called an "upsell") as well. (In fact, some 20-30 percent of those who call will order the second offering.)

The product is then delivered. Once they've had a chance to use the product and realize its value, a bond is created. A few weeks later, the buyer may be sent a catalog with similar products. Again, a high percentage (up to 20 percent) of sales are made. (This far exceeds the successful one to two percent direct-mail response rate, because the mailing is a highly targeted list.) By creating an ongoing series of audiotapes (or some other form of "continuity programming"), the marketer is in touch with the consumer on a monthly basis and has the opportunity to sell other quality products. (The trust between the marketer and consumer cannot be abused.) The marketers are using infomercials as only one aspect of the marketing process, which draws out and identifies their target audience.

Recap

What you want to do is take your concept and see how many different products you can create from your core idea. The more products you can identify that have distribution channels the more revenue you will create and the greater awareness you will generate. You also want to create as many channels to your audience as you possibly can, so that you can offer multiple products. Why go to all the effort to research, produce and then sell one product when, with a well-thought out product development and marketing plan, you can expand everything you are trying to accomplish into multiple products. Now that I've given you a free $1000 consulting session, I want something from you in return. Please use this information wisely to create products that people can really use–programs that inspire, teach and motivate. Products that benefit people's lives. If I catch you marketing something really stupid, I want the $1000 back!

Now go get 'em.

SO MANY QUESTIONS, SO LITTLE TIME
PART I

Producing has two separate tracks. The "creative" track requires looking at things in new ways. The "get it done" track requires accomplishing physical steps in the right order. Asking yourself the right questions is invaluable. Use these questions. Write your own. When the questions are all answered, the project is probably done!

Were we not in so much of a hurry, there are many questions we would ask ourselves before dashing into a project. Actually, getting it done happens through asking yourself the right questions. Your own well-thought-out answers can help lay the foundation for the entire project and guide you on your way.

While writing my last book, *Film & Video Financing*, I went through chapter upon chapter of dense information on strategies about getting a production financed. What it really boils down to is finding your own palette of approaches and techniques. And these can be discovered by putting yourself through a question-driven process.

For that reason, this column and So Many Questions: Part II are kind of like a producer's SAT. Think about these questions, cut out this article, and paste it on your refrigerator, car dash or your new Panasonic LQ-4000 rewritable optical laserdisc recorder (Whoa! I'm starting to sound like fellow Contributing Editor Scott Billups).

The whole process of producing is finding the answers to the right questions through meeting people and asking for–and getting–support. Producing consists of a series of small steps. If you think about them beforehand, you can save a lot of time–years perhaps. That's why it's important to find out what you need by asking yourself these questions.

Before flying into action, write down answers to the questions that follow. If any remain unanswered, that means you still have preparatory work to do. Let your mind be creative in answering the questions. Write down any and all ideas. Perhaps you can use a tape recorder, then transcribe your ideas later (this prevents the act of writing from getting in the way). First time around you are in the information hunting and gathering stage, so don't be critical of the answers you get.

Go through this process more than once, and give yourself plenty of time to answer each question. By putting the questions into your subconscious, you will be working on them constantly. You may get answers at strange times, so have a scratch pad nearby to write them down. Sometimes you may not get a specific answer, but will have a subtle feeling about what to do. Pay attention, and give yourself a chance to interpret it. This can be helpful in reaching your goal. Once you've devised answers to all your questions, evaluate them.

From consulting with hundreds of producers of home videos, it is my experience that they find it difficult to be honest about the real marketplace value of their project. Producers frequently fantasize about the wealth their project will create. That's what keeps them going. However, we need to make sure that what we tell ourselves is possible. Honesty to oneself and to one's partners, investors and others is critically important.

Here are the questions. They apply mostly to home video oriented projects. But if you are working on industrials or television projects they will also be useful. Here we go.

The Project

What do I want to make?
Why do I want to make it?
What do I hope to realize in terms of financial return?
Why?
Will I be able to stick with this project for the next year? Two years? Five years?
Do I have the ability, resources and contacts to produce this project myself?

Partners

Who would be an ideal partner(s)? Why?
What kind of skills should he or she have?
What would attract him or her to this project?

Packaging and Presentation

Have I consulted with marketing and publicity experts to predetermine the hooks and promotable elements in my film or video? What are the hooks? Which hooks can be amplified? What new hooks or elements are needed?

Budgets and Rights

What will it cost?
Has my budget been professionally prepared?
Am I certain it is accurate?
Have I made assumptions about deferrals or special deals that could fall through? Did I delete them from my budget?
Have I cleared all the rights in the project (story, book, music, talent, etc.)?
Do I know the exact cost of these rights?

The Market

Is there a market for my film or video?
How do I know that?
What does my project offer that will attract a distributor?
What does my project have that will interest an audience?
What does my project have that appeals to the media and generates publicity?
Will people want to see my video more than once? Why?
What are the elements (actors, story, marketing, etc.) that will make it successful?

Income Projections

What returns can I expect?

What other videos have had similar performances?

Have I researched the market for this specific project?

Do I know the video's income potential in each market?

Do I know how revenues flow back to me from rights sales and licenses?

Do I know the deductions and fees subtracted by distributors and agents before the money reaches me?

Is there a significant upside or do expected revenues cover the budget and no more?

Development

Am I good at developing properties?

Have I the skills for developing profitable, worthwhile projects, or am I better at getting it produced once it's selected? Is there someone I can partner with who's good at development?

Do I have the time and resources to develop a property?

Should I try to raise the development money?

Do I know how risky this is?

Do I know how to structure a development deal with investors?

Am I able to incorporate promotable elements within my story or video idea? What are they?

Resources

Do I know how and where to commission key art and/or package art for my project?

What skills do I need in my support team?

Am I (or do I have) a charismatic salesperson with highly developed communication skills who can pitch the project?

Do I have a lawyer in place who can turn "letters of interest" into formal agreements?

Do I have an accountant to prepare the financial structures that are necessary?

Do I have a production company with a track record to handle the physical production of the video?
Do I have letters of intent from the principal participants that can be converted to contracts?
Do I have a financial vehicle which I can use to raise financing?
Do I have a professionally prepared budget that accurately reflects both above-the-line and below-the-line costs?
Have I examined each and every line item to find potential savings?
Have I identified the banks that finance video production?
Have I contacted the guilds and unions? Have I been able to make any special deals?
Have I found a postproduction facility that will cut a deal?
Am I willing to negotiate for everything? If not, do I have someone that is?
Have I explored deferred payments with everyone involved in the production?
Have I identified the best distributors/clients for my project?
Have I decided whether to approach them with my package, or will I wait until my video is finished? Why?
Do I know what impresses a banker? Can I make a presentation to a banker in his or her own terms and leave my normal exhilarated pitch at home?

Income Projections

Are my income projections based on similar projects? Really?
Am I able to put my desires aside and objectively assess the financial upside of my project?
Has my project been financially researched by someone experienced with each market and with how cash flows (after deductions) to the producer?

Deferrals

Who will defer some or all of his or her salary?
What are the facilities that will exchange services for equity in the project?
Where do people stand in relation to one another in the flow of revenues?

Who comes first? Who comes last? Who shares at the same level (equity partners, producers, deferrals, investors, interest, bank, loans, etc.)?

Investors

Who is willing to invest in my project?
Who–among my friends or family–will loan or invest money in it?
Who do I know that will introduce me to an investor or lender in my project?
Can my lawyer, family, co-producer or others refer me to potential investors?
Who has supported my work in the past?
What former employers will help in my financing search?
Do I know a banker that will loan money?
Can I borrow against my equity in a house or property?
Are there companies within or without the video business interested in participating in some manner in this project?
Are there corporate sponsors I can approach?
Are there manufacturers, airlines or service companies that may donate or invest by providing the production with equipment, airline tickets, hotels, food, clothes, cars, etc.?
Do I know a lawyer who will work for equity in the project?
Are there any blocks between me and the money I need to raise? What are they? What do I need to do to make those blocks go away? Am I willing to do it?

International Pre-Sale Agents

Which distributors have handled similar videos?
Who are they? In the U.S., Europe, Asia?
Will they pre-buy rights?
Historically, what income have they generated, what advances or pre-buy payments and deals have they made?
What producers were involved in these deals? (Have I found and talked with them? What was their advice?)

Is my attorney watching over the project and all negotiations?

Do I need to make pre-sales in order to fully or partially finance my project?

Have I found a reputable foreign sales agent?

Is he or she someone I feel good about working with on my project?

Does he or she attend all the major video markets?

What kind of sales record has the agent generated for his other producers?

Am I confident my sales agent knows the major foreign buyers, and isn't simply sub-licensing through other agents?

Do I have a trailer, key art or other materials my sales agent can use?

Have I explored domestic pay television, satellite companies, and pay-per-view for financing?

Does my project really have value in the foreign markets? Why?

Obviously, some of these questions will not apply to your specific projects, but I'll bet they made you think more deeply about your projects than usual. Most of us wait until the last minute to think about things that actually require some serious thought long before we charge into production. I hope these questions sparked your thinking.

Next time, we'll continue the adventure. Until then, go get 'em.

SO MANY QUESTIONS, SO LITTLE TIME
PART II

Here are some of the questions we should ask ourselves before dashing into a new project. In fact, I've learned that getting a production done is really the result of asking yourself the right questions. The path from program development through production and marketing is basically a series of small steps, each of which needs care and attention.

These questions can help you with the answers and resources you will need for your project. If you think about them now, and answer them thoughtfully, you'll be in much better shape as you move forward. Give it a try.

Risk Capital

Am I offering a fair deal to my investors?

Is it competitive with other investments they could make?

Am I aware of how important my own integrity, enthusiasm, and ability to create a vision are in obtaining investments?

Are my investors also in the video business and can they help get distribution?

Do I know what my investors really want?

Do I have more investors lined up than I really need? If not, then why?

Can I get the names of potential investors for every "no" I receive?

Has my lawyer explained state laws and SEC regulations about raising money to me?

Do I understand how limited partnerships work?

Have I structured my deal in a competitive and equitable fashion?

Do I understand how letters of credit work?

Is it desirable to have someone else raise money for me? Why? Why not? Have I prepared a "hit list" of potential investors?

Am I willing to network with virtually everyone I come into contact with in my life?

What am I doing to get visibility for my project?
Are there television, home video, corporations, or other buyers that might want an equity position in my project?
Have I found a foreign sales agent?
How many markets do I wish to pre-sell to finance my production?
What markets will give me an upside?
Have I identified co-production partners?

Pre-Sales

What is my pre-sale strategy?
Is there really an opportunity for pre-selling rights in my video? Why?
What percent of my budget can I really expect to raise?
Have I found a reputable pre-sale agent?
Pre-Sales (Cont.)

How long has he or she been in business?
Have I pre-sold domestic pay television?
Do I have a U.S. distributor in place?
Do I understand how cash flows back to me from the sales agent?
Do I understand how revenues from distribution come back to me?
Deductions?

Distribution

Is it my best strategy to engage the financing and support of a distributor before production or when the video is finished? Why?
Is it realistic to think a video distributor will "pick up" my video once it's finished?
Who might? Why?
What is the greatest advance I can expect to get from the distributor? Why do I think that?
What have these companies recently paid for other similar videos?
Who will negotiate my deal with a distributor, financiers, and/or investors–a lawyer, a producer's rep, or me?
Are they experienced?
Who will negotiate special deals like sponsorship, facilities deals, deferments?

Are they experienced?

Are my negotiation skills strong enough?

Am I, or is someone else, able to conceive all the financial elements necessary to put my project together?

Can all the pieces be tailored to fit financially and legally, and can I still offer my investors (if any) an attractive return? (Am I able to clearly map out this strategy?)

Have I found investors, actors, facilities, distributors, and others–all of whom have a real stake in my project–who can continue to promote the video to ensure profits once the video is completed?

Are my deals with my distributors equitable?

Is everyone appropriately awarded for the risks they have taken or will take?

Financing

Have I taken the time to design a strategy, game plan, and "hit list" for my financing efforts?

What do I think the best route or combination of routes is? Why?

Are my partners strong, and do they really bring something to the party? Are my attorney and accountants experienced in the video business?

Is my investor deal appealing?

Does it communicate that I'm looking out for my investor's interest?

Resources

Do I get good feelings from the people involved in this project?

Do I expect that we will work well together?

Do they have something special to contribute?

Are our skills complementary or supplementary?

Can other people I've met better handle these jobs?

If I know someone isn't "right" for a project, am I willing to move him or her off of it?

Do I have an agent that can help me secure actors?

Home Video

Who are the best distributors for my video? Why?
What elements in my video are particularly attractive to distributors?
Why? Is my budget appropriate to the genre and the expected revenue
potential of my video? Why?
Does my video meet the expectations of its audience?
Is there a strong script?
On what schedule is the production budget paid out?
What are the basic contract terms in a home video contract?
What am I looking for?
What kind of deal do I want?
What rights am I specifically not granting to a particular distributor?
Why? What are realistic home video revenues?
How do I calculate them?
Over what period of time will I receive them?
What is the retail price?
How does retail price affect royalties?
Is there a best time to release my video?
In what territories world-wide does my video have the most potential?
Why?
Do I know exactly what delivery materials I must submit to the dis-
tributor before I get paid?
Are there any conflicting holdbacks that will keep me from releasing
my video for a period of time?
Do I have the rights to all the rights required by my video?
When do I expect royalty reports and royalty checks?

Video Sponsorship

What's more important to me: getting production funds or a market-
ing commitment? Why?
What are sponsors looking for?
What are the benefits my project can offer a sponsor?
What can I give to a sponsor?
What are all the things I might want from a sponsor?
How could a sponsor use my video?
Can I justify and calculate the number of consumer impressions my
video will deliver? How?

69

What companies could use my video as a premium? How?
Do I have contacts with an advertising or product placement agency?
Why does the value of my project increase to a distributor when I have a sponsor attached?
What makes my video sponsorable?
Can I create a different version of my video for a sponsor?
How can I do this?
How can I create a second distribution window after a premium deal window expires?
Do I have the time to find and conclude a sponsor deal?
What are some marketing ideas for my video?
Who are the target audiences? How does the video serve them?
Are there manufacturers whose products can be included in my video?
How can they use my video in their promotions or sales presentations? What is its value to them?
What would they be willing to pay or provide?

Summary

Do I have the energy necessary to make this video? Am I able to deal with rejection? Is my intent strong enough to go through everything it will take to make this video? What will sustain me as I find the answers and carry out the actions associated with these questions? Why do I want to make this video? (Spend at least an hour answering this question. You may be surprised by the answers you find.) Write down or record the answers no matter how silly or profound they may be at the time. Go back to your list of answers one week later and see if you can find the real answer in your list–one that you can look to in the months to come for strength and inspiration.

Good luck and much success in your search for financing.
Now go get 'em!

FINANCING

WOULD YOU LIKE TO INVEST IN MY MOVIE?

This was originally written for "New Screenwriter & Director" magazine of London.

This question might as well be embroidered on the baseball caps of independent filmmakers because it's repeated frequently enough. But unfortunately it's not the first question that should be asked.

The first question really is a series of questions:

"Have you prepared a package?"
"Do you have a great final draft script?"
"Do you have recognizable actors?"
"Any other promotable elements? A well-known theme song? Based on a best-selling book? Based on a true life story?"
"What is your budget?"
"Do you have a shooting schedule?"
"Will the producer and director really deliver on time and budget?"
"Who is your distributor?"
"What are your income projections?"

These are only the most basic questions. Only when they are answered in depth are you really ready to talk to people who finance movies.

This process of asking questions requires patience as the project is written, budgeted, designed, cast and marketed to distributors, investors or other media buyers. On one hand, you must be enthusiastic, and on the other, thick-skinned enough for the numerous rejections you will encounter. If you don't have experience in financing then team up with a partner who's raised financing before. Sure you'll have to give up some of your profits to a money-raising partner but your project will get in front of the right people and you won't have the arduous task of dragging your project around for years. Get a partner and get on the learning curve.

Who's Your Audience?

Frequently I hear filmmakers say their film is for "everybody." That makes marketing real tough because you can't market to everybody. Instead you market to those audiences who you think will most enjoy your film and who will spread the word to their friends. If the wrong audience is duped into seeing your film, you may suffer the consequences in the weeks to come.

Before raising money, you need to know what genre your film is, who the target audience is, why they will want to see it, and whether your film contains the necessary marketing elements to hook an audience. Without considering these aspects, you may create something that the marketing, distribution and publicity people cannot sell. Distributors will make an investment in your film only when they see the profits they will reap. The more aware you are of how to package your film for a specific audience or to work within a particular film genre, the greater your chance for financing.

What's the Genre?

Knowing your film's genre may dictate the budget range appropriate for the audience size. You do not want to spend too much on a film that may have a limited audience. Conversely, you may need to spend a great deal in order to satisfy the production quality for other genres. Science fiction and action/adventures with special effects cost far more than adult dramas. Audience sizes range greatly. If you raise too much money for a project that has a small audience, your investors will suffer the consequences. On the other hand, if you can demonstrate to investors that you will produce an appropriately budgeted film with highly promotable elements that will generate good word of mouth, financing will come easier. To do this, you must know how to increase the production value of your film by "doing more with less" during production and then increasing its value more through marketing.

Use similar techniques to enhance the perceived value of your film in your investors' eyes while financing your film. Market your film to your investors using mock-ups of movie posters, advertisements, and video boxes. This will help them envision the finished product. Let them dream a little with you.

Investor's Money or Distributors' Money?

For indies (independents), going to private investors is clearly the most expedient method of financing, particularly if you are working with relatively low budgets and can prove that you can recoup the investment (and then some) from worldwide theatrical, home video, cable and television sales. Your projections however must be realistic. Use examples of films that are similar to yours. (This does not mean relating your film to *Jurassic Park* just because your film has dinosaurs in it.) Be conservative.

Private investment allows you much more freedom to get your film made. The investors are likely to be unsophisticated about the movie business (or they wouldn't have invested in a long-shot independent film) and will be more likely to stay away and let you make your film in peace.

However a smarter strategy might be to get what is called a "negative pickup" from a distributor. How does this work? The distributor gives you a contract that commits to paying you X dollars when you deliver the film. (Naturally you have to stick to the script that was submitted and the cast and not change critical elements and to deliver the film as promised.) You take the contract you've made with the distributor to a bank. They will discount the contract and give you a percentage of what the distributor has promised... say 50 percent to 70 percent. The money from the bank allows you to make the film. The bank is repaid when the film is delivered. The good news is that since you've got a distributor that put money into your film, there is a strong likelihood that they will do their utmost to make your film a success (and recoup their investment and reap profits). <u>Private investors can only give you money and are unable to help you market and distribute your film.</u>

Best Case Scenario

On the other hand, if you are able to finance your film with private money, and receive major attention at film festivals, then it is possible to create a bidding war among distributors and get a better deal. (A "negative pickup" deal on an unmade film from a distributor is going to be very tough on the filmmaker because the risk is very high.) A well-made finished film that garners good reviews and maybe even has some international appeal will get respect from the distribution community.

The downside is if you create a bad movie. You will neither find a distributor nor be able to repay your investors.

Confidence

So knowing all this, do you feel a little blue? No. You can't feel defeated at this early stage or even show it because winning investors requires confidence and enthusiasm in great quantities.

How do you feel enthusiastic when there are so many pitfalls before you? Easy. <u>With every step, you are getting closer to your dream</u>. With every step, you are creating something wonderful out of nothing. With every step, you are enjoying what you are doing. And your movie <u>is</u> coming together!

You've prepared a strong package, a fabulous idea, a strong script, a great crew, superb actors, a savvy lawyer and accountant, and a distributor with experience in marketing. This confidence inspires confidence in others and is a critical requirement regardless of where you are looking for financial support.

You will also instill confidence in all the other participants. Because you are enthusiastic, everyone will feel enthusiastic. "*Hey, this project is a good idea! I want to be part of it!*" And at precisely the right moment–not too early and not too soon, just when the alchemistic cauldron begins to heat up and the package is finally ready–the filmmaker can then go out into the marketplace for the final ingredient: the money.

Many producers make the mistake of asking for "help" and looking to the investor to make it all happen. *"I need you to invest, otherwise it may not happen."* No investor wants to be in this position. He wants to feel secure, and what better way to give him this feeling than by not really needing his money.

The right moment arrives when a filmmaker can say with certainty to an investor: *"It's happening. The train is moving down the tracks. Do you want to get aboard?"* He gives the investor a choice of investing. The filmmaker makes it clear that everyone is committed to the project, that investment is really not a problem (even though it is) and that <u>the investor is free to not invest</u>. In proximity to a passionate filmmaker, in a moment of shared vision, an investor may surrender to the moment. Then the filmmaker must quickly close the deal and get busy making the film he or she has dreamed of.

Critical Mass

But how do you get your package together? Where do you start? There are two approaches. The first–which is not possible for most independent filmmakers–is to get the biggest star and/or director you can find. Everything else will come together quickly. Great approach. Few have the clout to do this.

The second approach is to use "critical mass." Critical mass means you build the elements to leverage other elements. If you're a new filmmaker, it may be more difficult to get the big star first, so you get a high concept that interests a good writer to write a good script that excites a director who begets the big star. You get what you need one step at a time.

<u>Start where you can succeed and build from there</u>. The more success-ful you are every step of the way, the more confident you feel and the better equipped you are to go to the next stage. Producing is taking

lots of small steps–focused small steps–so at the end of your journey, you have a complete film.

But I Am Creating Great Art!

Well, maybe. But whether you are or not, it is important to enjoy the process. Don't wait for the day that your film rewards you by grossing $100 million because chances are it won't. But if you enjoy the day-to-day process, your payoff comes daily.

Stay Focused

Keep your focus and goal clearly in front of you. Having the intelligence to separate your goals from distractions is basic. Continuing to take the right steps in an efficient and effective manner is the day-to-day work that must be done. You must have a realistic idea of how and where to start (appropriate to your station in life and what you can really do) and accurately assess your ability to inspire others. This focus and the sense that you will accomplish your goal elicits more support and agreement than anything. People want to believe, they want to be led, and <u>they want you to be the one to bring it all together</u>.

With a prepared package and your newly found confidence, it's time to start pitching. But not everyone is marching to the same drummer. Different people will be moved and influenced in different ways.

Take Your Best Shot

What amazes me is that filmmakers will go to great lengths to light, stage, direct and photograph their scenes but do not put all of this know-how into making presentations. Filmmakers are very creative, visual, charismatic people. Why not employ all the tools of your trade when raising money as well?

Pitching to Right- and Left-Brain People

It's important to know who your audience is when you are pitching your project and how they receive information. Everyone is different and you need to be alert to determine the best sensory modality to emphasize. Some people favor the *intellect*, others favor *feelings*. Some are *visual*, others *auditory*. Obviously everyone uses all their senses however if you can "speak" in their modality your communication will make a much greater impact. Tailor your presentation to their sense modality and you will increase your effectiveness.

While this is overly simplistic, let's assume that there are basically two types of people in the world: each perceives the world very different-ly from the other. One primarily uses his or her right brain, the other primarily his or her left. You'll probably might meet both as you pack-age your film.

Right-Brain People

•   Your *actor* is interested in the <u>emotions</u> of the character he or she is to play.

•   Your *director* is interested in a compelling idea and the best way to <u>visualize</u> it.

•   Your right-brained *investor* responds to the emotions, feel, look and textural quality of your film.

Left-Brain People

•   Your *banker* is interested in <u>analyzing</u> your contracts and the concrete ways in which the loan will be repaid.

•   Your *left-brained investor* wants to know <u>how quickly</u> his or her money will be returned and <u>how much profit</u> the film is likely to gen-erate over <u>what period of time</u>. "Give me the numbers," he'll say.

In talking with your actors, director and composer, you may use evocative language because this is the mode that best suits their perceptions. You paint a picture with your words. You describe a vision for the film, its mood and tone.

When you are talking to investors, you may have to radically shift gears. Your banker and investor may not be interested in the "dramatic arc" of your film's story. That's not what they want to hear. They want just the facts. Schedules, cash flow charts, spread sheets, market shares, release dates, and bottom lines–the very stuff that drives artistic people crazy is what left-brain people will rely on in order to evaluate your project.

Successful filmmakers are aware of the modes of perception of their investors and pitch accordingly. Filmmakers understand their audiences' modes very well and can lead them by their senses through the cinematic experience. Clearly this is a valuable area that requires further thought and investigation.

About Investing

One great problem with the business of raising money is that you really can't, with any sense of certainty, show your investor how and when their money will be returned. Profit is unknown. *"Well, it depends on so very many things...."* is not what your investor or banker wants to hear. It makes him real nervous.

Our business is very, very speculative, and the outcome is beyond the filmmaker's control. *How does he or she know that the film will receive the right marketing campaign? Will the film be released at the right time? Will we get an honest count from our distributor?* Most investors have heard about (or worse yet, some have been burnt from) a movie deal gone bad. No wonder investors seem scarce.

The Delicate Bubble of Belief

So what is a filmmaker to do? I suggest that you block such horrible thoughts from your mind to protect the sanctity of an investor's tranquillity and confidence. Besides, it's far more enjoyable for you to use your storytelling skills to talk about "this wonderful film we are making" than to dwell on tragedies that could be. The investor is warmed by your enthusiastic glow and it's hard to "*say no.*" Focus on the world of possibilities and happy endings.

The dance between filmmaker and investor begins. Observe the unspoken rules so that the delicate bubble of belief is not broken. The filmmaker's job is to sustain the vision for what is to be. Like a magician, the filmmaker keeps everyone believing. His/her vision is a dream that he/she's trying to make come true through the efforts of others. "*If we just keep working together and you keep paying for it, we can do miraculous things!*"

The more people who support the filmmaker, the more real the venture looks to everyone, and the more real the vision actually becomes. The filmmaker's art is alchemy: mix in enthusiasm, talent and money, and voilà!–a feature film comes out of the smoke.

Now go get 'em.

WHERE DO YOU GET THE MONEY?

Where do you get the money? Isn't this what we all want to know? With this column, I begin my one-on-one approach to financing, production and marketing solutions. My goal is to empower producers to develop opportunities and create successful strategies to get video programs made and marketed.

The most arduous of all steps is financing. And even money-raising cannot commence until a "package" is fully loaded with such items as script, talent, director, and business plan. Then the investor must be seduced with incentives and inspired. Video financing is like spinning plates in a circus. If the plates stop spinning, you lose your job. Financing is very creative, and no two deals are the same.

Home Video Companies

Private investment is not necessarily the most desirable form of financing. Private investors can't help you get their money back, since they have no business involvement in your program. Home video companies can. They have a financial stake in your program and will distribute it.

Home video companies should be one of the first shopping stops on your financial "hit list." The manufacturer sells your videos (through wholesalers) to video stores (for rental) and to mass merchants and bookstores (for sale). Naturally your program must have elements that are promotable and will appeal to a large audience. Otherwise you won't interest a large home video company that is looking to sell no fewer than 50,000 units per title. Most titles are movies. Only a hundred or so "specialty titles" sell in this range.

What you'll be looking for is an "advance against royalties," which you can use for production. A video company will want approval of the script and its realization. A common payment schedule would give the producer 25 percent upon signing an agreement, 25 percent upon principal videography, 25 percent upon rough-cut approval, and another 25 percent upon delivery.

The home video company will "recoup" its advance from the producer's royalty. Let's say the tape royalty is 20 percent of the wholesale gross receipts, and the tape is sold for $19.95 retail. With an approximate wholesale price average of $10, the producer will receive $2 per unit. If the producer was advanced $50,000, then the tape will have to sell 25,000 units to recoup its production advance. If the tape doesn't sell 25,000 units, then the producer will not see another dollar. The home video company will also ask to retain all other rights, such as television rights, which will help them protect their "downside." The good news is that the producer got the show made (and earned a production fee). The bad news is that all the upside potential of ancillary markets resides with the home video company. Whoever takes the financial risks, reaps the benefits. But what about financial arrangements that could leverage the financial "upside" more in the producer's favor?

The Educational or Business Market

Let's say that you had an idea from which two tapes could be created for two distinct markets through two different distributors. Consumer tapes priced below $29.95, and educational (or business) programs at $59, $99 or even $500. Both programs utilize the same source material, but you've found ways to "position" the material in two entirely different ways. For the home video version, you get a $50,000 advance. In your contract, you retain the "educational or business" version rights (as well as book and audio rights). For the educational version, you create a longer program and/or include a study guide or workbook to justify the higher price. You receive a second advance from the "educational distributor." Each program has a different title and is packaged distinctly.

Think about multiple markets, and you will expand both your revenue streams and communication opportunities. Also think "lines." It takes as much effort and money to market a series of tapes as it does a single program. And once you've found a market, why not sell them additional tapes? Create two or more tapes at the same time.

Let's suppose that the producer cannot raise enough money for the production from these distributors. Where does he or she go?

Private Investment

Many films and videos are financed by family, friends or business associates through limited partnerships. Each limited partner or investor puts up some money in exchange for a portion of the net profits. The traditional deal gives the limited partners or investors 50 percent of profits and the producer 50 percent. (The producer may share his or her 50 percent with talent, crew and others.) When the royalty checks start to come in, the investors are paid back their investment first. Sometimes they are paid an additional 15 to 30 percent before the 50/50 split. Sometimes the split is skewed in the favor of the investor, say 60/40. Sometimes investors are allowed to make back twice their investment then receive a small ongoing share of profits, say 10 to 25 percent. There are endless creative ways to cut the pie that compensate the investor for the risks they are taking.

If you privately fund a production and you've made a terrific program that many distributors want, you are in a much better position to leverage a better royalty deal and hold onto ancillary rights. This increases your upside if you have also made a reasonable deal with your investors.

Facilities as Partners

Why go through the hassle of raising money, however, if you can convince a facility with cameras, editing suites and videographics to be your business partner? Many facilities will be willing to engage in "soft dollar" financing. This works by the facility assuming "soft costs" (overhead, profit margin) and the producer paying "hard costs" (editor's time, tape stock, etc.). A facility may be willing to finance as much as 30 to 60 percent of your below- the-line expenses in exchange for an equity share (30 to 60 percent of the profits). Assume that the below-the-line budget (excluding producer, talent and writer's fees) is $100,000 and that a facility puts up $50,000 in services. You pay them

$50,000 toward the hard costs. They may be entitled to a 50 percent profit participation (after you've received your deferred fees).

Or you may pay them back in full, give them a 10 or 20 percent "bump" (interest on their investment), as well as an equity position of 10-25 percent of profits. If you run out of time before the project is finished, you may have to beg more editing time rather than go back to your investors. Since the facility is your "partner," structure your deal so that everybody wins. Companies with postproduction and or duplication facilities are open to worthwhile projects. But again, these must be projects that truly will earn out in the marketplace, and your business and distribution plan must clearly show how this will be accomplished.

Next time we'll discuss other opportunities that can include other co-production partners, sponsors, television, premiums and other media forms. Feel free to be as creative in your thinking about how to finance your program as you are about your production design.

Now go get 'em!

SHAKING THE MONEY TREE

As I write this, I'm once again raising money. Will it ever end? No. Better get use to it folks, money-raising is part of producing. No money, no production. The more comfortable and skilled you can become with the process, the easier the money-raising will be.

I continue to use each and every finance technique that I describe in this book. It pays to read and reread these ideas again and again. It will spark your imagination and help you with your own financing.

Have you been shaking that money tree? Where Do You Get the Money discussed deals with home video and non-theatrical (educational and business) distributors, private investors and facilities. This column deals with other co-production partners, sponsors, television, premiums and other media forms and the roles they may play in financing. You're going to have to be as creative in the way you put your deals together as you are in the way you produce your programs. Developing a taste for financial strategies will greatly influence your success.

Co-Ventures

Co-venturing is one of the best ways to finance your programs, because the risk is spread among other parties. An ideal co-venture might look something like this: an investor, a production company, and a distribution company each put up one third of the budget. The production company may put up fees or overhead, while the others put up cash. The normal distribution deal would allow the distributor to recoup its production advance in "first position" at the royalty rate (which is very slow) before giving the producer "overages" from which the producer and investor would recoup in "second position."

You can do better than this when you bring in two thirds of the financing. In the co-venture, everyone stands in the same position for recoupment and profit. In the one-third/one-third/one-third co-venture, the distribution company would receive and deduct a small distribution fee, duplication, marketing and advertising expenses from gross revenues. Then each partner would be paid back their investment at the same time. No one partner would stand in line before another, and all would share equally (one-third) in profits. What I like about this deal is that everyone has the same goals and is treated equally. Too frequently do producers and their investors stand last in line.

You also might go to television to raise financing. PBS, TBS, HBO, Showtime and many other cable (and network) systems need programming. They will either provide an advance, or pay upon broadcast for the television rights in your program. That still leaves all home video and other rights to exploit. While they may not cover the entire budget, they may supply a significant portion of your financing. Some systems, like HBO, are putting up a few million for small made-for-movies, but retaining all rights. The question before a producer is "do you want to get it done?" or "do you want to try to retain some rights for 'upside' profits?" Most just opt to get their programs and videos made because they feel financing is scarce, but it doesn't have to be this way.

Premiums

Like their cousins, the personalized coffee mug and baseball hat, videos have entered the premium market. Why? First, they have a very high perceived value. Consumers know videos cost $19.95 or more. If they can get one free-with-a-purchase, or as a low-cost purchase-with-a-purchase, they feel it's a great deal. Many advertisers and their clients have been using videos to draw in new consumers for their products, because video can deliver a very targeted demographic. Burger King's video promotion using Teenage Mutant Ninja Turtles sold well over 10 million units. With new videos coming out every few weeks, kids and their families develop a Whopper habit–which is the real goal of this premium or incentive program.

These big premium deals are few and far between for most producers. There are, however, many companies that would buy 5000 or 10,000 or even 100,000 videos if they felt it would expand the market for their core product. A premium deal in the bag can help finance your program. How does this work? Say you are making a one-hour how-to program. You make a deal with a company that you will cut a "special version" (half hour) of the program for them. It will have special packaging and a promotional spot on the tape. They pay you $1 (it could be a tad more or less) over cost for 50,000 units. That's $50,000 you can put into the production. They have a premium, and you have some financing. You own the sole rights to the long version for the video markets. Everyone wins.

Sponsors

Producers everywhere look to sponsorship as a means to finance video, but most miss the point. Unwittingly, they pitch sponsors to put up production money. Wrong! Not that important! Producers say, "Wiese, are you crazy?" and I say "No." Producers aren't thinking of the big picture. Why get only $25,000, or $50,000 toward your production budget when you can get millions in advertising and cross-promotion? And it's much easier to get a "yes" out of sponsors.

First, realize that sponsors have their own agendas. They are trying to sell their services and products. Unless your video can help them do that, they won't be interested. If they are interested, go for cross-promotion. Say you want to produce a series of children's tapes. The sponsor wants to introduce a new product to kids so the kids will use the product early in their lives and develop a loyalty to it. Why not have the sponsor commit to promoting your video in their next multi-million dollar print and television campaign? (And you can also sell them premiums.)

Such a campaign would have built enormous public awareness about your children's video–far more than the paltry $75,000 that most video companies would spend on video marketing for your program. With that awareness, you should be able to strike a much better advance deal with a video distributor once the sponsor's promotion ends. And consumers who didn't get the video through the sponsor's promotion may buy it.

Sponsored Financing with a Twist

Last year I produced a comedic Monopoly-like board game called Goin' Hollywood, in which the players are producers trying to get their movies made "any way they can." The game was launched regionally in Los Angeles. We were actually involved in two businesses. The first was selling board games through WaldenBooks and gift stores. The second was selling advertising. Since we had many "power spots" (famous locations and businesses) on the board, we sold "ad space" for them to such places as Mondrian, L'Ermitage and Chateau Marmont, and to magazines such as Premiere, Variety and Hollywood Reporter. Rather than take money which we certainly needed, we learned we could get much more value out of our "ad sale" by taking free hotel rooms and catering at the hotels where we held our "game playing" press parties, and by bartering for full-page color ads in the magazines.

Press parties and ads were expenses we would have incurred anyway. By bartering the ads, we accomplished much more. (Since the real cost of the hotel rooms and ad space was less to the sponsors, we were able to barter much easier that if we were looking for cash.)

These are only a few of the kinds of creative financing, bartering and cross-promotion that you need to think about as you pull all the elements together for your video programs. Every time you find a creative way to finance, it may lower your risk, improve your marketing opportunities, and increase revenues. Now go get 'em.

WHAT INVESTORS WANT

Producers should cultivate the art of listening. There are many things an investor may want (in addition to financial return). If you can really hear, and learn what these things are, it will be easier for you to reach your goal

When I first started raising money for documentaries, I was very surprised by what some investors wanted. It had little or nothing to do with their investment–they really didn't care whether their money was returned or not. They were interested in what the film had to say and in getting a message out. Some were just interested in participating with filmmakers.

Unsophisticated investors (meaning those that haven't invested in films or videos before) go through your prospectus, listen to your presentation, and scrutinize you very carefully. They ask many questions that you must be prepared to answer. They certainly will have questions that you will need to answer. Many questions will go unasked but are very important to address during your presentation.

Here are some things investors like and need to hear:

1.   The video will make a lot of money, more than their investment, and maybe a whole lot more than that. (How can you demonstrate this? Will it be sold to the corporate market? To the consumer market? By direct mail or through direct response ads? How many will be sold and at what price? Over what period?

2.   There will be a large publicity campaign that will generate enormous public excitement and awareness, and lots of people will want to see the video they've been hearing about. (How can you demonstrate this? Is there a hook that suddenly interests a large segment of the population? Today that might be something about police violence or on a patriotic subject. Before you make your video, you must think about publicity which will help the video find greater distribution.)

3.	Your video is a class act with high profile elements. There are well-known, prestigious stars, directors and/or writers in your video. (Is your video based on a best-selling book, a life story, a high profile news event, a literary masterpiece, or a corporate training breakthrough? What makes your video stand head and shoulders among the competition?)

4.	Your video will be shot in exquisite locations, or will be loaded with special effects, or will have some visual element that is really terrific, or all of the above. (Do you have footage of that great volcanic eruption, or whale footage, or great spaceship fly-bys?)

5.	They can participate or get involved at some level. Can they visit the set, go to parties, go to the premiere, meet the actors? (What can you offer that gives your investors some participation but doesn't crimp what you have to do during production?)

6.	They have a choice about investing in your video or not investing in it. They don't want to be pressured, or coerced, or sense that the video's existence depends on their money. They do not want to feel that without their money the video won't get made. This puts too much responsibility on the investors. It's the producer's job to get the video made.

Some Other Thoughts

1.	Money attracts money.

If you already have some money in your pocket (especially your own), it will bring a sigh of relief to your investors. No one wants to be first (unless there is some financial reward for doing so). By sharing the risk with other investors, everyone's comfort level rises.

If you have done your homework and put together an admirable package and an honest agreement, you will find investors. If your project has integrity and if you are offering a fair deal to investors, you already have an advantage over other producers beating on the same doors. Honesty is very attractive to investors, who know it when they see it.

2.   Don't confuse money with quality.

There will be lots of videos that look better than yours because they have bigger budgets, but that doesn't mean they are better. Investors recognize that good videos can be made about powerful subjects on smaller budgets.

A good video is competitive in the marketplace because audiences for good videos are growing. The number of video festivals in this country boggles the imagination. There are VCRs in over 70 percent of all homes. People use video in business. They watch video for entertainment. Schools use video for education. Tastes are changing, movie audiences are getting older, and they are demanding more from movies. Audiences often turn to video during their leisure and work hours. They want better, more intelligent material, and videos that bring meaning, knowledge or new skills to their lives.

Independents have one significant advantage over networks and large video companies: they can make goods videos for little money. This is attractive to investors because there is tremendous upside in producing quality videos for reasonable budgets. Independents know that the limited money they are able to raise must go into the video and be seen on the screen. The fewer fees taken out of the budget, the better the investment package appears to investors. No investor wants to fall victim to a "hit and run" producer. If you make quality videos, you will attract quality investors.

3.   When you want a hundred people to show up at a party you invite a hundred and thirty.

When you line up your investors, you overbook because some may fall through and not deliver on their pledges. Some will have "cash flow" or "stock market" or "personal" problems when it's time for you to pick up their check. If you have commitments for more money than you actually need, it does wonders for your self esteem. That attitude attracts even more investors. People run to abundance and run from scarcity. If you have more money than you need, you have leverage in your distribution negotiations. You won't have to cave in on deal points. If you don't have all the money you need, the money does the talking and you lose some of your negotiating strength. If you don't need the money you can make tougher deals, which benefits your investors.

4.   A money raising technique:

Whether investors say "yes" or "no" to your project, be sure to get other names and contacts from them. If they say "yes," they'll be inclined to think of others who might like to invest. If they say "no," they may feel guilty and at least will want to give you something for free–like someone else's name. Fine. You can use every contact you can get.

5.   Make sure your lawyer complies with all state laws and SEC regulations in preparing your investment documents.

If you proceed in an unprofessional, haphazard manner, you can be shut down and suffer terrible consequences. For example, you are not allowed to advertise your project in newspapers or magazines. In some cases you must qualify your investors–they must be able to afford the risk–and they may be required to have earned over $250,000 per year for the last several years. Discuss this with your attorney to learn whether he or she must screen and qualify every potential investor.

Summary

It baffles the brain to understand what investors want. I continue to be surprised. The main point is to get out there and talk about your project. Your enthusiasm is a greater magnet for finding investors than your idea. (Really!) It's not only about money, it's about doing good work, making a difference, and sharing knowledge. Frequently, some of the higher human aspirations will emerge in the form of investors. And no sense being shy about asking for money–you don't get weird when you ask for videotape stock. It's simply another resource. Money is more abundant than you think. Now go get 'em!

INVESTORS, WHERE ART THEE?
PART I

You're in a jungle. You hear sounds from every direction. You see evidence of animals being here, but you don't see them. Investors are like that. Everywhere we go, we see the results of money being spent. Where does this money came from? Your job is to find the investor. It's a jungle out there.

More than the latest chip camera, more than the new hi-def monitor, more than the beta version of a graphics program, producers want to know how to raise money for their projects. The next few columns are designed to help producers in their search for the illusive grail: financing.

The first step is not getting the money, but preparing a package, a pre-production presentation that outlines the project, cast, budget, schedule and distribution as well as a marketing plan that predicts anticipated returns. This requires that the producer be good at writing, designing and packaging the video project, be enthusiastic, be thick-skinned enough for the numerous rejections he or she will encounter, have some experience in financing (or have partners who are), and some idea about where the money is and how to go about getting it.

Private Investment

Going to private investors is clearly the most expedient method for funding video productions if the projects have the ability to return the investment (and hopefully some profit.) Private investment allows you much more freedom to get your video made because anyone with money can help you. Distribution, however, may still be a problem, and investors will have to be convinced that distribution will be forthcoming.

Confidence

Winning over investors requires confidence and integrity. For many, this confidence comes only after they have prepared a strong package, a fabulous idea, a strong script, a great crew, superb actors, a savvy lawyer and accountant, and a distributor with experienced marketing skills. This confidence inspires confidence in others and is a critical requirement regardless of where you are looking for financial support.

The producer also instills confidence in other participants. Everyone is confident that the project is a good idea and therefore will commit to it. At precisely the right moment (not too early and not too soon) when the alchemical cauldron begins to heat up and the package is finally ready, the producer goes out into the market place to secure the final ingredient: the money.

The right moment arrives when a producer can say with certainty to an investor, "It's happening. The train is moving down the tracks. Do you want to get aboard?" He gives the investor a choice of investing. The producer makes it clear that everyone is committed to the project, that investment is really not a problem (even though it is, or the producer wouldn't still be talking to investors), and that the investor is free to not invest. In the heat of the excitement, many investors surrender to the moment. The producer must then quickly close the deal.

Many producers make the mistake of saying "help" and looking to the investor to make it all happen. "I need you to invest, otherwise it may not happen." No investor wants to be in this position. He wants to feel secure, and what better way to give him this feeling than by not really needing his money.

Critical Mass

If you assemble your pre-production package, slowly and carefully, you can achieve a critical mass that will improve your odds. "Critical mass" means you build the elements to leverage other elements. If you're a new producer, it may be more difficult to get the big star first. So you get the script or video idea that begets a strong director that begets a big star. Start where you can succeed best, and build from there. If you can get the big star first, that helps you leverage a director and financing. The more successful you are every step of the way, the more confident you feel, and the better equipped you are to go to the next stage. Producing is a process of taking lots of small focused steps so at the end of your journey you have a complete video.

Keep your focus and goal clearly in front of you. Having the intelligence to separate your goals from distractions is basic. Continuing to take the right steps in an efficient and effective manner is the day-to-day work that must be done. You must have a realistic idea of how and where to start (appropriate to your station in life and what you can really do) and accurately assess you ability to inspire others. This focus and the sense that you will accomplish your goal elicits more support and agreement than anything. People want to believe, they want to be led, and they want you to be the one to bring it all together.

With a prepared package and your newfound confidence, it's time to start pitching. But not everyone is marching to the same drummer. Different people will be moved and influenced in different ways.

Right-and Left-Brain Pitches

It's important to know who your audience is when you are pitching your project, and to tailor your pitch to his or her perception. Although it's never as simplistic as what I'm about to describe, this may give you some useful ideas.

Let's assume that there are basically two types of people in the world; each perceives the world very differently from the other. One type primarily uses their right brain, the other their left. (Actually, most people shift back and forth between both parts of their brains, but let me continue.) Here are some examples of these two kinds of people you will encounter during your production.

Right-Brain People

Your actor is interested in the emotions of the character he or she is to play. Your director is interested in a compelling idea and the best way to visualize it. Your right-brained investor responds to the emotions, feel, look, and textural quality of your video idea.

Left-Brain People

Your banker is interested in analyzing your contracts and the concrete ways in which the loan will be repaid.

Your left-brained investor wants to know how quickly his or her money will be returned, and how much profit the video is likely to generate over what period of time.

In talking with your actors, the director and the composer, you will usually use evocative language because this is the mode that best suits their perceptions. You paint a picture with your words. You describe the vision for the video, its mood and tone.

When you are looking for investors, you may have to radically shift gears. Your banker and investors are not terribly keen on the mood and tone of your video. That's not what they want to hear. They want just the facts. Schedules, cash flow charts, spread sheets, market shares and bottom lines. The very stuff that drives artistic people crazy are what they rely on in order to evaluate your project.

Different people perceive the world differently. If you want to communicate successfully with these different people, you need to understand how they perceive the world, and tailor your presentation appropriately. People perceive the world in a variety of primary modes, and frequently switch between modes: kinetic, acoustic, visual, etc. Successful communicators are aware of the modes their audience is accessing. Successful producers are aware of the modes of perception of their investors and pitch accordingly. Videographers understand their audiences modes very well and can lead them by their senses through a video experience. Clearly, this is a valuable area that requires further thought and investigation.

About Investing

Many investors will be in their left brains when they are thinking about the use of their money. One great problem with the business of raising money is that you really can't, with any sense of certainty, show your investor how and when this money will be returned. Profit is an unknown. "Well, it depends on so very many things..." is not what your investor or banker wants to hear. It makes him or her real nervous.

Our business is very, very speculative, and the outcome is beyond the producer's control. How does he or she know that the video will receive the right marketing campaign? Will the video be released at the right time? Will we get an honest count from our distributor? Most investors have heard about, or worse yet, gotten burned from a movie or video deal gone bad. No wonder investors seem scarce.

Delicate Bubble of Belief

So what do most producers do? They block such horrible thoughts from their minds to protect the sanctity of their investor's tranquillity and confidence. Besides, it's far more enjoyable for the producer to use his or her story-telling skills to talk about "this wonderful video we are making." The investor is warmed from the producer's enthusiastic glow, and it's hard to "just say no." If the investor looked too deeply into what could go wrong, it could be depressing and might convince him to do something else with his money. It's better for the producer to focus on the world of possibilities and happy endings.

So the dance between producer and investor begins. There are unspoken rules to be observed so that the delicate bubble of belief is not broken. The producer's job is to enthusiastically sustain the vision for what is to be. Like a magician, he keeps everyone believing. His vision is a dream that he's trying to make come true through the efforts of others. "If we just keep working, and you just keep investing, we can do miraculous things!" The more people the producer has lined up, the more real it begins to look to everyone, and the more real the vision actually becomes. The producer's art is a kind of alchemy. He mixes in enthusiasm, talent and money, and voila! A video cassette comes out of the smoke. Now go get 'em.

INVESTORS, WHERE ART THEE?
PART II

Like Ulysses, the producer's quest for financing leads him into mysterious territory, unknown landscapes, and into the domiciles of strange creatures.

Sometimes, however, the search involves waiting, and in some mysterious way investors are drawn to you. Imagine financing your video without ever leaving home.

Four times this kind of strange thing happened to me. I've been packaging a television and home video series about spiritual masters, which includes such extraordinary people as The Dalai Lama of Tibet, and other Eastern and Western teachers who address contemporary issues. The series explores how to live a spiritual life in the modern world. This, I believe, is a very difficult project to fund because the opportunity for huge paybacks are small unless of course we have a surprise blockbuster. But financial rewards are not what this particular project is about, and perhaps that's what people are responding to when they want to contribute.

Serendipity Reigns

Out of the blue (I love that phrase) came two calls. People had money they wanted to invest in film and video. "Did I have any ideas?" The first caller was looking for other kinds of investments besides real estate. I told him about a few commercial projects and then sheepishly about Masters Among Us, a spiritual masters series. This one took hold. Rather than invest, he offered to go out and find corporate contributions. Today, he faxed me a redraft of our proposal that he thought would be helpful. A former theology student and successful businessman, he was looking for something else to do. He found it.

Call number two was from another man looking for interesting opportunities. Besides real estate, he had bought a high-end video camera and has partnered with a top news cameraman. The spiritual masters project interested him as an investment with the possible caveat that we hire his crew for some of the shoots.

Then I received an unsolicited call from a former investor. Every year I send him a royalty check from Dolphin, a film I made 12 years ago. He told me that he just ran across a check I'd written in 1986 behind a drawer and "would I write him another one?" Certainly. When he asked me what I was up to, I told him about spiritual masters and the Dalai Lama who had agreed to participate. He told me that he is now on the board of directors of a foundation that gives money to spiritual media and the arts, and that I should apply for a grant!

And lastly, a friend of mine was talking to a friend about our project. She surprised him by saying she'd like to invest a very large sum (when another investment pays off). I've been in this business long enough to be skeptical until the check is in the bank. But the point I'm trying to illustrate is that something else seems to be happening. None of these financing sources were solicited. They just happened!

My sense is that strong intention ("this project is going to happen") combined with serendipity ("how I don't know exactly") and a lot of hard work are the ingredients of this success.

Every week we refine and strengthen our presentation package. With every new contact, spiritual master or crew member, investor or contributor, video, television or audio deal, we strengthen our ability to get the project made. People feel this, and want to be a part of it.

Even if you believe that there's a little magic happening here, you can't stay in bed and wish it to happen. You have to do the conventional things to find financing. I contact former investors, ferret our new possibilities, look for facilities deals and distribution and marketing opportunities. Still, there is this nagging feeling that there is another level on which this project is coming together. There have just been to many serendipitous occurrences.

Time Allocation

I have become more conscious of my time. I only have a limited amount, and I want to use it well and make it count. I don't like to spend time developing projects, unless I am confident (and committed) that they will get made. I certainly don't like to try to raise money where the chances of getting "no's" are high. I want results.

The Three-Strike Rule

I've developed and produced enough home video projects to know where to go to find financing and distribution. Over the last few years, I have developed what I call my "three-strike rule." After three, unsuccessful pitches to video distributors, I move on. Three rejections (by qualified buyers) means the marketplace is telling me "no thanks." I figure I should know who is most likely to buy the project. Of course, you have to pick your three pitches very carefully. You don't pitch a spiritual masters project to an exploitation distributor. (However, given my recent experience, this may not be such a bad idea!)

Videos have a shorter gestation rate than films. I like that. They are quicker to develop, cost far less to produce, and are released into the marketplace months later. The financing arc on a feature may take years; with a video, it's only months. If you like instant gratification, videos will suit you.

At any one time, I have a dozen videos (or TV programs) in development, a handful in production, and many more in release. Features move forward very slowly (or not at all), although the financial rewards and visibility are much greater.

What Flavor Investor?

There are two kinds of investors. One is unsophisticated in the video business; the other, may be a video distributor who knows the video business inside and out. Which is better? Who do you go for first? If financing is your goal and you feel capital is scarce, then you take what you can get from either type of investor.

Conventional wisdom suggests it's more advantageous to get financing from an end user, like a broadcaster or home video company. The thinking goes that if the end user invests in a video, he or she is motivated and capable of getting the money back by making sure the video is successfully distributed. The power of self-interest is not to be underestimated. If your financing doesn't come from an end user, you must rely on other resources.

A second argument frequently made for going to end users for financing is that it's usually easier. An end user understands video deals. It doesn't matter if your end-user investment partner is domestic or foreign, because he or she will protect their own downside–either through their own distribution efforts or by selling it to others.

The other school of thought suggests that nonvideo-industry financing, or the private investor route, is best. This type of investor is less sophisticated and makes fewer demands about the kind of video produced.

Many, many videos have been financed by private investors. Now, however, some savvy investors are staying away from videos because they know the marketplace is flooded and easy profits are harder to come by. Today the competition to sell to the video rental market is greater. A retailer no longer buys most B titles, but prefers As which are feature films almost solely produced by the studios. Video rental stores don't want to stock hard-to-market B films and videos when they can have A pictures (for the same price) that bring greater visibility and higher rentals. For an investor in independent B videos today, the risk is heightened, and the rate of return diminished. Why shouldn't he/she look for other kinds of investments?

Nevertheless, making a financial killing is not necessarily the motivating factor for some investors. My *Videography* column, What Investors Want, explores what will motivate your potential investors.

Until next time, don't go get 'em, let 'em come to you.

HOW DO YOU MAKE THE MONEY BACK?

I can't say it enough–you have to understand distribution agreements inside and out. Be sure you understand how the money will come back to you (and your investors). You have to be absolutely clear about this, or you and all your partners are in deep trouble.

Ah, distribution... the word sends producers running in fear and/or loathing. Unfortunately, many of them don't really want to face distribution, and they dive into production only to face it when they surface for air.

What's so bad about distribution, and why does it get such a bad rap? The experience of many producers is that distribution revenues fall short of expectations projected in the business plan. Informing investors of this fact is always unpleasant.

Recently, I've given a lot of thought to this whole issue, because–like all producers–I think there's got to be a better way. I'd like to set up a home video distribution label, so I won't have to go hat in hand to distributors every time I have a program I want to produce.

I've worn the producer's hat, the distributor's hat, and many hats in between. I have these recurring dreams of hundreds of smiling investors raving over my last video, patting me on the back, and filling my hands with wads of money for my next project. Then I wake up.

Why can't this dream be real? The context in which our business exists goes something like this: "We all know there is the 'business' part of show business. It's tough, ugly and full of cheats. You can't blame me for wanting mine now, can you?" All negotiations seem to end with "I get mine now, thank you." High paid lawyers structure deals that only nuclear physicists can understand. Everyone (the distributor, the investor, the producer, and the star) wants to stand first in line for profits (if any). Since everybody knows that there never are any profits, they want a big fee now. Hence, ridiculously large budgets.

Financing and distribution deals are definitely not about setting up win-win situations. "Somebody's got to win, somebody's got to lose" is Hollywood's distribution theme song. We need distribution deal structures that benefit distributors and producers and their investors. How hard could that be?

Distributors have convinced producers that without them producers don't stand a chance. Even if you leave the office for the next distributor, the deal you're offered is essentially the same. I don't care whether it's a royalty deal, a distribution fee deal, or a joint venture, when you run the numbers the basic video distribution deal is 80/20. That's 80 percent for the distributor and 20 (or less) for the producer. The distributor makes a profit long before the producer (and the investors). Why? "Why not?" responds the distributor. "Without distribution, you'd be nowhere." Only hit-making producers have been able to retort, "Hey, without my program, you'd have zip to distribute!" But most don't have this clout.

Suppose, however, that producers everywhere woke up one morning, and the entire context of the business had shifted. Let's imagine that The Creation of the Product is everything, and producers began saying "Listen up Mr. Distributor, without our programs there'd be no distribution business." By making the product supreme, all deals become subservient to the creators, the producers and their investors. Those who contribute to the creation of The Product–be it money, creative services, a script or other elements–are the real benefactors at Gross Receipt Time.

Well, that's not really going to happen in our lifetime, but here's a deal structure that does make sense. Suppose investors, producers and distributors came to the table, and all agreed that what each of them contributed had pretty much an equal value. And let's further suppose that each partner (the distribution company, an investor, and the production company) agreed to put up one third of the budget.

The distributor agrees to pay for manufacturing and packaging the cassettes and for marketing. The distributor's money would be recouped first. And because the distributor is providing a very real service and is risking additional monies on manufacturing and marketing, he is entitled to receive an equitable distribution fee (say 15 percent). Thereafter, the actual marketing and distribution costs are deducted, and all the three partners share equally in thirds.

What I particularly like about this structure is that everyone has the same goal. Everyone stands under the waterfall. Since everyone's goal is the same, everyone receives equal treatment. There is no preferred standing.

Let's run the numbers between both deal structures. We'll first look at a traditional deal.

Twenty Percent Royalty Deal   (50,000 Units Sold)

Price of tape:	$ 19.95 Retail	
	$ 11.37 Wholesale	
Producer's royalty:	$ 2.27 (20 Percent)	
Gross receipts:	$ 568,500 (received by distributor)	

Minus:
Producer's royalty: $13,700 in royalty	-113,700	($100,000 Production budget plus overages [to share with investors])
Duplication costs:	-112,500	($2.25 Per tape)
Marketing costs:	- 75,000	($1.50 Per tape x 50,000 units)
Net to distributor:	$267,300	(Effective 47 percent fee)

What's happened with this standard structuring is that even with successful sales of 50,000 units the producer only makes $13,500 above and beyond the production costs. If he's raised the money through a

50/50 limited partnership the investors get paid back their $100,000 investment (the budget). Then the producer and investor split $13,500. Each gets $6,250. Big deal.

But look what wealth rains on the distributor. He pays duplication and marketing costs and nets $267,500. Yes, the distributor has overhead, sales staff to pay, and rent - but he still comes out way ahead of the producer and the investors, who've had their money at risk for a very long time.

The "Thirds" Partnership Deal (50,000 Units Sold)

Price of tape:	$ 19.95 Retail
	$ 11.37 Wholesale

Gross receipts: $568,500

Minus:
  15 percent distributor's fee
                    - 85,275

Duplication costs	-112,500	($2.25 Per tape)
Marketing costs	- 75,000	($1.50 Per tape)
Production budget	-100,000	
Net to partners:	$ 195,725	
Each partner:	$ 65,241	

If each party puts up $33,333 (a third of the production budget), then each one nearly doubles their investment. And they do so all at the same time. Meanwhile, the distributor is still rewarded with $85,000 as a fee for the distribution service, which can be applied to overhead and yield a profit.

I'm a producer. I value the product that my investors have allowed me to make. I'd like to see them recoup their investment, and then some. With a win-win deal, everyone gets results. And when the investor wins, there is every likelihood that they will invest again. When I set up my distribution company, I'll let you know. Until then, go get 'em.

THE CHICKEN OR THE EGG: FINANCING ISSUES

You're making a painting. You start with a sketch, an outline. You add some general colors, and you begin to add definition. Finally, you do the details, the highlights. The truth is you really start everywhere at once because you have to see the finished product in your mind's eye before you even start.

Producers are confused about where to start. "Do I look for distribution first? Or do I look for financing?" You look for both simultaneously.

I am currently putting together a series of six one-hour programs for television and home video. This documentary series is best suited for PBS broadcast, and then will be packaged as a six-part set for home video. The series will be promoted as an "event" with a book, audio and home video release, all timed day-and-date with the television broadcast. There is foreign sales potential as well. (This model is akin to The Civil War, the recent series that was literally a multi-media event, with simultaneous home video, book and broadcast release dates.)

Production financing for such a project comes from many sources. Here's how you start.

The Value of A Good Name

The first step is lining up "name" actors (recognized men and women that have some popularity with viewing audiences), because obtaining distribution is critical. Name actors are what will interest home video distributors. In turn, their sales to the home video buyers will be easier with recognizable names. Most consumers will hear or read about the programs (before they actually see them), and names will entice them to tune in or purchase the video, book or audio. So the first thing to do is secure name talent.

Not so easy. Because without financing or distribution in place, why would actors (or their agent) even want to talk until a "serious" offer can be made? Normally they wouldn't unless: (1) they believed in the project (and they do), and this is where quality helps; and (2) we had a track record, and they believed that we'd be able to pull it off (they do). No star wants to lend their name to a project that may not succeed. Talent puts you into a position to get "serious" with distributors and investors.

The Relationship Between Broadcast and Home Video

A broadcaster is very important because PBS exposure, for example, is a kind of "theatrical release" for a home video. A nationwide broadcast can capture enormous publicity, which in turn sells video cassettes. While we may not be able to count on PBS for cash (they take years to find sponsors to underwrite programming), we may be able to get a broadcast date if the series was offered to PBS at a very low price. (Start to see how all this fits together?)

Okay, now a brief recap. Stars are interested in the project, but not signed. PBS is interested in the stars and the project. Several home video companies are ready to negotiate. This brings us to the Book Deal and the Audio Deal.

Book Deal

Our book agent tells us that he knows three or four publishers who are willing to give us an advance on a companion book to the series. These advances range from very large amounts to very small sums and are based on whether PBS airs the show locally or nationally.

Audio Deal

The same thing goes for the audio cassette deal. The audio company, however, believes that the talent involved is the main driving force for audio sales. They like the possibility that a companion book may be published, because a book's penetration into stores may help to leverage an audio cassette with the same title. Audio is a small piece of the financing pie, but every little bit helps.

Pay and Basic Cable

We are also approaching the cable networks. If they give us a license fee for the program, it may take up any shortfall from the home video company. Then we could forgo a PBS broadcast. And even if the series airs less on cable than on PBS and reduces public awareness, the objective is to get the series. This is another possible scenario.

Foreign Sales

There are some foreign television and home video sales to be made with the series, if according to our foreign sales rep the names are recognizable internationally. These names will also have to work in the U.S., which is the primary market for the program. Foreign pre-sales (to home video and television) may make up as much as 40 percent of the financing.

Time for another recap. Each market represents a possible piece of the financing puzzle. Everyone is interested, but won't commit until the others do. It's a matter of getting everyone ready to say "yes" then closing all the deals at the same time. Broadcast and home video distribution deals will lock the stars.

Investors

Distribution and broadcast deals will bring in financing, because they will provide comfort to any investors if we still need their money to cover production cost. With distribution in place, investors can be approached. Their involvement will be predicated on the question, "Who's distributing the program?" It's unrealistic to expect anyone to invest until that question is answered. It's most likely that investor money is going to come after distribution is in place at the tail end of the financing maze. (Most producers unknowingly begin looking for investors. It's very, very difficult to close deals for the reasons just mentioned.)

If, however, we sell off all the rights (home video, pay TV, all foreign rights), there may not be any upside (positive reason) for an investor. That is if we receive advances for these rights in order to finance the series, that may be the only money we (and the investor) will ever see unless the series is a big hit. That's a risky proposition and may not offer enough upside for an investor. The ideal situation is to sell as few rights as possible to raise production financing (and assure distribution), but not so much that there's no upside left for an investor.

One way to piece it all together is to selectively sell off territories. Pre-sell U.S. to home video and television, and then pre-sell foreign rights in England, Japan or France. Then take in investors. The upside for the investors are the unsold territories, such as Italy, Spain, Germany, Australia and a number of other key territories. The investors will look to those territories (and overages, if any) as their primary source of recoupment.

Contributions

There are also people who may want to support the series with a non-profit donation. Some people like the content and inherent message in a series. In order to take in non-profit contributions, we have to financially structure the series as a non-commercial project. (What that means is that we can't have any investors. The minute we accept non-profit money, we can't also have "profit participation" for investors. It's one or the other. Although some producers have played it both ways, we won't. Get your lawyer's opinion on this matter before proceeding.) We sometimes receive individuals' funds indirectly through a non-profit organization. The contributor gets a tax benefit and writes a check to the non-profit foundation, which deducts a five percent administration fee and then writes a check to us.

Summary

A lot is involved but if you know the true potential of your project and understand what elements leverage other elements, you can save a lot of time. You put your effort in those areas that will produce the greatest result. You identify the players and understand their motivations for either licensing, advancing, pre-buying or investing in your program. We're still in the midst of putting this one together, and significant progress has been made in a few short weeks. I'll let you know when it's in the bag. Until then, now you go get 'em.

PRODUCTION

DIRECTING MY WAY OUT OF A PAPER BAG

Directing actors is one of the most exciting and stimulating collaborative parts of the filmmaking process. I love it! If you get a good script, and cast it well, you are 80 percent of the way there!

The Monster in the Paper Bag

Fear. That's the big thing. A director friend of mine told me that he's always terrified but that he uses the energy from his fear to move forward and get things done. He said that all directors are like that. It's just what you do with the fear. Hmm.

Yes, I can relate to that. Since I've recently written a feature script (based on my novel) that I want to direct, I have come face-to-face with the fear that he's talking about. In a moment of honesty, I took a look at my own directing skills and saw they were lacking. Where I was most stuck, most fearful, was working with "actors." For the past several years I have taken the bull by the horns and enrolled in a whole lot of courses and workshops in Los Angeles to work out my own directing process.

I was surprised to learn, having met many working directors in these workshops, that most of them are afraid of actors. It's nothing new! Now we are not afraid of producers, DPs, producers, special effect artists or even makeup artists. But then why actors? I think my fear came from not really understanding how they do what they do and how to direct them to do it better.

Now I don't mean the kind of directing that calls out "make it bigger," or the "when you get to this chair fall down in it and begin to cry" school which is called result-oriented directing. I mean the type of directing where you help create an authentic moment, an event which you record with a camera.

I realized that until I understood a lot more about how actors achieve these wonderful moments in real time that I would always have this unconscious area in my experience that would forever haunt me–especially when I had to direct a dramatic scene with an actor (or actually even a non-actor).

How Do Actors Do That?

I mean what is it that they do exactly? And how do they do it? And how do you talk to them? And if you get too touchy-feely and, God forbid, you upset one of them, might they rush off to their dressing room and put you behind schedule and overbudget? (Been there!) So that's why a lot of us hide behind the camera and fiddle around with the technical stuff. Actors make us damn uncomfortable. Give me a camera that won't talk back. Pity the director who gets into it with an actor and lets the whole crew know that "he really doesn't know what he's doing" anyway! You know what I'm talking about! The fear of being found out, that you don't know what you are doing is the fear that keeps us from learning. The double bind with our craft is that to learn directing you have to do it, learn on the job, hop in the fire. There's no other way.

I also had another agenda going. Being a film book publisher, I first set out to find what directing books are already on the market and I came up with a very short list. Sure, some authors write a chapter or two about it, but there are few books about directing actors in films! Most of the books talk about how to "direct the camera" and little attention is paid to the actor. (This, by the way, is the most common complaint made by actors. Most directors don't talk to them very much and those that do, do so in such a way that the actors don't know what the director wants.)

Workshops for Directors

The first thing I did was sign up for a number of directing classes and workshops in Los Angeles. I took four. Two were a complete waste of time as they were given by instructors who wanted to show off rather than teach the rest of us their techniques in an understandable manner. They kept the knowledge to themselves, as if it's a mystical art that only the initiated can learn. (Not!)

The other two classes blew me away and I am forever grateful to the instructors Judith Weston and Mark Travis. (So grateful, in fact, that I have published a book from each of them. Judith Weston's book is entitled *Directing Actors: How to Create Memorable Performances for Film or Television*. Mark Travis's is called *The Director's Journey: Collaboration between Director, Writer and Actor*.)

Judith's class puts the director (or producer) in acting situations so that you can feel (the absolute terror!) what actors go through. Mark has directors work with actors on scenes and then critiques the directors on their directing. Both give you a very extensive and full arsenal of techniques and approaches to getting the performance that you want. I am happy to say that my fear of directing actors is completely gone. I'm cured! In fact, I take absolute delight and thoroughly enjoy working with actors. I love what they do and how they do it!

My Approach

From the workshops I've taken over the past few years and the dramatic directing experience I've garnered, here is the process that works for me. Naturally you'll find your own style and approach but perhaps this will give you some ideas you can incorporate into your work. My approach is very fluid and organic. I don't necessarily go through all these steps as I will describe below, or even in the same order, but you'll get the idea.

The First Meeting

When the actors first come into the room, I make sure my energy is warm, open and enthusiastic and that I pay a great deal of attention to them. I am already prepared, my script pages are organized (I have copies for them), and I give them all the juice. I make sure I know their names.

After a minute of chitchat, we get settled and I tell them very generally what I am trying to do. It is very important to establish a relationship right at the top that they know <u>is a collaboration</u> and that you are looking to them to contribute to the material. I explain that I have some ideas about the script, but that it is really an <u>exploration together</u>. That sets the stage and most actors are tremendously appreciative of this approach. First, it lets them know that you appreciate their process and their art, and secondly, that you are very open to what they may bring to it. I tell them let's have fun and let's explore the material.

The First Read

Next I ask that they give me just a straight read of the script. I don't ask for a "flat" read nor do I ask them to get into it. They are not ready. This should be non-threatening just to get everyone familiarized at the same time with the script. We put our chairs in a circle so that everyone is equal. I do not direct from behind a desk nor is my chair different from theirs. (Everything you do needs to support the notion that you are all equal and in it together. The director's job is to watch and adjust and draw them out when they get stuck.)

Sometimes a word or an idea will need clarification after the first read. (If lines have to be changed, and you have the authority to do that, then you can do it now or make notes to change something later. If there are changes, they should be minor and of the nature that will help the actor do something better. But you do not want to even suggest that *"Hey, if you don't like something, we'll rewrite it"* or you'll may spend weeks in a hut like Francis Ford Coppola had to do on *Apocalypse Now* with Marlon Brando!

I don't like to get into a whole lot of psychological babble about what the whole piece is about (even if I am the one who wrote the script). If they ask a question like–*"What's my character going through here... I can't tell?"*–I answer with *"What do you think?"* Often their own answer is more interesting than my right answer and I am willing to go with their interpretation (unless it's really off base), and secondly, if it's

114

something they created, then it will be much more authentic. You can't talk an actor into believing something; she has to create it for herself. So I try not to ever tell actors how a character is "feeling" or "thinking" about something. I'd rather let them discover it and most of the time they will.

After we clear up a few basics, we may read it another time. I always find at least one thing to compliment them on, something that they are doing that I like. An actor will "save" that interpretation and probably give you another version of it again. So I might say something like: *"I really liked that little thing you did on this line, when you took that quick little glance at him when he wasn't looking."* If, on the other hand, I don't like the glance, I might say: *"You know, it's really great the way you avoid making eye contact during this speech. In fact, try doing that throughout and see how it feels."* Be supportive and you'll get what you want.

On Its Feet

It's expected that the actors have learned their lines for a day's shooting, so I expect that they know their lines for rehearsal as well. The next thing I do is get the scene up on its feet. I may give some very simple blocking and staging directions. It depends entirely on the scene. I may already have ideas about how close or far I want them from each other, how they move about, the visual dynamics of the scene, what's going on in the background and so forth, but I also like to see what comes naturally. Remember, we are creating an event here and if it comes about organically through their working it out, it will be much more authentic and believable.

The same principle applies here: if I like what I see, I keep it. What doesn't work for me, I replace with something else. Saying *"I really hate it when you..."* or *"It really looks stupid when you..."* is a sure way to stop the creative process. I say, *"Hey, here's an idea I'd like you to try..."* and use this to replace what I didn't like. Always keep it moving forward, always keep it positive.

Stuck Points

Sometimes you get moments that aren't working and you don't even know why. The more you work on it, the worse it gets. Something isn't clicking. What I do then is turn to theater games and exercises, or improvs, or finding "similar situations" in the actor's own experience.

For example, maybe the actor isn't connecting with the emotions you are looking for. You might, very gently, talk to them and ask if something similar ever happened to them. *"Did anyone really hurt you by leaving and not telling you why?"* (Now that's happened to all of us at some time.) I ask the actor to recall that moment and to tell me about it. Then I ask them to do the scene again. Usually the real experience they are recalling will <u>inform</u> the scene and it will come to life.

Or say it's an intimate scene. Here you've got two people (the actors) who just met each other and they are suppose to have been lovers for the last year. Well, the intimacy of their relationship isn't coming out because, in truth, they have no relationship. What do you expect? They just met. They are touching and looking at each other but it's not happening. They are not connecting.

I may have the actors do an exercise where they sit facing each other, and first one, then the other actor, (both with eyes closed) touches each other's face and describes what they are feeling. After about 10 minutes when they've each had a turn, we do the scene again, and whammo, the intimacy of the exercise comes alive in the scene.

Or I may try an improvisation. I'll tell them they can use or not use the lines in the script and they can make up lines if they like. Whatever they feel. Anything goes. Say they are two lovers and they are having a fight. To increase the dramatic tension, regardless of the text, I will tell one actor that their job is to get out of the room, and tell the other that their job is to keep the other person in the room. This will immediately change the staging and raise the stakes. Great ideas and moments are sure to emerge that can then be reincorporated into the scene when you return to the script pages.

The Process

The great thing I am discovering about directing is that if you keep it process-oriented then you make incredible discoveries about the material. It becomes a kind of musical jam session where you are exploring the limits and boundaries of the script's subtext. The director is the eyes and ears of the process and the final arbitrator of what will go before the camera. But you are all in this together.

Now frequently you won't have the luxury of a rehearsal which I think is an ultimate shame. Even if you have time for a little rehearsal, the moments and shared experience can quickly be brought back alive once the cameras roll. You'll have a much stronger and more authentic performance.

Blocking for the Camera

Once you've got the scene blocked out (and you may want to do this in collaboration with the camera operator), then you decide how you are going to cover the event with the camera. You discuss camera style and lighting.

Since you are always under the gun in terms of time, I try to figure out a master shot for the entire scene. I don't mean the conventional, nail-the-camera-down wide shot. My master shot may be a moving shot throughout the whole scene or on a dolly or handheld. I probably don't expect to ever use the whole shot and I may start and stop the camera, but I want to get as much of the *performance* as I can without stopping and starting because it has the real power to deliver. If you break a performance up a lot with the camera shots, you will get all kinds of inconsistencies and continuity problems that may take even longer to solve. It all depends on the complexity of the shot and the lighting, but if you start with the approach of *"How much of this can I cover with one shot in one lighting set up?"* you'll have a leg up on the time element. (Watch a Woody Allen movie. He does this all the time. He's going for the performance, not camera tricks.)

Shoot It with Hi-Band 8mm

Now if you are in rehearsal, it's sometimes valuable to shoot everything with a Hi-Band 8mm video camera. Don't worry about costumes, lighting, backgrounds or any production values. Just worry about how you are going to shoot it. Use the camera like a paint brush and try different shots with your actors once you've blocked out the scene. Make sure your cuts are going to work. When you get home, you can watch the tape which is really your video storyboard. You can prepare for the shoot by taking notes based on the video storyboard and have a much clearer idea of what you want to do.

Objectives and Motivations

If you give each actor something very specific to do as their objective, you will get a lot closer to getting good performances. *"Your objective in the scene is to get him to hug you."* (The lines may be doing something entirely different than this.) Now the actress has a whole pallet of ways to get him to do this from "seduce" to "demand" to "flatter." These are called "action verbs." Give your actor their objective, and one action verb (at a time) and see what happens. If you don't like the performance, try another action verb that may bring you closer to getting the result you want. Do not, I repeat, do not say to the actor, *"Okay, now walk here, and when you get to her, I want you to cry and hug her."* That's result-oriented directing. Don't get so panicked for time, like most directors, that you start directing like this. It takes away the collaborative process and puts all the burden on the actor who may or may not come up with what you want. They will do the result and it will probably look pretty bad.

The Five Elements

I have primarily been talking about directing actors and the director's job to create an event for the camera. Of course, the director also has other tools to work with:

•   The story structure and its dynamics, pacing and rhythm

118

- Lighting

- Casting

- Camera coverage

- Editing

Each of these areas merits a full discussion as well and the director must make many conscious choices to obtain the desired results. Naturally, the finished film or video will be the synthesis of what happens at every level to recreate the event. However most of us are more versed in working the technical side of directing than the human side. Hopefully this article has been useful to you in getting reinspired about the human dimension of our work. So with that in mind, go get 'em and happy rehearsal.

P.S. My two favorite directing coaches who will help you shape your own approach are Mark Travis (The Travis Group [818] 508-4600) and Judith Weston ([310] 390-1315). Their workshops are some of the most beneficial work I've done in years. They are rare resources for anyone interested in improving their directorial skills. Run, don't walk, to their doorway.

THE BALI SHOOT

Are there advantages in using low cost, high-end consumer Video 8 cameras for documentary production? That's what I was trying to find out late last year, when I borrowed a CCD-9 camera from Sony and two wireless microphones (one professional, one consumer) from Nady Systems to take on location to Bali, Indonesia. I planned to shoot a travel series pilot there.

I've produced many video and film documentaries. Like other producers, I've learned that whenever you bring lots of gear into a shoot the logistics can suddenly become more important than the subject matter. The things you want to shoot have to wait until you are set up for them. But with Video 8, I didn't have to worry about such things as white balance before shooting. Not having to give the camera much attention meant no one else did either, making it inconspicuous.

I Passed For a Tourist

I've made many trips to Bali during the last 20 years, so I knew to a great extent who and what I wanted to tape, and, to some degree, the conditions I would encounter. I had taken 16mm cameras into that country a decade ago, which caused quite a stir. Normally you need a press pass, and then are assigned a government liaison to make sure you don't film any bare breasts. This time I wanted to enter like a tourist, even though I had 40 rolls of Video 8 cassettes on me. Fortunately that tape is small, and I was able to spread it through my luggage, put it in my pockets, and pretty much hide all 40 hours of raw stock. Imagine trying to do that with 16mm film!

Rather than hide the camera during the customs process, I shot as we went through it. I taped the guards, the immigration officials, and, when our luggage came off the plane, the customs inspector. He was so self-conscious about being videotaped that he concentrated on making sure he looked official. He gave everything a cursory look, but didn't think to question my camera. Later, I saw many tourists with video cameras, and realized why he thought nothing of mine. (Perhaps my anxiety comes from working in New York and Los Angeles, where you need a permit to shoot professionally in your own home!)

Accompanying me was Geraldine Overton, a CBS staff photographer (now also my wife), who specializes in portraiture of television stars. Besides occasionally shooting Video 8 herself, she took stills that I planned to incorporate into the video program.

Sometimes we took a tripod; I later wished we had used it more often. It is extremely difficult to hold the Video 8 camera steady. It's so lightweight, only 3 or 4 lbs. with batteries. Unlike VHS cameras, it doesn't balance on your shoulder. A tripod is needed especially for panning. An amateur Steadicam JR for such cameras was introduced after my trip; I wish I'd had one with me.

I developed a hand-held technique for interviews when I didn't have a tripod. I started by composing a slightly wide head shot of my subject, and then while still shooting moved the camera away from me so that I could maintain eye contact with that person, keeping them relaxed. Occasionally I would look back into the camera to make sure it was level, making adjustments if necessary.

We also took a reflector, which twisted down into a large pizza-size carrying case. The villages in Bali are surrounded by high trees and dense foliage, and the midday equatorial light is dreadful. The reflector gave us a fill light when the sun was high.

Do's and Don'ts

I learned many things about shooting Video 8 through my experimentation. Turn off the automatic focus function. If there is something in the foreground and you are panning foliage, the automatic focus will go crazy–shifting back and forth with every move. The only time I used the automatic focus was in low-light situations where it was impossible to focus, and when I knew that there would be no other objects that would throw off the focusing function.

In many instances, I left the automatic iris on. If the subject was back-lit, I switched to manual to expose the subject and not the background. This is very hard to do correctly, especially if you are trying to match scenes within a sequence. The adjustments looked good through the viewfinder. However when I returned to Los Angeles and replayed some of the scenes, I learned that some were either under-exposed or overexposed. Perhaps a larger portable color monitor on location would have afforded me greater accuracy.

Here are some additional do's and don'ts:

• Although the camera is superb at shooting in low light, it will look decent only on the original tape. If you try to transfer or dub it down during editing, it will loose all color and appear very grainy. Nevertheless, the low-light ability of the camera can be a bit seductive. I shot classic Balinese nighttime shadow puppet performances, sitting directly beside the puppeteer as he worked his "actors" against a shadow screen. The sole illumination was from an oil lamp a foot or so above his head. This dim light, however, was sufficient to capture the audience, performing puppets, puppeteers and musicians in silhouette as I alternately shot from in front of and behind the screen.

• Shoot primarily close-ups and medium shots. Long shots won't hold detail unless they have strong graphic elements.

• Compose scenes with bright primary colors. This will focus the viewer's attention. Beef up your shot through strong colors and contrast.

• Again, beware backlit situations. The camera will read the background, so use the manual iris to correctly expose your subject's face.

• Keep your subject close to the camera when shooting dialogue scenes for maximum sound quality. I had some problems with the wireless microphones, so I really didn't get the chance to see what they could do.

•   Carry the camera so that it can be pulled out and turned on quickly. I used a woven basket backpack. In five seconds, I could be rolling. Sometimes I just carried the camera by its superbly designed hand strap. One day we climbed Mt. Batur, a volcano. We started in the dark at 4 a.m. with the camera recording only the sound of our huffs and puffs. It was hard enough to get ourselves up the side of the volcano, and that's when I appreciated how lightweight the camera is. My Video 8 tapes were one hour long. Each day, the camera, a few batteries, and two extra tapes were all I needed. In only a few instances, where I shot performances or rituals that were hours long, did I need more than one tape per day.

•   The camera's automatic functions, low weight, and ease of operation enable anyone to be your "second unit." I let local folks do some shooting so I could include myself in certain scenes. In typical 60 Minutes style, locals shot profiles or over-the-shoulder shots which I could eventually use as cutaways.

Can I Charge It?

Batteries were a major problem and a source of frustration. The international battery charger I brought took all night to charge a 30-minute battery and died after a few days. Our major concern was always whether we'd have enough power. I met a Frenchman who also had a Sony Video 8 camera, and he graciously took my 45-minute battery which is twice as heavy as a 30-minute version and charged it overnight. I tried to buy his charger but to no avail.

I finally found a 20 lb. device that converted Indonesian power to the U.S. standard, which was too big to carry with us. I used the device with my U.S. battery charger, and we would leave it in a bamboo house with electricity. This allowed me to charge a battery or two a day. Since I took four or five batteries with me, I would make sure they were all charged before heading out for extended trips. Batteries gave about two to three hours' worth of power, and they never lasted as long as the manufacturers claimed. Not using the automatic zoom or focus, by the way, saves power.

The camera, meanwhile, held up very well. I was sorry I couldn't get the wireless microphones to work. I don't know whether this was a function of the particular equipment I had, or if I just didn't test them well enough. There were situations where I really needed them. For example, recording dialogue in long shot showing two people in a crowded, noisy market was impossible. You had to be on top of the camera to be heard.

Upon returning to the States, I used a Video 8 VTR to transfer to Betacam selected scenes from 12 hours of tape. The resulting five hours of time-coded Betacam became my masters. I transferred this to 3/4" with time-code on window dubs, and edited it. The audio held up remarkably well. The video usually did too, unless it was poorly exposed, shaky, or shot with low-light.

Technically speaking, the most successful sequence was of women harvesting rice. Our presence made little difference to them. I was able to cover their work from every angle, including holding the camera high above their heads as they separated the rice from the chaff by beating it against boards. At 7 a.m., the light was excellent. The women wore bright colors, and the sound was great. All conditions were optimal.

In contrast, one of the most memorable moments in Bali made for unsuccessful images. We were at a special religious ceremony where village priests performed rites by which ancestral spirits blessed newborns. Incense smoke spiraled up toward a full moon. Women chanted and a gamelan orchestra (whose music I describe below) played gently in the background. Villagers sat beneath huge altars adorned with offerings and prayed while priests sprinkled water on them.

The only light sources were a single incandescent tube located high in one of the altars, flaming incense, and the full moon. Although I could capture all the images, there wasn't enough light to make it through the transfer process. The addition of a small camera light would have helped, but would have been inappropriate. The secret of such shoots is striking a balance between ideal technical conditions and being invisible and unobtrusive.

By the way, gamelan music indigenous to Indonesia includes the deep low tones of gongs and the high-pitched sound of flutes. Its dynamic range can be difficult to record without distortion, but it came out remarkably well on Video 8's audio track.

The Future

About half of what I shot under the best of conditions was acceptable quality for broadcast. My next trip to exotic lands will include some lights, a portable generator for charging batteries, the Steadicam JR and I hope a Hi8 camera. More gear will probably mean adding another person to the crew, which will impact on what is being documented. Nevertheless, these added elements are important to get professional quality.

Another key ingredient to this kind of production is low-cost, high quality graphics and effects. In terms of basic shooting, however, my Bali experiment proved to me that the Video 8 format, properly used under ideal conditions, offers major advantages for documentary production. It's an essential piece of the desktop video puzzle.

ZEN & THE ART OF STEADICAM JR

I returned to Bali and Java with a remarkable piece of gear (we videographers do love gear) which I hoped would bring a transcendental quality to my subject matter and allow me to spend less time shooting and more time just "be-ing." It worked.

It was a whole new kind of visual language. I had a sense of freedom, unrestrained movement, and a spirit-like point of view, and I knew that the tape I was shooting would convey it all. Moving with a Canon Hi8 A-1 Mark II mounted on a Steadicam JR, I walked around the world's largest Ninth Century Buddhist monument, and shot its 400 life-size Buddhas and nearly two miles of bas-reliefs depicting the life of the Enlightened One.

I was on a trip to Java and Bali. Although I'd been to Bali frequently since 1970, this time had special significance. Not only was I there to try out the Steadicam JR, but also to find adventure and capture some compelling video. Geraldine, my wife, is a photographer. Each day we would plan what we hoped to shoot, but often we wound up simply going on impromptu adventures with friends–Indonesian painters, shadow puppeteers, or shaman.

Steadicam JR is a wonderfully designed gadget, specially created for lightweight camcorders. It took some time to initially rig the camera to the Steadicam platform, even though the instructions are very thorough. Maybe it's because the camera and rig just feel so darn strange at first–even when they're balanced correctly.

Los Angeles-based Cinema Products Corporation manufactures and sells Steadicam JR. They also supply a terrific padded case for it that will also fit the camera you choose to mount on it. Although I thought it would take some time getting the rig unfolded, plugged in, and turned on, it really wasn't bad–15 seconds and I was rolling. I incorrectly assumed that once you get the camera balanced you're set. Instead I found that you do have to tweak the rig occasionally, which is painless. One hand holds the camera and the other gently turns or tilts a small ring under the base of the platform that floats the camera in the intended direction. The human body and arms do the rest. It is a great adventure to be able to keep both eyes open and see everything around you while also viewing and composing your shots on the rig's liquid crystal display (LCD), rather than squinting one-eyed through a viewfinder as you try not to stumble.

The Tai Chi movements I learned years ago suddenly came in handy. "Ward off with right hand," "stork spreads wings," and "carry tiger to the mountain" far better describe the kinds of Steadicam moves you can make than "pan left and tilt" ever could. I never did, however, get very comfortable with the toggle switch in front of the handgrip that turns the camera on and off. I frequently bounced the shot trying to stop tape. At four pounds, the Canon A-1 Mark II is about the heaviest camcorder that will go on a Steadicam JR–allowing only a small battery. I thought this might be a severe handicap but it turned out not to be. Initially, as with every new mount, there is the tendency to try to move too fast, which I did. (Look ma, no hands!)

The nice thing about the Steadicam JR is that it gives you the ability to get more involved with the activity you are shooting. For one thing, people can see your face and you don't have to look at the screen all the time. Documentary purists believe that success is measured by how little your camera influences what you are shooting. They know that the act of observing affects the observed. Others, however, have no qualms about "directing" and manipulating documentaries. I draw from both schools, but feel I've discovered the seedlings of yet another approach. I'm not quite sure I'd recommend it for producing "traditional" documentaries or industrials, but I do feel this approach can reveal profound personal insights.

Steadicam JR lets you participate. Video has the same effect that Polaroids had in primitive cultures–instant feedback. Often a small group gathered behind me to watch the images on the magical LCD. Once all my subjects ended up behind the camera, resulting in an empty scene!

Even though Steadicam lets you participate, you still must make a choice about what and what not to tape. And since you are experiencing and recording simultaneously, you don't always know if what you are shooting has any long-term value. Part of you must think so, however, or you wouldn't be pushing the button. Consider: What we chose to shoot we automatically imbue with meaning. Further meaning comes in post, selecting, editing and juxtaposing our recordings of reality. This is the part where we try to make sense of it all.

One technique I experimented with to capture impressions of Bali and Java was writing down daily incidents and moments as if they were a dream. The important thing was to take this attitude when recording these experiences. Often we may not understand their meaning and value until we've turned these gems over in our minds and let every facet reflect.

"Something here invites the unconscious to come out with great intensity," I wrote. "I feel it every time I'm here. There is a thin membrane between dream and reality. Sometimes you are not quite sure what side you are on. Reality is our own selection of images projected on our own internal screen. Our unconscious feeds our inner projector with images that instruct and call attention to what we need to learn. Sometimes we are not always paying attention, so we'll have to sit through the same experience again to get it."

In using Steadicam JR, I gave up the sense of distance I get when looking through a camera. I entered reality with both eyes wide open. The establishing shot is an objective shot, a kind of "witness," which tells us where we are going. If you think–"oh, I've been too tight, I better make an establishing shot," you've just lost it. You are no longer in the experience.

In a foreign country, the senses can often be overwhelmed. Everything is alive and seems relevant. With newness, there is no desire to filter out what you are seeing. Nothing is taken for granted, it's all important, and it all comes rushing in. The mind tries to process and record it all. You are awake like never before–eyes burning, ears ringing, skin tingling, nose aroused, and heart pumping. Everything is happening right now.

When I was a young filmmaker, I had hoped to make my living by recording and sharing my experiences. Using Steadicam JR returned me to that feeling. It goes where you go. Sometimes you follow it, but it's very difficult to synthesize and organize what you are shooting as you go. This is especially true when you are a stranger in a strange land, and you don't know what's happening next. If you are shooting a "how-to-change-a-tire video," you could easily edit it in the camera. That's because you already know how to organize the material. Life's not like that, it doesn't unfold in neat three-act plays.

What if we let the Steadicam JR float into the experience guided by the unconscious, and we just followed? Don't think, don't pre-edit, just be. A Zen approach to Steadicam taping. To shoot successfully you have to "be." You have to let go into the experience. When you do, remarkable things happen. My ideas in this area were encouraged recently while screening the first episode of a PBS series for Spring '92, titled Millennium.

I loved the show, specifically because the narrator struggled to make sense of his own journey amid alien cultures, and to discover indigenous tribes and their wisdom. It appeared as if much of what "just happened" was taped and later edited to make sense, but there really wasn't much of a "story." He was thrown off-balance, and so was the viewer. I felt this was a very honest approach. You come away from this program with disturbing questions that haunt you the next day.

That off-center feeling is what it was like to be in Java and Bali. Not everything I wrote down was covered by Steadicam footage, but combining those images with narration will reveal many things. The piece still needs to be edited. I am like a tightrope walker, shooting with a Steadicam JR, trying to refine the process. Now it's your turn. Shoot and let me know what you find out. Until then, go get 'em.

IN FRONT OF THE CAMERA
WITHOUT A NET

Sometimes I find myself in situations where the best thing to do is to just give up. I relax, knowing that in a short time, it'll all be over. Here's one of those times.

When I was asked to appear on a local television show for a series on entrepreneurs, I should have asked more questions. I guess I was flattered. But no... I plunged ahead and thereby came up with material for this article.

On the phone the producer and I agreed that I would discuss the subject of "How to <u>Produce</u> the Project You Love" with two women hosts for this their second television show of a series on business and entrepreneurs

I arrived at the studio at the agreed upon 9 am, and the producer was nowhere in sight. I examined the gray walls and filthy floor of the "green room." The women hosts arrived but still no producer. I went through the notes I'd written in advance, showed the hosts the "case study" products I'd brought, and as we planned who would do what, I learned I was the *first* guest they'd ever had. (Hmm, a little miscommunication from the producer.)

Rushed, tense and in a tailspin, the producer arrived, gave me a cursory "hello" and then she went off toward the control room. I chased her down the hall and showed her the videos I had brought for "roll-ins" as we discussed. She decided against using them.

On the stage there were three chairs set on a raised platform against a dark blue curtain, almost the color of my suit. (I began to imagine my appearance as a decapitated head floating in space.) The producer told me to sit in the chair in the middle. I quickly realized that I would have to twist back and forth every time I was asked a question by a different host. From the camera's point of view, this might look very strange to television viewers. I politely suggested that I sit on either side and address both hosts to eliminate the head turning. The producer would have nothing to do with this suggestion. I would sit where I was told. ("Okay fine, just let it go. It's not your show, Michael. You're the talent.")

Two minutes before the cameras were to roll, the producer told me to discuss "How to <u>Finance</u> Your Project." I said we had already discussed what I was to do and that I'd prepared something different. She said, "No, you'll discuss financing" and then threw a curve ball to the hosts. "You do the intro and you do the close." Completely opposite of what they had just prepared to do.

The stage manager's hand counted down, "Five, four, three, two, one," and the red lights went on.

At this point, there was nothing to do but let go. *It's not my show. Let them do what they want.* I was determined to some energy going with the hosts, forget about the cameras, the bad lighting, the bad staging, the rude producer, and the fact that I'd now rather be cleaning out my sock drawer.

The interview went well. I used the props I'd brought. I connected to the hosts who I sincerely believed were interested in what I had to say. When the show was over, the producer stepped between me and the hosts, told me she had only two minutes and had to talk to the hosts. She literally turned her back to me and said "thank you." I never received a copy of the tape which she promised me.

I understand all too well that producing is really a job you easily prepare for. It's on-the-job training. More and more producers and would-be producers are walking into studios unprepared for the job. You just have to leap in and do it.

However there are two approaches. The first is exemplified by the producer above. Afraid to show what she doesn't know, she put up a smoke screen of rush, importance and rudeness. She kept people away by her confrontational manner. No one could challenge her and she would keep control. The second approach is much more vulnerable. Simply admit what you don't know and seek help from the crew and staff around you. Use whatever resources you can to figure it out. Unfortunately many first-timers go about it from the first approach and close themselves to learning. They are not building a support team for the future but rather burning bridges.

Tips for Producers

Hopping back behind the camera (where I am more at home), I'd like to offer these tips for working with non-professional actors (who more and more producers of cable, documentaries, public affairs, or interview shows are having to contend with).

Having just been in the hot seat, I respect the value of these tips much more:

• Create an environment (physical and emotional) that will make your talent comfortable. There is no formula here just good sense. Be sensitive to each individual's needs. Maybe a relaxed chat about what you expect of them will help. Maybe they'd like a drink of water. Maybe a tour of the studio will be helpful. The sooner they feel at home, the better the results.

• Enroll the crew to introduce themselves, preferably with a handshake. Be warm and informal. Include everyone as part of the team. Make it a group effort as quickly as possible.

• Wait to sit the talent in front of the camera until your lighting setup is almost done. Sit them down and briefly tweak the lights. You do not want them in anticipation too long, yet you do want them feeling comfortable in front the camera before you start.

• Adjust the light so they won't squint. They can also look into the light briefly (with their eyes closed!). This will close down their pupils and make them less likely to squint when they do open their eyes.

• Talk to them and they to you in normal speaking voices to get sound levels. Be playful if that's appropriate. Keep it natural.

133

• Let them know you have plenty of tape and it's cheap. That there's no problem if they make a mistake or wish to do something over again. Say "We've got lots of time" (even if you don't). If you're relaxed, it will help them relax (here's where pre-production planning and doing your homework really helps).

• If they do make mistakes, blame it on something technical so they won't get flustered. People try hard to please. The harder they try to please the more unnatural their appearance.

• Have releases signed <u>after</u> the taping. It may be too confrontational before to read legalese and only makes the taping "more significant."

• When interviewing someone, make them feel and let them know you are on their side. Let them know you may interrupt them or redirect them from time to time.

Tell them you will play "devil's advocate" from time to time. You will challenge them as if you <u>don't</u> believe them (even though you do). This will get a rise in the energy of their response. Experiment with this but make sure they know it's part of the "game." Some talent really do well rising to the occasion of the game and the results are great. Other people don't get it and this technique may not work.

You have to feel and intuit what's going to work best for each person. If you make time to chat with them before the cameras roll, you can predetermine your approach.

• If possible, give your talent something to do. Give them a prop or ask them to do some action that they normally do. We can actually learn more about someone by watching what they <u>do</u> rather than listening to what they say.

• When slipping a lavaliere mike down a woman or a man's shirt, have someone of the same sex handle these duties. Make fun of this little job. It's kind of intimate to have a wire slipped under your clothing so make a game of this as well. Keep the talent relaxed!

• It's the job of the interviewer to focus so much energy on the guest that they get into the material and forget that they are on television.

When the interviewer is not seen by the camera, I like to position the interviewer as close to the lens axis as possible so that you see more of the guest's eyes. This is more intimate for the viewer. The interviewer can sit directly under the camera lens as well. Experiment. I don't suggest that the guest look into the camera. They may get so nervous that they lose naturalness.

• The interviewer should not break eye contact nor look at a monitor to direct the shot. Taking attention off the person answering the question will appear as a slight break or loss of attention in the guest's dialogue. Get the shot set up and have someone else direct a camera move if necessary. Or if the interviewer is also the director, he/she can tap the camera operator if a move or reframing is desired.

• Guests do not know whether or not they should use their hands. I think hands increase expressiveness. Even if you are in a close-up, you can feel more energy if they are encouraged to use their hands. If they hold their hands together, tension gets stored.

• At the end of the interview, thank them for their contribution. And tell them how good it went and how much you appreciate them regardless of whether you think you will use the material or not.

In Front of the Camera Techniques

If you are ever called for your "15 minutes of fame," here are some techniques you may wish to employ for your own relaxation. (I used every trick in the book to chill out during my recent appearance!)

• Get to the studio early. Park, relax, have some tea or juice. (No milk. It clogs up the nasal passages, and is sticky in the mouth.)

• Chant or hum low notes in the car. This relaxes the back of the throat. When the lights and camera go on, your throat will naturally tighten, but not as much if you do some singing exercises first.

• Before the lights go on, sit where you are going to sit during the interview. Or stand at the podium in the room where you will speak. Imagine it filled with people or cameras. When you actually get in place for the taping (or presentation), you won't register the surprise you might otherwise feel because you will have pre-visualized it.

• Walking to the set, or sitting in the chair, <u>feel the earth under your feet</u>. Make a conscious effort to stay connected to the ground. Stay in your body. It will support you. Do not get stuck in your head. Use your hands. Don't lose the power and expressiveness of using your whole body to communicate.

• Don't wear stripes with 45 degree angles. No ties or blouses with these designs. Don't wear pure white. It's too bright for the television camera. Bring several selections of clothes. Once you inspect the environment, you and/or the director can decide what you should wear.

• Drink water before you go on.

• Go to the bathroom before you go on. Be careful. (When I was a segment producer, I had a male guest who thought he could make a pit stop 30 seconds before he was to go on a live talk show.) He got away from me at the rest room door. When he came back, I noticed he'd wet himself. But I didn't dare let on or we'd have no guest. I grabbed the floor director's head set and told the director only to do close-ups of the guest. The studio audience may have been aware of what had happened, but the home audience never knew and the guest stayed cool. Whew, a close call!

There are probably dozens of other techniques you can call upon, however the thing to remember is that you are working with other human beings, complex creatures with a myriad of feelings and emotions. The closer you can get to what makes them tick, the better your footage and the more interesting it will be to your viewers. Awakened by these profound insights, I encourage you to try them out. If you have some you'd like me to try out, write me a letter.

Until then, go get 'em.

WHAT DO EXECUTIVE PRODUCERS DO, ANYWAY?
PART I

I started my career in the trenches (writing, shooting and editing). In this article, I am probably trying to figure out what I've been doing during many of the last few years.

Do they get the money? Do they put in their own money? Just what do executive producers do, anyway? Nobody really seems to know the answer to this question (except perhaps executive producers and they aren't talking). The executive producer credit is usually prominently displayed first (or last) in a video production; no doubt they're important folks.

We know what the producer and director do, they produce and direct. But the whole art of executive producing is rather mysterious, so let's shed some light on it.

Meta-Management

Executive producing is the art of "meta-management." I use meta in the sense of its dictionary definition of "standing above or behind," the way an executive producer stands behind the producer and director.

Besides obtaining the money (however that happens!), there are other aspects to the executive producer's job. The most important of these is people. And whenever there are people, there are relationships. The management of these relationships falls into the executive producer's domain. This is also true of directors and producers, but for executive producers it's on another level–the level of meta-management.

The executive producer is responsible for all the key relationships. On one side, you have the business relationships between financiers, facilities, distributors, marketers and broadcasters. On the other side, you have creative relationships. The executive producer may hire the

137

producer, director and writer. The concept for the program may be something that the executive producer found or developed. The executive producer is often the first person to get the project financed, fully packaged and made. (In some instances, producers bring their packages to executive producers to get them made.)

In my most recent work, I developed concepts with a broadcaster. Some originated with the broadcaster; others I found. Some we selected, developed and then "green-lighted" for production together.

Money, Money, Money

People in our business can't seem to say the M word enough. When we say that the executive producer "handles the money," what does that mean? It means that he or she is responsible for the money. It doesn't necessarily mean that the executive producer puts up the money. Rather, the executive producer is responsible for the project's financial status and for delivering the program on time and within budget. For this, of course, he or she looks to and depends on other people.

Since you depend on other people, as a producer I've learned that it's very important to make sure that all the agreements are in place. This is also the executive producer's job, but again at a meta-level. Without agreements people get crazy. I know you know what I mean. We've all been in situations where agreements weren't clear. We know how terrible that feels. All the energy goes into thinking about who's getting what.

The first thing I do is create clear, written agreements with my creative partners in projects. These agreements are usually a short letter or deal memo (which may later be expanded into a long-form agreement) stipulating what the project is, each partner's responsibilities, fees, payment terms (usually triggered by performance), credits and profit participation (if any). When people start to work on a project and things aren't spelled out for them, they may feel they are on very thin ice. This makes for very insecure and inauspicious beginnings. The first thing an executive producer does is clarify the relationship in basic terms: money, money, money. Once done, there's a sigh of relief, and the creative work begins wholeheartedly.

I don't often get into the fine points (in legal jargon the boilerplate) of an employment or rights acquisition contract. That's for the lawyers to do. And they may go back and forth for days, weeks, or months. That's their job, and I want no part of it. I want my relationship with the director, actor, or producer to be "creative." And so do they. You can't be negotiating with someone out of one side of your mouth, while trying to instill inspiration, confidence and security out of the other.

Nevertheless, the executive producer is called in for things that others deem as unpleasant–such as negotiating, or renegotiating, or simply saying what needs to be said. I've been held up (as in "this is a hold up") by disgruntled facilities and freelance directors. Misunderstandings about money are common in our business. Here are some variations on a theme that executive producers frequently encounter. And it's always about money, money, money.

A shoot or postproduction schedule runs longer than anticipated. Even though the original employment deal was a "buyout" (a flat fee for the entire project), the director (non-union) wants more money. The director took more time than expected, then held up the video masters as leverage (until he was advised by his lawyer otherwise). An out-of-town production facility and staff producer didn't get along. The producer refused to pay for poor quality work. The facility was not going to send the camera originals until they got a check significantly larger than what was agreed upon.

The producer in both cases left the job incomplete. Call in the executive producer! I refused to be held up for ransom. But I did agree to be fair and that we'd work out an agreement we could both live with. And I'd do it fast. But only after the masters were returned. How do you do this?

You have to get into the head of the party that feels wronged. I've been there, so I know what they are feeling. They are scared they are going to get burned. The first order of business is to assure them through your own personal integrity that they will not. I say something like this:

"Look, the first thing I want you to do is return our tapes by Federal Express. When you've done that, call me back and I'll be here to renegotiate your fee. I'll probably pay you most of your overages (over budget items), but you'll have to justify the expenses to me. You'll probably get less than what you're asking for, however, but I'll end up paying more than what was agreed at the outset. We'll both give up something. The hassle we're having now will go away, and we'll both feel good about the outcome."

It works when you set up a context for both people to agree. Both parties do agree, and disputes are settled. From this foundation of trust, it's not uncommon for people to work together again.

I am unwilling for messes to persist for very long; I don't like the feeling. I was willing to go to the effort, however uncomfortable, so that the party that was feeling wronged (for whatever reason) wouldn't be hurt financially and we'd get closure right away. Even though things had gone askew and there was some misunderstanding, we'd both come out of it with a good feeling. To have a successful career in video, you want to create good will and long-term relationships.

To accomplish that I had to not only know my needs, but the other person's as well. This comes from knowing what you want. You can't get it if you don't know what it is. Then, somehow (naturally), the getting comes rather easily. You may have to guide, teach, cajole or demand. But you know what you want and need and can communicate that to others, you'll get it.

Don't Cross This Line

There is a line, however, which is not to be crossed that I am learning about and have experienced recently. That line has to do with where the executive producer's job starts and stops before it enters someone else's sphere of responsibility. If you hire a producer, then the producer's job is to produce. If an executive producer has to step into producing (or directing or writing or whatever), then this is an acknowledgment that they've hired incorrectly. The first job of the executive producer is to hire correctly. If you don't do it correctly, it's time to get another day job.

When you've hired someone, you've already agreed on what they will do. Their domain has been established. You have to live with that decision unless things really go off track. Otherwise, you have to back off. Your job is now to be as supportive as possible, and to bring your talents, abilities and insights into play only when they are required or requested. But, most of the time, you don't want them to be required.

That was a hard one for me to understand. "What do you mean you don't want to hear from me?" screamed my wounded ego. "Because, you dummy, you've already hired the best people to deliver the goods. It's not your job," I replied.

I frequently want to do something, just to make sure I still can. But that's not doing the job I have now. Now I realize, "If you want to direct, then direct!" Executive producing is not the place to be confused about what hat to wear.

To be continued. . .

Meanwhile, raise some money and executive-produce.
Now go get 'em!

WHAT DO EXECUTIVE PRODUCERS DO, ANYWAY? PART II

In the last article, we discussed the mysterious art of executive producing and the responsibilities of managing people, money and relationships, of creating agreements, and of production intervention. Now there's more!

Setting Limits

The executive producer has the final word. He or she is responsible for every aspect of the production and is held accountable to his or her employers, be they broadcasters, home video companies or corporate entities. Every project has restrictions, which may relate to budgets, schedules, formats or content. The executive producer (and everyone who works with him or her) must also conform to these limitations. The limits must be clearly defined for everyone. If you or your employees ignore these limitations, you won't work again. They'll take away your "executive producer card," since you are the one your employer hired to keep everything on track.

Giving Rope

Concurrent with the role the executive producer is asked to play in "limiting" the perimeters is another role that requires that the producer get the greatest contribution possible out of the cast and crew.

I try to give the people who work with me a lot of room, lots of rope. This has been difficult to do sometimes because I also want to feel in control of my projects. Yet I also want to see how much responsibility someone can handle.

I've been given jobs where I had lots of responsibility. I've had jobs where I wasn't given any. In the former, my bosses got ten times what they paid me. In the latter case, they got no more than what they required. Most people who work in our business do so because they like work that allows them to express their creativity as fully as possible.

If you let people do more, they will, and if managed the project's quality will exceed its budgetary price tag. Ours is not factory work. In fact, it may be one of the last businesses in the country where there is still a work ethic. People in our business care about the quality of their work and will deliver quality because their own integrity calls for it (regardless of what they're paid). Producers, directors, writers, crews and actors want to excel. They want to create a "break" for themselves, and want the chance to really perform. When I've got funding for a project, I'm delighted to offer an opportunity. I know that if I give creative people their shot, nine times out of ten their work will go beyond my expectations. If you allow people more responsibility than they've had, you have the chance to really see them do something terrific. If you confine them, the results will be restricted. Your employer doesn't care about how you get the job done or what philosophy you use. They want results. As an executive producer, you have to deliver, on time and on budget.

This means you have to trust your people and to communicate clearly what the limitations are. And at the same time, you must trust them to do more, to give more, and to produce the greatest results they can. An executive producer has to be prepared, from time to time, to pull everyone back, to remind them of the limitations. It's not a free-for-all. (Sometimes you have to yell "Stop!" If you don't, you'll still be working on it on the due date.)

Interventions

On one occasion, I had to intervene against a director's wishes after three days of shooting. We were out of tape and drop-dead tired. The crew had long gone home, and it was time to return the gear to the rental house. The director was holding onto my pant leg begging for "one more shot," as I dragged him out of the studio in the harsh reality of dawn. It broke my heart, but I had to say, "I'm sorry, but we're finished now."

Another time I required a producer to cancel several days of new shooting because I felt we had more than enough already in the can to finish a terrific show. I suggested we edit what we had and then see if we needed more. We didn't.

The Creative Process

The most important thing to realize about other people is that we all see things very, very differently. I mean that in the extreme. We take it for granted that just because we speak English we understand what everyone means. This is not so. This assumption can lead to enormous problems and frustration. If you start with the premise that humans perceive things very differently, then you can at least try to understand how other people think and work.

Creative Differences

Prior to most voice-recording sessions, you prepare a script. Then you go into the studio, and you follow the script. On one occasion when the talent also had final creative control of the project, the talent refused to use the script even though that person had a hand in writing it. The talent said, "I can't work this way. I have to see how I feel, and then just do it." No amount of cajoling was going to move that mountain. The path of least resistance was to go along with it. I could see that this was the way the talent worked, and that this was the way it was going to be. As executive producer, I had to relax and support the talent in being creative in the studio regardless of my own feelings that most people do not work this way and that it is very expensive. My role was to create a supportive environment so that we could get the best material from the session as possible.

Another example: The director is also the interviewer on a documentary. The show has already been rough-cut prior to the host shoot. We are to shoot a few lines of interstitial material with the host, which will connect the various segments. The cameras start rolling. Instead of going through the script, starting with the first paragraph and moving forward, the director begins interviewing the host. We are not getting any material that's been written! Twenty minutes later, I find a moment to interrupt. I ask the director to join me out of the room, away from the host and crew. I ask the director why no script material is being recorded and to please get to the script. I don't want improvisation. The director is enormously upset and defensive. The director said my interruption sabotaged a strategy the director was using to relax the host, and build up that person's confidence. She said we were getting what we needed anyway, even though it wasn't written. I disagreed. I said that not only was the host (an amateur) as relaxed as she was going to get, but that none of the material was usable as it did not fit into our approach to the documentary. The director didn't seem to hear me. I figured I'd really blown it. Not only were we not getting what we needed, but I had sent the director into an angry rage. Within minutes of returning to the cameras, the director started working on the script. We got what was written.

I'm still second-guessing myself on this one. Rarely do I interrupt shoots. Here I felt compelled to do so. Did I overstep my bounds? The director became enormously upset and felt betrayed. Yet I didn't believe we were going to get what we needed, so I intervened. That's the executive producer's prerogative. Sometimes you use it. Sometimes it's unpleasant.

Yet another example of how differently people work and think. I came to a documentary shoot to see how things were going. The director knew exactly what he wanted–in fact to such a degree that it was staggering. Not only had he previsualized every scene, but he knew exactly how much footage to shoot at the head of a scene for a voiceover. And he knew what he wanted the voiceover to say and how long it would run. He knew how he would cut it, he knew exactly what to shoot, and that's what he was doing. He was not overshooting coverage "just in case." I'm rarely that clear on how everything will go together, so I shoot somewhat more coverage. What he was doing was going so well there was nothing for me to do–so I left.

The executive producer is not the director, nor the producer. So the executive producer is not to direct or produce, but rather manage the work of the producer and director in the most supportive role as possible.

Here are some goals for executive producers to hold in mind:

- Cast the right people for the right jobs and as part of a team.

- Make sure abilities are complementary and not supplementary.

- Get as much creative work out of people as possible.

- Keep the team spirit alive.

- Give people "creative rope" when it will enhance the project.

- Make people feel good about what they are doing.

- Smooth the path for everyone. Play a supportive role.

- Be a leader and the final arbitrator. Provide the last word.

- Be the liaison between the financial, marketing and production groups.

- Anticipate problems and solutions.

- Hold the vision of the entire project from start to finish.

- Make sure the program is consistent with marketing and promotion goals.

- Learn how much or how little to be around.

Until next time, go get 'em.

PRODUCING TO MAKE A DIFFERENCE

In the beginning of my career, I felt the power of film and wanted to use it responsibly. Over 25 years later, I am still struggling to do meaningful, contributory work with the skills I've acquired. The greater my commitment to do quality work, the more possible it is.

Younger videographers take note: Stick with your original dream. It is possible! You may not get there in the first year, or the second year, or even the second decade of your career, but you will get there. Therefore it's important to choose subjects worthy of your time and effort.

Here I am deviating from my usual focus on marketing, distribution and financing. With this column, I thought it might be appropriate for us to reflect on what we hope to achieve with our experience, technical skills and financial resources.

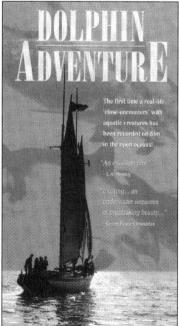

When I started making films (you remember them) at art school in the mid-Sixties, I saw film's potential to take us into altered states of consciousness, and to make social and political change. I told myself that I'd never make a TV commercial. And for more than ten years that was so.

In 1978, I made *Dolphin Adventure*, an hour-long documentary on inter-species communication between humans and dolphins that made a plea to end dolphin slaughters. Although it was shown on 33 networks throughout the world and at an International Whaling Commission meeting, it was only in recent years that Starkist and Bumble Bee promised not to buy tuna that was caught in a manner that killed dolphins. I felt a great sense of victory, and although there's certainly more work to be done about gill nets, I wrote my investors about the triumph and thanked them for their support.

But then my work took an unexpected turn in the Eighties. I got tired of the up and down (mostly down) emotional and financial curve of independent life. I was lucky to produce one independent short or feature documentary each year, and my learning curve was directly tied to these few projects. I wasn't learning unless I was producing and trying out new things. To top it off, someone sent me their resume listing hundreds of commercials and films they'd worked on. "Incredible," I thought. "Is this possible? Think of the learning!"

So I got some real jobs and went down paths I had no idea I'd ever pursue. I produced dozens of superficial segments for variety television. I produced nearly 100 political campaign spots for senatorial and gubernatorial races. I filled Showtime/The Movie Channel's pay-TV air with over 1200 promotional segments. At Vestron Video, I acquired, produced and/or developed more than 200 home video programs. That's a lot of product! I ended up replicating the resume I was so impressed by as an independent. But other than that, what did I have to put on my reel? Not much that made me feel really proud.

On the other, hand, the learning was fantastic. I spent tens of millions of dollars of other people's money learning. But the end result was simply a lot of entertaining stuff, a lot of persuasive and promotional programming.

When I think back, however, I am still most fond of *Dolphin*. Why? Because the result had some impact in saving dolphin lives. I feel this way although *Dolphin* still hasn't repaid all its investors after ten years, and Vestron Video programs have grossed over $60 million. My Vestron programs were basically diversionary entertainment. Other than the National Geographic programs, most don't seem to make a difference.

Since Vestron and Showtime weren't arenas where I could "produce to make a difference," I had to find other outlets for that side of myself. I did that through writing, lecturing and participating in organizations outside work. But I was divided and living two lives. My desire to contribute and my desire to earn a living were not integrated. (I knew visionary engineer Buckminster Fuller quite well before he died. I once asked him how to integrate one's ideals and work. I saw the enormous contributions he'd made, and he seemed to always be working at his vision. He told me not to fret, that sometimes you have to earn a living. That made me feel better.)

I think too often our attention is on how to earn a living, or how to gain more experience, or how to use a new piece of equipment. We forget the enormous power of our medium. This is a shame, because the world's in trouble and needs our expertise. Not that we have all the answers, but we can join with experts and help them communicate their ideas and solutions to the world's problems. They need us. We need them. And the world needs the contribution from both of us.

I'm not suggesting that we all quit the jobs we enjoy and that put meals on the table, but I am suggesting that we find ways to do something more with our skills and hi-tech equipment.

ECO, Earth Communications Office in Los Angeles and Nashville, is a consortium of about 1000 motion picture and television professionals: actors, writers, directors, producers, lawyers and others who are finding ways to get the environmental message into their work. Lots of actors, like Tom Cruise, Olivia Newton John, Rosanne Cash, John Ritter, and scientists, such as the U.N.'s Dr. Noel Brown and The Smithsonian Institute's Dr. Thomas Lovejoy, are participating.

ECO's members have an impressive list of accomplishments. They've enlisted every major motion picture studio in Hollywood to start recycling programs. ECO members have produced and distributed public service TV spots to hundreds of television stations and movie theaters, organized major awareness events, and drawn together environmental experts to speak on water, energy, recycling, pollution, the ozone, deforestation, the Amazon rain forest ("Big Green"), and many other environmental topics. Script writers get the message into sit-coms and soap operas. Record stars are including fact sheets on their CD jackets about things people can do to save energy and water. They are also demanding that their record companies stop wasting resources by manufacturing oversized CD packaging. You don't have to join ECO to start thinking about environmental and social issues, but in a short time ECO presentations inspired me about what I could do to make a difference.

A single person can make a difference. And media producers–with access to millions of people–can effect even greater change.

I've consulted with a number of organizations and quite often their approach to media is quite weak. After all, they are concerned with issues, and they may not be as experienced with creating "television events" as Greenpeace or The Sierra Club. There are organizations that you can work with and would welcome your experience. There are probably several just waiting for you to call.

In cooperation with these organizations and their experts, you can use your production and organizational experience to help them deliver their message. You can ask for donations of time, equipment and materials and get it because a lot of people–who don't know what to do–are just waiting to be asked. You could write news releases or articles, produce PSAs, news segments, electronic press kits or even documentaries for local and/or national broadcast. You could create training programs. Or help experts prep for and get on television. There's no end to how your experience could benefit getting the message out there.

At the beginning of each year, I review my goals. This year I made a specific "work" goal to "do well by doing good." Besides getting involved with ECO, I found an opportunity to produce six PBS specials that will also have home video distribution. Not only are the shows assured of being broadcast but they are "how-to" programs which empower people with information that will improve both their lives and the environment. I couldn't be happier. Not since *Dolphin* have I found an opportunity to earn a livelihood and produce to make a difference all at the same time. It feels great.

These are little things you can do. There are big things you can do. It all counts. I encourage you to look at your life and your resources and find an opportunity where you can produce to make a difference. Now go get 'em!

MARKETING

INFOMERCIALS: WHERE'S THE INFO?

Infomercials really have one purpose: to sell product. They may do this by entertaining and informing, but ultimately there's a "call to action." Orders must be taken, or you're out of business. Give the audience info during the infomercial, but leave them with the sense that there is more to be learned by purchasing your "product"–which may be videos, audios or books. Then deliver products loaded with information adding to their knowledge.

I said I'd never work in television, never work in New York (or Los Angeles), and never do an infomercial. Never say never. It doesn't work.

But why infomercials? I hate infomercials. I don't watch infomercials. I'd never order anything from an infomercial. I don't trust them. I think they are manipulative. They are snake-oil's first cousin. I don't like 'em. But I have a vision....

I love special-interest videos. I've developed, produced, marketed and consulted on 300 or more home videos. Children's, music videos, comedies, documentaries, how-to's and genres that haven't even been named yet. They're great. Unlike movies, you can produce them quickly. Five months, six months–boom, they're done and out in the world!

But here's the rub. Video stores don't care about special-interest videos. They want movies. Well, maybe if it's a Jane Fonda video or a Shirley MacLaine video, they'll buy hundreds of thousands. But usually not. To sell special interest videos through retail stores, you have to first sell the wholesaler who has to sell the retailer who has to sell the customer who is a very busy and distracted creature and will, at best, only give you a few seconds of his or her time. It's tough. Real tough.

Infomercials, however, are a perfect medium to preview original programs. The viewer is clicking around the dial and–Whammo–something interesting appears. What is it? An infomercial. Let's watch. Your video product is pumped directly into someone's living room. No layers of middlemen. As a producer, marketer and video publisher of original, special interest programs, infomercials have great potential.

In 1991, I developed and produced a series of television and video programs for Los Angeles PBS station KCET called Lifeguides. These are empowering videos for the professional and the individual. They were made available through 1-800 numbers following the shows. And they were sold during PBS' pledge nights, through direct mail, and through retail outlets. One of the shows really took off. *Diet For A New America*, based on the Pulitzer-nominated book by John Robbins, made some chilling connections between our animal-based diet and degenerative diseases (cancer, strokes, heart attacks, diabetes, etc.) and the environment. Everyone I've talked to changed their diet after watching the show, and many people bought multiple copies of the program to give to their friends ("call 1-800-765-7890"). The video received the Genesis Award for "Outstanding TV Documentary on PBS" and has become an advocacy piece for vegetarian, environmental, and animal rights groups. This is what I want to do with videos! But, it's real tough, as those of you who have produced social documentaries well understand.

Mission Statement

It's a new year. I wrote a mission statement for 1993. I've found it enormously helpful in managing my work. Besides eliminating the day-to-day distractions, a mission statement becomes my value-filter through which I can judge my priorities. I try to spend most of my time taking steps toward my goals. It also has the added benefit of attracting worthwhile projects. Try writing one, and see for yourself.

Here's mine:

"Our mission is to empower and improve the quality of human life and the environment by creating worthwhile and educational communication tools."

So, it made sense to look to the infomercial—the perfect preview medium—to try to display and sell the kinds of videos alluded to in my mission statement. Shortly after having this notion and writing my mission statement, I was contracted to produce a series of health-oriented infomercials (the product, a bundle of videos, audios and books.) Each infomercial is based on the work of health professionals.

Here's some of what I learned:

• You need a concept that's memorable. ("The Juiceman," "Hooked-On-Phonics," "Where There's A Will There's An A.")

• You need an appealing, charismatic personality who either introduces the product or who has created the product. (Jane Fonda, Kathy Smith)

• Testimonials by celebrities seem to be important, especially if the celebrity says they are not getting paid to tout the product (e.g. Martin Sheen in Tony Robbins' infomercial.)

• Testimonials by real people are great. Use enough people, and there will be somebody to relate to for every type of viewer in your audience.

• Credibility is very important to overcome people's fears about the product, about ordering from television, about getting their money back, etc.

• The product must be simple and easy to understand.

• Americans want quick results. The product must offer quick results.

"Thin thighs in 30 days" is a promise too good to be true. Sign me up.

The basic structure of an infomercial is:

• Grabber–An emotional, personal element that gets attention.

• Problem–An undeniable, horrible problem.

• Product–Here's what will bring relief, deliver results, make you richer, sexier, or healthier.

• Solution–How you too can change. The benefits.

• Close–Why and How to buy, incentives, the cost.

• Guarantee–If you're not satisfied... money-back guarantee.

Concepts and rules I don't buy:

• It's better if you can't find it in stores. (Sometimes people see an appliance or product in an infomercial, and don't order it. But the first time they see something similar in a retail store, they buy it there.)

• You have to appeal to greed (real estate courses) and vanity (cosmetics, hair restoration products). These are lesser human qualities. I'd like to appeal to higher desires such as education, better health, improving relationships, etc. Ultimately people realize that more stuff won't make them better, happier people.

• Don't let your customer get away. Keep the 1-800 number up as long as possible.

Most of these are principles that apply to all kinds of marketing. My problem with many infomercials is that they employ these principles to sell products that have little value.

Many infomercial marketers' mission statements must be: "Our mission is to make money by selling product with little or no value." I think we can shoot a little bit higher than this.

The "hit-and-run" feeling I have when watching many infomercials is frightening. I feel an electronic hand reaching into my back pocket. The good news is that the FTC (Federal Trade Commission) is taking a very hard look at the infomercial business. The bad news is that it has had to come to this. The government should not censor infomercials. The producers and television stations should consciously produce responsible programming, without having to be told to by the government.

What's happening is there have been many consumer complaints. Producers have made outrageous claims about their products. The products don't perform. People don't get their money back. The product wasn't shipped in a timely fashion. Poor business practices hurt everyone who is using the medium to market products.

I'm basically a communicator concerned with producing communication pieces that say something and empower people. An infomercial or a television program that doesn't give you something–unless you order the product– really goes against the grain. Why can't an infomercial teach something, give something away, create a bond of trust between the viewer and the presenter? If they buy the product, fine. If not, they still got something of value. Maybe the next time they invite you into their homes they will buy something.

From a marketing point of view, what I do like about infomercials is that you know right away whether or not it works. You test an infomercial in a market or two, and instantly know the results. Either the product was bought, or it wasn't. If the test was successful, the infomercials are rolled out, more time is bought, and more product is sold. The best performing infomercials can sell 10, 20, 30 or 100 million dollars of product in a single year! The flops are instantaneous.

It costs about $25,000 or more to buy enough television time to test an infomercial. With testing, an infomercial can be re-edited and rebroadcast in less than a week to produce more sales. Revamping and publishing a magazine ad takes months. Television is fast. The Home Shopping Network, a kind of continuous infomercial, monitors in real-time the dollars coming in per minute. If sales fall below a certain point—zippo—the old product is history, and a new one is introduced!

When a video is the product, it can be duplicated as the orders come in and shipped very fast to customers. (The packaging must be prepared in advance however.) This means a producer doesn't have to have thousands of dollars tied up in inventory. If the infomercial is a flop, there isn't the problem of liquidating a warehouse full of products.

Who buys from infomercials? Some reports say people between the ages of 25 and 45 with incomes over $20,000. The best selling times are on the weekends and at night when people are less distracted. That's why the airwaves are filled with infomercials on Saturdays and Sundays. The job of the infomercial media buyers is to try to buy the best times to match the demographics of the product to the demographics of the viewing audience.

Not just car wax and cubic zirconias are sold through infomercials. Major national advertisers—car manufacturers and telephone companies—are airing infomercials. In all likelihood, this trend will continue. I only hope that the product really delivers, and that producers start to communicate something through their work. If they are called infomercials, let's see some more information coming through. How about some informational products that improve our educational and health care systems? What about giving somebody something for nothing?

And as I triumphantly step down off of my soapbox, I turn to you and ask "what's your mission statement?" Now go get 'em.

WHAT I'VE LEARNED ABOUT INFOMERCIALS

A Hit!

The first one struck out. The second one is a hit, and already bringing in millions of dollars in its first few months. If I stop producing infomercials now, I'll have the best batting average in the league. (The best infomercial producer around bats .333). But I'm a neophyte infomercial producer, and only make them because they are an effective delivery system for special-interest videos.

When I was VP of original programming at Vestron Video, my job was to identify, develop, produce and manufacture videos that we would sell to wholesalers. They, in turn, would sell to retailers, who then would sell to consumers. It was a tough business, with lots of selling. Think of an hour glass. There are lots of videos at the top and lots of video buyers are the bottom, but getting through that narrow opening in between (selling the wholesalers and retailers) is a large part of the game. It works when you have "A" titles, but even then it's expensive.

Infomercials provide a half-hour opportunity for consumers to "sample" the product. Like CDs played on the radio, audiences can sample the music and then purchase the album if they choose. The longer someone watches an infomercial, the more likely they will be to buy the product.

Infomercials are a kind of "theatrical exposure" for special interest videos. The enormous exposure on television brings tremendous public awareness and creates consumer pull when the video reaches the video stores.

The McDougall Program

The McDougall Program infomercial (on which I was executive

producer, writer and director) runs currently on the air on independent stations and cable networks throughout the country. It looks like it may air for a year or more. It sells health information.

Dr. John McDougall runs a health program at St. Helena Hospital in St. Helena, California. He works with people with life-threatening diseases and chronic illnesses, and his treatment includes what is essentially a vegetarian diet. It's not uncommon for his patients to lose weight, lower their blood pressure and cholesterol, and get off medications after two weeks on the diet. Some diseases are actually reversed. This infomercial is kind of a "doc in a box." It's the same 12-day program his patients experience at the clinic, and includes three books (one is a recipe book), an audio tape series, and a video–all for $150.

The opportunity to produce infomercials (and the video, book, and audio products) came at a time when I had just redefined my company's mission statement.

Our mission is to empower and improve
the quality of human life and the environment
by creating worthwhile and educational communication tools.

Infomercials are a perfect marketing vehicle for the health communication tools we produce and publish. An infomercial is part of the distribution and marketing plan. Once an infomercial has run its course, the product is sold in retail outlets with the advantage of having millions of dollars of television exposure.

In my PBS documentaries, I provide hard information. I had hoped to do this with infomercials as well. My rough cut included many of the specific principles of the McDougall Program. Cut out meat, dairy and oil from your diet. Eat fruits and vegetables, and exercise. It appeared too simple. If viewers felt they fully understood what to do, then they didn't need the program. By editing out some of the hard information and by emphasizing expert and real-people testimonials, viewers felt The McDougall Program really offered some life-saving, disease-preventing information.

Claims

When producing infomercials–especially about health–it's critically important to be able to substantiate every claim through sound scientific research documentation. We have two credible medical sources for every claim that we make. If the claim is too speculative, even in a testimonial, we don't use it. Not only are the television stations very leery of programs with outrageous claims, they simply won't air such a show for fear of liability. The FTC (Federal Trade Commission) is especially diligent in making producers back up their claims. The consumer must be protected from fraud.

You can only make claims for results that the average viewer might expect to receive from your product. We have testimonials from people who lost 200 lbs. on The McDougall Program, whose sexual potency returned, or whose breast cancer went into remission. We couldn't, however, use these "miracle stories" because this is not what the average person can expect will happen to them.

What did happen was that people did lose weight, reduced their cholesterol and blood pressure levels, got off medication, and began to feel better–so we emphasized these benefits.

Credibility

One element that contributes to the success of the McDougall infomercial is its authenticity. The testimonials are extremely credible. People speak from their experience of using McDougall's information. Almost any skeptic's concerns are defused by the experts' opinions and real-life testimonials. Whether they are young or old, male or female, viewers come to believe that McDougall offers something that works. McDougall himself looks directly into the camera and tells you about his program.

I believe that you have to be authentic. You have to tell the truth. You have to have integrity. People already do not trust television. In fact, statistically, only 15 percent will respond to a television offer. (These numbers are increasing.) The other 85 percent who might be interested want to see it, touch it, and test it in a store before buying it.

Many infomercials are shot before live television audiences to build excitement, or in studio living rooms. Neither approach felt right or "real" for McDougall. To build credibility and believability, I shot the infomercial documentary-style in people's homes, at the clinic, and during Dr. McDougall's radio show.

Strategy

As producers, we come in touch with a lot of information. It is our job to synthesize it, make is visual and auditory, and make it easy to understand. What I now look for are experts/presenters and information that can empower people's lives. Then I see whether it is best presented in a video, a set of audio tapes, books, or all of the above.

Do not think infomercials as a business unto themselves, or you may be very disappointed. The airwaves are very crowded. Top infomercial companies review hundreds of ideas every month. Very few are produced. Media time is getting harder (and more expensive to buy). Major advertisers are entering the field.

Instead, producers should think of infomercials as but one marketing element in a larger strategic plan that takes advantage of the great exposure infomercials can bring to a product.

Until next time, find a worthy project to do as an infomercial–something that really contributes value to people's lives. Now, go get 'em.

YOU CAN MAKE DESKTOP VIDEO–
BUT CAN YOU SELL IT?

The advice in this article is basically that you need to find the most appropriate distribution channels for your product and make sure that the production value you deliver matches the expectations of your audience.

The title of this column is the crux of the problem. Not a day passes when our consulting office is not asked this question by telephoning producers. And it's always the same problem. They've written, shot or produced material–and they don't know where to sell it. The right time to ask "Where can I sell it?" is when you're first onto a hot new project–not six months later!

I am convinced that you can use desktop video to create broadcast quality television programs. I recently called upon the hardest working man in desktop video," fellow *Videography* columnist Scott Billups. In the course of a few days, we shot, edited, mixed and mastered a half-hour television piece without leaving the room! Furthermore, production speed is hitting an all-time high, while production costs for quality product are plunging.

These savings, however, do not mean that producers no longer have to keep their eye on the marketing outlets for their work. They still have to recoup their blood, sweat and cash somewhere. So, "how do you sell it?"

I turn the discussion back on the producers and ask, "Who is your audience? How can you reach them? What are the distribution channels?" Most of the projects these producers offer are not going to be sold through video stores because they are not movie entertainment. And video stores don't sell much of any other genre than movies. You have to look to other markets to sell most how-to's, documentaries, business or corporate training videos, or the myriad of other hybrid videos which do not yet have a genre.

163

The business is closer to video publishing than to movie-making. Producers are creating communication pieces–the value of which is usually contained in the information within the video. You can learn how to do something by watching.

So, the questions become "Who is the audience?" "What would they pay for this kind of information?" and "How will they hear about (and subsequently buy) the video product?" You need an answer before you can market your videos.

Video purchasers generally get their information about new video releases through direct-mail pieces, magazine/journal ads, or television spots. For example, the Lifeguides documentaries that I produced last year for PBS are marketed through: (1) direct mail pieces to professionals and institutions; (2) reviews, publicity and ads in journals; and (3) a 1-800 number solicitation immediately following the television broadcast. It takes several channels to reach the marketplace.

Your exercise is to find out how your specific audience receives information. Hopefully, your program is priced high, and the marketing costs are low. Sometimes the costs of marketing are too high for low-priced programs, as you can see in the accompanying Direct Marketing Chart.

Pricing is a key issue.

Even with relatively low desktop video budgets you still have advertising, marketing and duplication expenses. (Fortunately, you may not have to duplicate until you have your first batch of orders.) Does your video contain information that is valuable enough for someone to want to pay for it? If so, how high is the perceived value, $19.95?, $99.95? What will people pay? How does the marketplace value other videos?

My advice to consulting clients: If you have a great idea for one tape, what about a series, a product line? Marketing costs are the same for one tape or a dozen tapes. With a line of video product, your average order rises, marketing costs fall, and you have an overall greater profit margin.

(Please note that the chart shows very general numbers. Use the outline if you wish, but you'll have to research your own actual numbers based on your own product and distribution channels. The costs could be higher or lower. The chart's numbers are for demonstration purposes only.)

Let's explore three venues for selling your tape. There's direct mail, where you send out a flyer. There's magazine "per inquiry," where the magazine gives you a free ad in exchange for a share of revenues. And then there's television advertising.

Let's look at two scenarios with a single-tape offering and a three-tape offering. The production budgets will be higher with the three-tape offering, as will duplication and UPS charges–but we'll also be able to increase the retail price on the three-tape offering while everything else stays the same! Your sales strategy might use all three marketing approaches.

Direct Mail

Let's assume we pay $1000 to have a flyer designed. We print and mail flyers, which cost 75 cents each, to a 30,000-name mailing list which we bought for $4,500. Marketing costs are $28,000. To recover these costs, we have to sell 2,043 single videos or 337 three-video sets.

A good response to a mailing might be two percent. The single-unit video sale requires nearly a seven percent response rate to break even. This is too high to consider. The three-tape offering with a 1.1 percent response rate to break even is a better bet. This analysis tells us you have a better chance of success with a three-tape offering than with the single tape. The marketing costs on the three-tape offering are 44 percent, almost half the retail price. Marketing is expensive.

	Direct Mail		PI:Per Inquiry		TV Spot		
INCOME	*1 Tape*	*3 Tapes*	*1 Tape*	*3 Tapes*	*1 Tape*	*3 Tapes*	
Retail Price	$19.95	$99.95	$19.95	$99.95	$19.95	$99.95	
Shipping/Handling	3	7	3	7	3	7	
Net Per Unit	$22.95	$106.95	$22.95	$106.95	$22.95	$106.95	
Duplication	-3	-9	-3	-9	-3	-9	
Order Processing	-2.5	-2.5	-2.5	-2.5	-2.5	-2.5	
UPS	-2	-4	-2	-4	-2	-4	
Credit Card Cost @ 3%	-0.6	-3	-0.6	-3	-0.6	-3	
Returns @ 5%	-1.15	-5.35	-1.15	-5.35	-1.15	-5.35	
Net Per Unit	$13.70	$83.10	$13.70	$83.10	$13.70	$83.10	
MARKETING EXPENSES							
Produce Mailer, Ad or TV Sp	1,000	1,000	1,000	1,000	4,000	4,000	
Mailer Cost/30,000	22,500	22,500					
List Purchase @ $0.15	4,500	4,500					
Subscriber/Audience Reach			30,000	30,000	100,000	100,000	
TV Spot Buys					1,500	1,500	
Total Marketing	$28,000	$28,000	$1,000	$1,000	$5,500	$5,500	
REVENUES							
Units Sold to Recover Mkt. (	2,043	337	73	12	401	66	
Resp Rate to Break Even	6.80%	1.10%	0.20%	0.00%	0.40%	0.10%	
Units Sold at 2% Resp.	600	600	600	600			
Units Sold on TV at 1/4% Resp.					250	250	
Gross Revenues	$13,770	$64,170	$13,770	$64,170	$5,738	$26,738	
Less 15% Magazine Royalty			1,083	7,329			
Net Profit at 2% Response	($19,778)	$21,862	$6,139	$41,533			
At 1/4% Response					($2,074)	$15,276	
Marketing as a % of Gross R	203%	44%	7%	2%	96%	21%	
* Based on 30,000 Magazine Circulation, 2.00% Response Rate, 600 Orders							

Per Inquiry

Another scenario that will produce results for little risk is the "P.I.," or per inquiry deal. Since advertising sales are the lowest they've been in a decade, there are publishers willing to cut deals just to get ad pages. Recently we made a P.I. deal with a magazine. We paid for the full-page ad design and mechanicals. In exchange, the magazine receives 15 percent of gross sales (not including shipping or taxes). They ran the ad for three months, and it was so successful they've just extended it for another six months. For us, there was little risk, and the ad produced supplemental sales revenues with no more investment than the cost of the mechanical.

In our video example, we pay $1000 for the ad's design and mechanicals. We make money (less 15 percent) very quickly with 0.02 percent response rate. If we get a 2 percent response rate, some income will go to the magazine publisher, and they may continue running the ad. Now is a particularly good time to try this strategy with magazines.

Television Spots

Television is much more risky, because you have to find a television audience that will respond to your tape offering. A highly rated show–even in a local market–might be prohibitively expensive. Let's assume we produce a TV spot for $4000, and we buy $1500 worth of ads to test our offering. Only on the three-tape offering do we make money, and this is with a 0.25 percent response rate. If the test is successful, more television time will be bought.

There's hardly enough space here to go into all the different strategies that could be employed for selling desktop video productions, but this will give you some idea of the possibilities. I invite you to combine these and other marketing avenues, especially publicity (which is sometimes free), in selling your desktop videos. Now go get 'em.

GETTING A BIG BANG FOR THE BUCK:
"THE ASTRONOMERS"

This is one of my favorite marketing examples. It demonstrates that you can take a very difficult subject (science videos!) and through the integration and synergy of various elements, inspire everyone's participation in a very esoteric product, and sell a lot of units.

It was a first! The home video and book release would occur simultaneously with the April 25th PBS broadcast of the limited series The Astronomers. The manufacturers of three different products–a television series, a video collection, and a book–would create national awareness for their individual products by working together.

As a consultant to PBS Home Video (which is distributed exclusively by Pacific Arts Video), I was assigned to coordinate the marketing plan for the video release of *The Astronomers.*

A Perfect Universe

This wasn't the first time I've worked on cross-promotions with publishers, record companies and broadcasters. At the outset, everyone usually says, "Yeah, great, we'll work together." But by the time the release rolls around, everyone is off on their own agenda, and the potential marketing synergy dissipates. The Astronomers was an exception. Everyone worked extremely well together. In fact, television and video producers of new works can look to The Astronomers as a kind of perfect case study of what can happen when marketers work together.

So far, the sales response from the field has been tremendous, and it looks like sales goals will be met or surpassed. What follows are some of the marketing elements and ideas which came together to create what at this moment looks to be a phenomenal success story.

The Astronomers is a six-hour limited series which profiles the lives and work of scientists revolutionizing our knowledge of the universe. The series is narrated by Richard Chamberlain and was produced on a $5 million grant from the W. M. Keck Foundation by Los Angeles PBS station KCET. It aired April 15th over PBS national and will continue for five subsequent Mondays.

Synergetic Relationships

Public Television is airing the series. PBS Home Video will sell the six-volume video "collector's edition" to video stores. PBS Video (the non-theatrical distributor) is selling the video to the educational and institutional markets. And St. Martin's Press is publishing the companion book. In our initial meetings, we emphasized a desire to promote The Astronomers as a "multi-media" event. In this way, each marketer could reap the benefits of everyone's efforts and could maximize their own sales through the tremendous, accumulative publicity and promotion.

If we worked together, we could economize, best employ our resources, and hopefully, avoid duplicating efforts. We could go to the press in a coordinated manner. (Three sets of publicists representing KCET, PBS Home Video, and the St. Martin's Press worked together so that three publicists weren't going to the same editors.) This meant that a publicity "hit list" could be divided, increasing efficiency and results.

Key Art

One of the most important coordinated pieces was the design of a single piece of key art, which was used for all media. (The book and the video used the key art on the covers. The broadcaster used the key art in newspaper ads.) To use different art would diminish consumer awareness and would be detrimental to all. The multiple impressions on viewers and consumers results in greater awareness. By the third time they've seen the art, they may respond by buying a book, purchasing a video, or tuning into the program. The key art was a man and a woman (astronomers presumably) next to the Palomar

Observatory dome looking at the moon. The beauty of this art is that it works well in both a poster or postage-stamp size, which can be used in both horizontal and vertical formats.

The Video

Each individual title sells for $19.95 retail. The six-volume set sells for $129.95. If you bought them separately it would cost $119.70. What would, in the words of a marketer, "add value" to the set, so that a consumer would spend $10.25 more for the collection? Answering this question was one of my tasks. Taking a lesson from The Civil War set, we licensed, re-published, and reduced a 48-page book, Your Personal Guide to the Night Sky, to fit inside the attractive video gift pack. Added value!

One primary promotable element in The Astronomers is the $1 million special effects. To get a bigger bang for the buck, we edited these effects together in a seven-minute "music video" –the ultimate space trip. Inside the "collector's edition" set, consumers will find a coupon to send away to get their free "music video." More value!

In addition, you receive other coupons which grant you a discount on 1) membership in the Astronomical Society of the Pacific, 2) a subscription to Omni Magazine, and 3) a discount on their own telescope. Even more value. Wow!

Selling the Sellers

A major ad and promotion campaign in The New Yorker, People, Omni, Premiere, Scientific American, Life and other national magazines should send customers flocking to video stores, bookstores and mass merchant outlets. But how do you get the video stores to carry the product?

You have to sell the sellers. With hundreds of new video products each month to choose from, and limited dollars, the video retailers must choose The Astronomers video product over someone else's. The goal of PBS Home Video is to sell units. In order to incentivize video stores to buy more titles, a large floor display with 24 titles was created. When the retailer bought the floor display, they got a free all-purpose telescope.

This did the trick! Store buyers wanted the free telescope to keep themselves, to give away to their sales people, or to offer to their customers through a drawing. Some saw how they could also use this free gift as a temporary floor display to help draw attention to The Astronomers videos. (To get the lowest possible price on telescopes, we bought in volume and told them a discount coupon would be inserted in every tape set. They went for it. After all, the tapes will reach an audience most interested in telescopes. In return, they agreed to stuff their telescope boxes with The Astronomers sales sheets. A perfect, target audience for videos. Everyone wins.

Cross Marketing and Coordination

There are numerous markets for a tape collection like The Astronomers. The most targeted are those with a strong interest in astronomy. These are the folks that would plunk down $129.95 for the entire series. But how do you get to them? In order for people to respond even to something they may be interested in, you have to get to them frequently and in many ways.

In order to take advantage of the six-week period when the programs would be on PBS, I wrote a "Special Astronomers Edition" of the PBS Home Video Newsletter. This newsletter is designed to create a dialogue between video stores and PBS Home Video. The notion is that if you give retailers good marketing tips and ideas on how they can more successfully sell the PBS line of home videos, you build loyalty. They will buy more PBS Home Video titles. The Special Issue was sent to 70,000 video outlets, and 350 observatories/planetariums, and 300 PBS stations. The newsletter featured marketing tips on how video outlets, planetariums, and PBS stations could work together.

Although each is driven by self-interest and has a slightly different agenda, everyone can win. PBS can attract more people who may potentially become station members (e.g. contribute money). PBS

Home Video can sell more videos. And the observatories can take advantage of all the publicity surrounding The Astronomers by creating workshops, seminars and other events as the public gets excited about astronomy.

Planetariums may get more attendees and members. For example, the newsletter suggests that local video stores call up their amateur astronomy clubs and invite them to bring their telescopes to the video store parking lot for a "Star Gazing Party." Such an event would certainly merit publicity in the local media and would help draw people into the video store.

A major event like this requires an extraordinary amount of planning; it doesn't just happen. Hopefully, some of these ideas will fuel your own imaginations when it comes to marketing and cross-marketing your programs. Now go get 'em.

DISTRIBUTION

DIRECT-TO-VIDEO MOVIES

Sometimes you need to get a reality check on what the rest of the world is doing. So I drove crosstown and spent a day among the movers and shakers of the non-Hollywood movie scene. Now we're not talking Sundance or Telluride if you follow my drift. We're talking money-making movies for the international markets. My time with these connoisseurs of the exploitative and violent arts was cut short by the outbreak of the Los Angeles riots. Who says there is no correlation between the media we create and the activity in our streets?

They haunt my sleep even now. I am walking down a long corridor. On each side, images press toward me–handguns, large breasts, uzis, wet breasts, sawed-off shotguns, perky breasts, zip guns, negligee revealed breasts, machine guns, the breasts of Oriental women....

Over 200 companies attended the American Film Market in Santa Monica, CA which I went to on March 2. I hadn't been there for several years and was told by friends in the film business that the quality of product and the number of companies participating in the film market had increased significantly.

One of my interests was to get a look at the opportunity for filmmakers who want to produce made-for-video features. The cost of producing and marketing highly promotable features and the scarcity of screen time mean that fewer and fewer films actually get to the screen. Home video is another matter. Many films that are never released theatrically can recoup some of their investment in the home video market.

Made-for-video features generally have little or no prepromotion: no advertising, no publicity, no reviews, no television appearances by the film's stars, and no theatrical exhibition.

The budgets range from a high of $1 million, but are usually in the $200,000 to $500,000 range. This buys about 20 days of shooting in

174

limited locations, and maybe a cameo by some "B" or "C" star. The only way these films are marketed is by fitting into a highly recognizable genre that has exploitable elements (e.g., sex and violence).

Although the American Film Market's catalog of film product seems to offer buyers a diverse range of titles including dramas and documentaries, what's really being sold are genre movies. Erotic thrillers and action/adventure top the list.

Those who want to produce a profitable made-for-video movie select an exploitable genre and then come up with a punchy title that suits the genre. Creatively they stick within the conventions of the genre. Genre audiences do not like their offerings mixed. Since they want to obtain as large an international audience as possible, they keep dialogue to a minimum. The pictorial elements are reduced to basic action and flesh.

The breasts and guns that haunt my subconscious were the images that besieged me as I walked the many floors of the Loews Hotel where sellers have booked bevies of suites and converted them into showcases with posters and video monitors displaying clips from their film products. It looks like if you aren't selling breasts or guns, you aren't selling anything.

The attendees are buyers from around the world, anxious to fill up television program schedules and home video rental pipelines. Some buy films for theatrical exhibition but most service the ancillary markets.

Having attended a number of the new media conventions each year, to me the AFM market appears to be a distinctly older group of buyers and sellers (mostly men) trading in violence and sex. "It sells," "It's what the buyers want," are the tired clichés being touted here.

There are exceptions to these genres being sold at the AFM but you really have to look hard to find this product.

I spoke with several producers who are producing their third or fourth picture. They shoot in 16mm film and transfer to video. They edit on

AVIDs or other non-linear editing consoles. They prepare NTSC and SECAM masters with split tracks (so that dubbing can be easily performed for foreign versions). Their films are represented by sellers at these and other world film markets (Cannes, Mifed, Mipcom, Monte Carlo) where the sellers license the video and television rights to the international markets.

Two producers I talked with have budgets in the $200,000 to $300,000 range. Their films are generally indistinguishable from numerous films already in circulation except by title. While we didn't discuss the individual deals, the producers told me that they would see a return of their investment plus $50,000 to $300,000. In both cases the producers provided their own financing (deferments and second home mortgages). They both were somewhat embarrassed by the genres they produced and said they "didn't plan to do this forever." They only wanted to make enough money to make the kind of movie they really wanted to make.

I've heard this justification for years in the film, television and video business. I've known people who've made great fortunes by producing exploitation films. Most of them professed to want to make other kinds of movies but I don't know anyone other than director John Sayles who has been able to do it.

My feeling is that you should identify your true passion and stick with it. Eventually you will be known for that area and will begin to see the rewards for your toil. If you really have passion for filmmaking, it will show up in your work.

I've carved out the "quality" area. I define "quality" as film, television or videos that make a positive contribution to life. And yes, it has limited the playing field but it doesn't matter. I can only produce a limited number of projects in a lifetime and already my plate is quite full. I couldn't do them all if I wanted to.

I do understand the fear that producers have about producing the kind of work they really feel in their hearts should be produced. They have to eat and it looks easier to go for the money-making genres. But are they really making a contribution? Can they sleep at night? We know, for example, that after two decades involving hundreds of studies there is a connection between on-screen violence and the violence in our society. We all know it's true but some producers are just making too much money to acknowledge it. They have nowhere else to turn (so they think) to earn a living but by glorifying dying. And they haven't learned to produce anything else.

I would encourage the producers of exploitation films, as well as the younger producers entering the new media arena, to really look inside themselves and ask the following questions: "What legacy do you want to leave?" "What do you want to be known for?" "What do you stand for?" "What do you want your children to know you contributed to the world?" When you get your answers, stick by them, and find a way to create your vision and leave something of your worth behind. You will be able to earn a living and you'll be able to get some sleep. Now go get 'em.

A Sex & Violence Exercise

Imagine that you are at a film market. You walk down long hallways of hotel suites which are inhabited by film salesmen. At the entryway to each suite, you stop, peek inside and see dozens of posters competing for your attention.

Read the following titles slowly to yourself and imagine movie posters appearing. What images do you see on these posters? Sense the emotions stirring in your body. Especially notice what happens in your genital and solar plexus area. These are the emotions and feelings that marketers are trying to evoke in video-store customers throughout the world.

Final Justice
Appointment for a Killing
French Silk
Caged Seduction
The Voyeur
Exotica

In a Moment of Passion
Heavy Petting
Acapulco Heat
Swimsuit
The Fraternity
Moll Flanders
Resistance
Inevitable Grace
Abducted 2
Cover Story
Cage II
Through Dead Eyes
Seduction of Innocence
Desert Steel
Street Warriors
When a Spider Bites
Squanderers
La Wars
Hunt for the Blue Diamond
Paid to Kill
Meltdown
Another 9 1/2 Weeks
Red Scorpion 2
Sexual Malice
Sexual Outlaws
The Great Bikini Adventure
Stranger By Night
Body of Influence
Sins of the Night
Secret Games II
Body Melt
A Killing Obsession
Resort to Kill
Erotic Time Machine
Harem Heat
Lady Chatterley in Tokyo
Death and the Maiden
Cutthroat Island

No Angel
Young Lady Chatterley
Angel of H. E. A. T
Skinner
Tender is the Hunter
One Man Army
Caged Heat 3
Killer
Jugular Wine
Masters of Horror
Fatal Past
The Silencer
Housewife from Hell
Whispering
The Seductress
Making the Rules
Murders & Acquisitions
Rift
Beyond Fear

(Note: These titles make up only a very small percentage of these types of films which are produced and sold each year. When is enough enough?)

WHAT ARE THEY BUYING?

VSDA is that great marketing Mecca where merchants from all over bring their video wares. It's always an eye-opener and there are always surprises. Here a producer, marketer or distributor can identify trends in the markets and see what their competition is doing that works.

VSDA, 1995

If ever there was an indication of what the direct-to-home video market is buying, VSDA is it. The letters stand for the Video Software Dealers Association, and their annual Las Vegas confab is that industry's largest event. An estimated 13,000 attendees gathered for this year's VSDA, including everyone from mom-and-pop video stores to such mass-merchant chains as Tower, Musicland and Blockbuster.

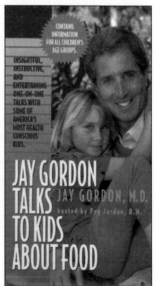

In years past I attended VSDA to see what response there was from buyers for Vestron Video offerings that I had spent the year acquiring, developing and producing. Now I'm attending as an independent producer trying to get a handle on the evolving marketplace. This year I was there with my children's nutrition videos, *Good Food Today, Great Kids Tomorrow*, which are part of the product mix from my infomercial of the same name. I was there to renew contacts, pitch a few ideas, and make sure my distributors were properly displaying my videos, which they were.

For retailers, VSDA is their once-a-year contact with the entertainment industry, and entertain they (the manufacturers and vendors) did! Wherever you turned, there were larger-than-life stuffed animals

(Barney, for kids) or larger-than-life stuffed bikinis (The Barbi Twins, for adults). Retailers lined up to get their picture taken with Beavis and Butt Head, *Playmate* centerfolds, and/or Lassie. Also appearing in person were former President George Bush, Hank Aaron, Paula Abdul, Alan Shepard and Mary Tyler Moore.

CD-ROM, however, was where the real spin was. Video retailers seem to be in agreement that sooner or later they're going to have to get into selling and renting them. In fact, Blockbuster has tested CD-ROMs at 57 San Francisco locations and will be expanding the test. Tower will add CD-ROM titles to 20 stores next month. At VSDA there was also a new media kiosk section demonstrating the latest set-top platforms and titles. It was a new experience for many video retailers.

The rush is on by developers, distributors and retailers eager to claim CD-ROM turf. A company called Vending Intelligence (Culver City, CA) displayed the world's first CD-ROM vending machine. Intended locations are supermarkets, college campuses, video stores, and book-stores. Their vending machine holds 952 CD-ROMs, including 48 different titles. You push a lighted panel and a prerecorded non-interactive sample of the disc plays. If you like it, you push a button and pay for it with a credit card. How's that for a video distribution outlet?

Depending on whose numbers you worship, there are about 10 million CD-ROM players (of various platforms) in homes today. That includes both game-oriented TV set-top devices (Sega, Nintendo, CD-I, 3DO) and computer desktop CD players (for Macintosh and PCs).

In the set-top category, Sega of America dominates the game market with about 1 million units sold since their launch in late 1992. They've sold about 5.5 million units of software ($275 million in revenues). Machines conforming to the 3DO system have sold about 150,000 units, and CD-I machines about 50,000. Software revenue in the computer CD-ROM market is several times that of the set-top category, but compatibility is still an issue. The installed base of computer CD-

ROMs to the set-top category is estimated to be four-to-one. Figures I've seen indicate that CD-ROM players are being purchased at an even faster rate than consumer VCRs were back in the '80s. According to the Optical Publishing Association, 1993 CD-ROM revenues were about $1.5 billion; in 1994, they totaled about $2.1 billion.

CD-ROM suppliers were much in evidence at VSDA, and appeared to be going after video retailers. Compton's New Media was there to open new channels of distribution. VP of Marketing, Bill Perrault (a former Vestron colleague), tells me they've sold more than 2.2 million copies of *Compton's Interactive Encyclopedia* since it debuted five years ago; 775,000 of those sales were in the last six months. Entertainment titles are getting the most attention, Perrault reports.

"The CD-ROM business is like the arms race," Rand Bleimeister, the new head of Virgin Interactive, told me at the show. "High production quality is the name of the game, and only those with deep pockets ($2 million or more per title) will be serious players."

The CD-ROM business seems to have more than a few similarities to the early days of video. For one thing, there are platform wars, reminiscent of the VHS-Betamax battle. This worries video retailers who ultimately want to rent and sell the new media and don't want to invest in the wrong platform.

The quality of many of the first wave of CD-ROM titles is generally very poor. Hottest titles reportedly include *Myst, Encarta, Compton's Encyclopedia,* anything by Living Books, *7th Guest, Just Grandma and Me,* and *Where in the World is Carmen San Diego?*

In the early days of video, there were a plethora of public-domain titles–black-and-white films and shorts whose copyrights had expired–allowing anyone to duplicate and sell them. In the early days of CD-ROMs, anybody with any image is rushing to put it onto a disc. Whether or not it's interactive doesn't seem to make any difference to these developers. The danger there is that consumers will be disappointed by these low-end products and will retract from the market.

CD-ROM genres are generally similar to those in video genres, with perhaps the exception of reference works. Because of quick access time, CD-ROMs are far superior at delivering reference material than is linear videotape. The other major difference with CD-ROMs is, of course, interactivity.

The jury is still out on how and whether or not CD-ROMs will be rented. I suspect they will be. The home-video rental business, meanwhile, continues to grow between two and three percent annually. Of the 75 million consumer VCR homes, nearly 42 percent are projected to be active video renters, renting nearly 10 titles per month.

Special-interest titles are what teleproduction professionals are most interested in, these titles typically being shot on tape by independent producers. Exercise, sports and children's titles predominated at VSDA.

On the plane ride back to Los Angeles after the show, I overheard one producer talking to some retailers about why CD-ROMs need to have a dramatic structure.

"Aristotle said you have to have a beginning, a middle, and an end. You need an antagonist and a protagonist. The only way you can make something interesting to someone is through drama. Drama equals conflict. The problem with CD-ROM developers is that they are logic based. Logic works on your brain, not on your emotions. But emotions are exactly what need to be elicited through CD-ROMs. That's why we need to tell stories and people will listen to stories again and again."

The conversation went on for about half an hour and ended when the video retailer said, "You've told me everything a CD-ROM shouldn't be, but nothing about what it should be!"

Exploring that, my friends, is the real task ahead for all of us. Now go get 'em.

HOME VIDEO:
BUSINESS BY THE NUMBERS

VSDA, 1996

Time for that yearly snapshot of the home video business. Over the 20 years I've been producing for the home video market, the landscape has continued to change. It's important to have a sense of what is happening in the marketplace so you can plan your business activities accordingly.

VSDA (Video Software Dealers Association) was held this year in Southern California. VSDA ([818] 385-1500) is an international trade association representing over 3200 companies throughout the US, Canada and 22 other countries. Its members come from home video retailers, independents and large chains, video distributors, the home video divisions of the major and independent film studios, video game and multimedia producers, and other related entertainment businesses.

VSDA's convention is held in July, the time of year during which many of the research companies release statistics and update their analysis of the video business. Here's some of their findings:

Home video is a mature industry generating $16 billion a year as America's number one leisure time activity. A White Paper commissioned by the Video Software Dealers Association found that VCR usage increased by eight percent in 1995 and consumers are renting 13.3 videos a month.

Overall Market

Alexander and Associates reported that total consumer spending on video in 1995 was $20.6 billion. This includes rental and sellthrough markets. This is 15.1 percent higher than what was spent in 1993 and 2.5 percent higher than 1994.

Rental volume decreased 8.7 percent from 1994 to 1995 and revenue fell only 5.2 percent because the cost to rent a video increased. The average fee in 1994 was $2.50 per night and in 1995 this increased to $2.61 per night.

On the sellthrough side, purchase volume increased 17.7 percent on the sale of 682.9 million tapes in 1995. The 1995 average purchase price was $14.20 compared to $14.74 in 1994. So although the retail prices are falling, the increased purchase volume of 17.7 percent is making up overall resulting in a sellthrough revenue growth of 12.7 percent.

What's happening here is that as the retail prices drop, volume picks up, and there is an overall growth rate of 12.7 percent. Still a very good increase for what is now considered a mature market.

In 1995, rentals accounted for 52.9 percent of the total video revenue, while sellthrough accounted for 47.1 percent. With tape prices falling and more theatrical movies slated for sellthrough, the sellthrough revenue will be accounting for a greater and greater percentage of the overall video revenues.

Video Revenue

	1993	1994	1995
Video Units Purchased (Millions)	462.5	580.1	682.9
Video Rentals (Billions)	4.5	4.6	4.2
Consumer Spending (Billions)	17.9	20.1	20.6

Source: Alexander and Associates

I was in the video business in its go-go days during 1983-87 when growth was phenomenal and retail video stores were mushrooming on every corner. But in those days the business was primarily rental. Prices, at $89, were too high to capture the dollars of any buyers except collectors. Today, nearly 12 years later, the public has finally come to accept videos, like a book, as a "sellthrough" product. They can afford to own it, and view it again if they like (or not). For years, the sacred word among video programmers was "repeatability." Unless a video was "repeatable" like music or exercise, consumers wouldn't buy it. This axiom is no longer true. After all, how many books do you own that you've read once or less than once? The analogy we constantly made in the good old days about "video being like a book" has finally come true.

However there are some differences. The titles sold through to consumers are generally the big theatrical hits that are also hits in the rental stores. With marketing expenditures reaching $20 million or more, the larger films are well-known to consumers by the time they reach the rental stores. Smaller films are not seen in most theaters, rarely appear.   Home Video certainly don't show up in the mass merchant's video bins. The White Paper supports the ongoing activity of the video rental stores (with the underlying sentiment: *"Don't worry too much about sellthrough boys. You're making a good profit at rentals."*) since an ongoing concern among the video stores is that the mass merchants (K-Mart, Costco, Price Club) down the street are stealing their business by selling video titles. This is particularly troublesome to the video store which may be renting a video for $3 (but what if you could buy it down the street for $9.95 or $6.95 or even $4.95?). The speculators are suggesting to the video retailer that in order to curb cannibalization that maybe they should devote no more than 20 percent of their floor space to sellthrough.

What About DVD?

DVD (Digital Video Disc) has just come out, however it will be five years before there will be significant sales due to the established VCR base and the cost to consumers of converting to another format. The first DVD machines will not be able to record.

Other Highlights

• Video accounts for more than 50 percent of the motion picture industry's revenues.

• In a poll of 4500 people, on a scale of 1 to 10, watching a video is America's number one leisure activity (7.1), is more popular than going to a movie theater (6.2), attending a sporting event (6), watching cable television (5.5), watching pay cable (4.4), or watching a pay-per-view movie (3.6).

• There are 27,000 video stores in the US. Chains at the national and retail level are continuing to expand.

• VCRs have an 87 percent penetration of US homes.

• More than 65 million Americans visit a video store once a week.

• The video business is still growing.

• Consumers spend three times as much on video as they do at the movie box office.

• Consumers consider renting a video a good value.

• A typical video store offers more than 8000 titles.

• In 1995, about 300 movies went directly to the video market without having a theatrical release. This is a trend.

Average Number of Videos Owned by Households

All Titles

	Animation	Other	Movies	Kids	Other
All Buyers	41	10.8	13.9	4.8	11.5
Heavy *Renter*	48	13.6	17.2	6.2	11.0
Light *Renter*	28	7.2	9.9	3.7	7.2
Heavy *Buyer*	81	18	24	10.4	28.6
Medium *Buyer*	47	13.9	16.6	5.7	10.8
Light *Buyer*	20	4.6	7.1	1.7	6.6

Source: VSM/Chilton Research Services

What's interesting here is that the heavy renters of videos are also the heaviest buyers. If you like videos, you rent and buy them!

The sellthrough king from 1992-1995 is Buena Vista (Disney) with 34 percent, followed by MCA (22 percent), Warner (20 percent), Fox (12 percent) and others (12 percent). The top-50 sellthrough titles include 19 that grossed more than $100 million at the box office. *Jurassic Park*, *Forrest Gump* and *The Lion King* each earned more than $300 million in theaters. Box office success does not necessarily mean home video sellthrough success. Seven titles on the top-50 chart were released to video years after their theatrical release or without being released theatrically.

Seventeen of the top-50 sellthrough titles are from Disney.

Top-50 Sellthrough Titles by Genre

Genre	Number of Titles	Percent
Action	4	8%
Adventure	4	8%
Animated	17	34%
Comedy	11	22%
Drama	2	4%
Erotic Thriller	0	-
Family	12	24%
Foreign	0	-
Horror	0	-
Romance	0	-
Romantic Comedy	0	-
Sci-Fi	0	-
Thriller	0	-
Western	0	-

Source: Video Store Magazine

Children's titles continue to dominate the sellthrough market. Animated and family release account for 58 percent of all titles on the list. Comedy also sells well with 22 percent. The genres that consumers want to own have broadened in recent years including adult-themed films such as *Forrest Gump* and *The Fugitive*.

There is a correlation between the low-priced titles which are not just big sellers but are also strong renters.

Release of Sellthrough Titles by Quarter

4th Quarter	38%
3rd Quarter	22%
2nd Quarter	22%
1st Quarter	18%

Source: Video Store Magazine

Top-10 Direct to Sellthrough Releases, 1995

	List Price	*Sales (000)*	*Box Office*
The Lion King	$ 26.95	27,500	$312.1
Forrest Gump	22.95	14,800	321.1
The Santa Clause (tie)	19.98	11,500	144.8
Cinderella (tie)	26.99	11,500	N/A
Batman Forever	19.96	10,500	168.8
Apollo 13	22.98	9,600	179.5
Casper	22.02	7,500	168.8
Miracle on 34th Street	14.98	7,000	90.5
Mighty Morphin Power Rangers Movie (tie)	22.98	6,100	17.2
The Mask (tie)	19.98	6,100	119.0

Source: Video Store Magazine

Summary

So let's see if we can interpret any of these developments in terms of what it means to us: the video producer. Shall we look at it in terms of good news/bad news?

The good news is that people finally accept video as a sellthrough product. They want to own them and collect them. There is a sense of pride. They value videos. However, for the most part, movies and kids programs are the genres that are the top sellers, not special interest videos (which are best sold through direct response and direct advertising, not retail distribution). In fact, the sales of videos will very soon outpace rentals in total income. Someday a video market may develop where you will see a title breadth and depth similar to the superstore bookstores with both best-sellers and independent presses. (In fact, in the superstore bookstores, best-sellers only account for 3 percent of gross sales.) My point is that there is room for everything, not just the blockbusters. But this day has not yet come. When it comes time to sell your video, hope for a fourth quarter window, but look out, the marketplace is flooded with products.

For the present, if you want to produce videos for mass audiences you should stick to family features, animations or comedy. But look out again, Disney owns the playground!

The bad news. If you want to see your products in the video and mass merchant stores, it has to have a very highly promoted name or title. No store will stock your title unless it has high-volume potential. In reviewing the special interest titles released this year, there were very few, and those that were released were branded titles. Exercise has become saturated. Here and there are comedy tapes. The direct-to-video titles are exploitation (horror, erotic thriller, martial arts) with budgets in the $250,000 range. An average seller is about 5000 units which domestically will allow a producer to recoup 30 percent or more of his budget, the balance coming from foreign television and home video sales. If you can sell 30,000 units or more then you are well on your way.

If, on the other hand, movies are not your thing, and you enjoy producing special interest titles in other genres, and, if you can get to your audience through a target mailing list, magazine or association, then direct marketing may be the way to go.

Until then, go get 'em.

SELF-DISTRIBUTION

The Kantola Brothers are hot. They're focused, and they're profitable. Model yourself after those who have mastered the playing field, and add years to your life!

The Kantola Brothers: self distribution has led their company to $3 million in sales.

With the plethora of low-cost production technologies available, there are a lot of producers out there who feel they could market and distribute their own programs. Everyone has thought of doing this at one time or another. You may have created something that no distributor will take, or feel that you could do a better job marketing your video title. Maybe you want to make more than the traditional video royalty.

For some, it's the right move. For others, the constant attention to customer service, marketing, promotion, duplication and shipping may be enough to drive them right back onto location. What follows is the story of one company, Kantola Productions, for whom self distribution was definitely the right move.

Steve and Rick Kantola formed the video production and marketing company that bears their name several years ago. As a two (now seven) person operation, they took destiny into their own hands and produced one, and then a line of, video programs–creating a quiet but successful distribution company. This year Kantola Productions, based in San Francisco, will have sales reaching approximately $3 million. How did they do it?

Using their story as a case study, I'll identify some principles that may help you in your own distribution efforts.

1. Start Small, Have A Strategy, and Bootstrap Your Way To Success. The Kantolas produced a video titled Toastmasters Be Prepared to

Speak in 1985. Rick was the Researcher/Writer and worked with an organization known as Toastmasters to develop the script. Steve served as Producer and is now Marketer/Distributor of this and an entire line of Toastmaster video programs. Toastmaster was not paid any fees during development or production. They do, however, now receive a royalty on tape sales. The Kantola's self-financed the $50,000 budget and worked with an experienced production team to produce the first half-hour program.

2. Make the Owner of the Content and Core Audience Your Partner.

The "how to" nature of learning how to speak in public is ideal for video because you can see how–and how not–to give a speech. It's informative, entertaining and dramatic.

3. Be Sure The Content Works Well in Video.

Viewers go through every step of learning how to give a speech, from speech writing, to practicing, and delivering their words. The video is a comprehensive approach to the art of how to give a speech–a skill needed by almost every business person today.

4. The More Needed the Skill or Information, the Greater the Market.

The initial program was sold at $79.95 and sells today for $89.95 with a 32-page study guide. When the tape was first produced, there were only a few similar tapes on the market, and those had higher price points.

5. Research Similar Titles–Look Before You Leap.

Today there are several $29.95 "speech" tapes in the marketplace, but the producers have inappropriately selected consumer distribution. This is a very tough way to go because: (1) there are many movie titles competing for shelf space, and (2) the producers must sell at a low price point when actually the market will bear a higher price. The consumer-oriented "speech" titles have had little success.

6. When You Get A Hit, Create Sequels.

Once it was clear that Be Prepared to Speak had found an audience, the Kantolas developed three new titles that could be marketed to the same buyers. These included Be Prepared to Lead, Be Prepared To Sell, and Be Prepared for Meetings.

7. Pick the Right Channels of Distribution.

Through Steve Kantola's efforts, 60,000 units of their program have been sold. And, as they get better at opening up channels of distribution, sales increase each year.

8. Keep Working Your Title.

Steve emphasized that they are "very careful" and "give full attention to all the details." He says, "when we started we were undercapitalized and had to be very careful. If we had started with all the money we needed, we probably would have made expensive mistakes early and been out of business today."

9. Start Small Until You Learn the Business.

The good news for producers, then, is that in most cases they have to start small. Lean and mean is a great teacher, because you must be innovative and employ low-cost guerrilla marketing techniques. You can't buy an ad in People magazine, so you have to get customers in clever and effective ways. The Kantolas started small, "in a low-profile office and without much of a phone system" and have built a very successful small business.

10. Self-Distribution Means Do It Yourself.

The two-person operation must go through all the steps from brochure design, copy writing, getting it printed, buying lists, and doing the mailings. (The Kantolas also hire graphic artists to tweak their designs and employ a mailing house in Oregon to do the mailings.)

194

11. Hire Professional Help When Needed.

They also do their own order fulfillment. When testing a mailer or sales offering, they may select as few as 2500 names from four or five lists. Strangely enough, Steve says, "Tests do better than roll-outs and no one knows exactly why." So even though you may identify a strong list, you may not get the exact percentage return as the test. Once the test is successful, then all the names from the list will be used. Lists that do not perform well will not be used any further.

12. Tests–Walk Before You Run.

Mailing pieces, in quantities of 10,000, may cost $1 each, or a total of $10,000. A one percent return would be 100 sales. For an $89 tape, the mailing would gross $89,000. A half-percent return would gross less than $45,000. Subtract other costs, such as duplicating, shipping and handling, overhead and program production, and you quickly see how little is left as "net profit." This emphasizes the importance of testing. The difference between the right list and the wrong list is the difference between success and failure.

As the business grows and you gain confidence in mailing hundreds of thousands of flyers at a time, the price for an eight-page color mailer can fall to 30 to 60 cents. Thus your cost per order will fall accordingly. A strong list and high volume mailer can increase your profit margin.

13. Identify as Many Distribution Channels as Possible.

Besides selling directly through the mail to individuals and corporate buyers, the Kantolas also sell through distributors–mostly catalogers–who feature videos in their own direct-mail catalogs. The catalogs buy the videos at a 40 percent discount.

Self-distribution works best once you discover several different channels of distribution. You then begin to market to each, gaining larger and larger entry into those channels. Kantola Productions videos are sold through these channels: 20 percent through display ads; 10 percent through catalogs/distributors; and 10 percent through joint venture and newsletter.

14. Know Your Buyer, and Market to That Buyer.

It is important to identify your buyer and find ways to communicate directly and effectively to that buyer. The more you sell, the more you will come to know who the buyers are. And in doing that, you can refine the copy and design of your mail piece and improve your ability to communicate the benefits of your program. Kantola has found that his video buyers are both middle and upper-level executives ("given the benefits, it's not an expensive product"), university professors, high school professors or "anyone who teaches public speaking."

15. Produce Programs That Have A Long Shelf Life.

It's cheaper to work out your ideas on paper before you start shooting. It's easy to be seduced by ideas during a cappuccino rush. Wait. Think about the criteria of your product. Is it a short, fad-type subject that–in two years –will be of interest to no one? Or is it "evergreen," and will be used for a long time? If your subject is of general interest, all the better. If it has a pre-promoted name, subject or celebrity attached, all the better again. There is nothing wrong with producing a tape on a "hot" subject, but you must have a marketing and distributing channel that can get the "hot" tape out before it turns "cold." You could be left with a warehouse full of Milli Vanilli.

In the Kantolas' case, they selected an "evergreen" subject that will be of interest all year long, for many years. Basically, the content (public speaking) is timeless. The only thing that may need to be updated from decade to decade is the clothes his subjects wear.

The secret to the whole operation, according to the Kantolas, is to stick to the basics. For them that is: (1) a name product (Toastmasters), (2) a title with great general interest, and (3) a low price point (in comparison to what a professional seminar consultant would cost).

16. Select A Marketing Partner.

Select a strategic marketing partner that can help you start off strongly. This partner may have access to content or proprietary information (for development into video) and to a mailing list, magazine or newsletter to get to a large target market. "Toastmasters," says Steve, "is a great organization. They helped develop the program. They wanted the exposure, and it was a good thing for their 170,000 members. They helped us bring the video to the market in the beginning."

17. Build A Database of Your Buyers.

Building from a core audience, Kantola began developing a mailing list of individuals, educators and businesses interested in his videos. As he developed new and similar titles, he could go back to his previous customers. He is always expanding his database. Now he sends out 1.5 million mailings per year. A one percent return would yield 15,000 orders.

18. Develop Customer Loyalty.

Kantola has focused on the kind of information his customers want. Experience has taught him who his buyers are so that he can send his mailer to the right person in the corporation.

19. Master One Line Before Going on to Others.

From the experience of developing one successful line, Kantola has also produced four business training videos in cooperation with the Wharton School of the University of Pennsylvania. The Kantolas are applying what they've learned to new lines of video product. Kantola Productions is probably just one of many quiet success stories. If you have a story to tell, please send me a letter.

Now, for the rest of you who may just be dreaming about "doing it yourself," I hope that you may absorb and test some of these principles and use them to successfully develop your own channels of distribution. Now go get 'em.

READ THE FINE PRINT!

Time and time again I hear from producers who've already made their deal. They were either so desperate to get a distributor or naive of the implications of what they signed that they made some rather obvious mistakes that they now regret. This article is a wake-up call regarding some of the simple things to watch out for in your contracts.

I am not a lawyer. I have, however, worked on hundreds of video-distribution contracts as a producer or consultant, and I have also been on the distribution side of the business when I was in charge of acquiring and producing non-theatrical programs for Vestron Video.

What I am about to suggest in this article can mean the difference between receiving healthy royalties from your hard labors or getting zip. This is information distributors don't want you to know!

When you receive the "standard" distribution contract from a video program distributor, you must not accept it at face value. Sure you've worked long and hard on your video and are happy to even find a distributor. But just because it's a "standard" contract doesn't mean it's okay to sign it. After all, you are "a special case."

The so-called standard contract is the deal that is most favorable to the distributor, but not to you. When you negotiate, you'll find that there is much more room in the contract than you ever expected. In fact, it very quickly becomes a non-standard contract.

In addition, there are "pitfalls" that you will want to modify or eliminate completely. To be specific, a pitfall is a deal point or legal language that's designed to put you–the producer–at a disadvantage. A pitfall means you will be paid less money, paid at a later date, or that you will have to give up important rights that you shouldn't. Although it is beyond the scope of this article to go into the minutiae of every word, phrase and paragraph, I have identified a dozen dangerous pitfalls that you should either avoid entirely, or–at the very least–understand the possible consequences.

It's not my intention here to give video program distributors a bad rap. Some distribution contracts are simple, straightforward, and provide real "win-win" situations for both parties. Other contracts really need to be brought out of the shadows and into the daylight. I feel strongly that some of these deceptive practices should be banished completely.

If the distributor wants your program badly enough, perhaps they will give you a "favored-nations agreement." This means that you, too, can receive whatever "best deal" they already have made with another producer. In this scenario, you reap the benefits of whatever a particular individual's lawyer negotiated for him or her.

As you read your contract, stay awake and watch out for the following:

1. What are the format rights actually being licensed? Are they for video, television, new media (whatever that may be), CD-ROM or interactive television? Define what rights you want to include. Define what rights you will exclude and keep for yourself. "Any and all electronic media rights" has no place in your contract.

2. Most distributors will want an "exclusive deal." But for what rights? And in what territories? If they only sell to retail stores and not through mail order or direct-response television, then you may be able to "exclude" these rights from your deal. If you grant all rights, then they will simply obtain third-party distribution for those markets that they do not directly sell to, which is something you could have done yourself.

3. Perpetuity is a long time. Your contract term should be limited to five to seven years for video.

4. Producers often get paid their advances on delivery. This means you are paid when you deliver the master videotape and other delivery items. Make sure you know very clearly what is expected of you. Delivery items may include the video master, but also a trailer, photos, a synopsis, et cetera. Perhaps the distributor should pay for some of these things.

5. Title rights. Editing rights. Do you want to give your distributor the power to edit your show or change your title?

6. Get "approval" rights on the video packaging and artwork. This means you can approve (or not) the look and copy on the box and sell sheets that represent your work. If you only have "consultation rights," it means you can say all you want but the distributor need not listen to you.

7. The distribution contract will specify a delivery date. Can you really deliver everything in 30 days? What's everything? This is where you must have a very clear understanding of what is expected of you. You would hate to have the distributor renege on the contract if you forget to deliver publicity photographs. A distributor will not write you a check until they get everything they need.

8. Read the language very carefully (and look throughout the entire contract) to make sure that there are no deductions from the gross receipts that would reduce your royalties. This is a real can of worms and some distributors will hide a line here or there that will reduce your expected royalty by as much as 50 percent.

9. Normally free copies of the videos are given to the press for promotion. That's great. But somewhere along the line distributors learned they could give "free goods" as incentives on other deals they were making with their wholesalers, and thereby not have to pay royalties to the producer. Limit them to a certain number of free goods.

10. To protect themselves, distributors will build into their contracts a clause that will limit the time you have to come after them for breach of contract, bad accounting, etc. They want to stop the clock at 12 months and say, "Hey, sorry, whatever we did no longer counts after this time." Get out your red pencil and delete this line.

11. I love how video distributors will give producers the right to audit the books (during normal business hours) but will not give them the manufacturing records so they can see how many tapes were actually manufactured. What's wrong with this picture? They either: (a) don't

want you to see that they are manufacturing one-hour tapes for $1.15 each or less; or (b) don't want you to know that they manufactured more tapes than they reported.

12. Say your distributor goes bankrupt or is bought out by another company. This has happened to me several times. The new distributor could care less about you. You have no relationship with them. I recommend that you put a clause in your contract that says the rights revert back to you and the contract is null and void if the company is sold. Some companies like to sign up lots of new programs to increase their company's "library value" with no real intention of distributing your video. This raises the value of their company when they put it up for sale. (If they don't release you before a certain date, then the rights should immediately revert back to you.)

Summary

This is a quick comb-through of a distribution contract. But it only catches a few of the major snarls and snags. Nevertheless, maybe it's scared you enough to get yourself a good lawyer when you negotiate your contract. I recommend that you hire an entertainment attorney, and hopefully, one who has dealt with your distribution company.

Any homework that you can do to understand and anticipate these pitfalls will help you work with your lawyer. I often negotiate the basic deal with the distributor and then pull in my lawyer for the fine points and the hard-core negotiation. This way I can remain the creative artist and let my lawyer be the bad guy. (Lawyers love this role!) I've had a lot of experience doing this. If you haven't, let your lawyer take the lead.

For distributors who are reading this article and are thinking, "Ah, hah! I never thought of that trick. I'm going to put that clause in our contract," just remember—what goes around, comes around.

I hope this has been a useful exercise for you and provides greater insight in how to create a profitable situation with your distributor. Good luck and happy negotiating! Now go get 'em.

CASE STUDIES
OF SUCCESS

BABIES AT PLAY:
HOW TWO FIRST-TIME VIDEO PRODUCERS MADE A SIX-FIGURE DEAL WITH A MAJOR STUDIO

The more experience we gain, the more we think we can identify principles to apply to future work that will ensure success. Right? Sounds good, yes? But every once in a while, there's a project that comes along where the rules just don't apply.

Every month my associate Ken Lee and I consult with dozens of independent producers. We provide them with information and advice on the entire arc of production (program development, budgeting, marketing, distribution, etc.). We help these producers "jump start" their projects. Many go on to successfully distribute their new video titles. Others, like the producers in the story you're about to read, go on to create an entire new business category!

Andrea Gennette (Executive Producer) and Tami Williams (Creator, Producer, Director) came to us about a year ago for consulting. We spent about five hours over the course of several months with them, helping to develop their project. By the time you read this, they will have delivered their masters to a major studio and collected a six-figure advance.

Gennette and Williams had produced industrials in the past but nothing for the commercial, consumer home-video market. They wanted our assistance in bringing their new concept to that marketplace. When clients come to us, we ask that they consider a brief list of questions: "What is their overall goal?" "Who is their target market?" "What resources do they have to support their project (i.e., marketing relationships, celebrity endorsements, financing, etc.)?" "What obstacles might be preventing them from achieving their goals?" We review their answers to these questions and provide clients with an overview of their projects' strengths, weaknesses and opportunities. Then we recommend resources to fill out their package.

Gennette and Williams's concept was incredibly simple. Williams is a working mom, and like most mothers with young children, she discovered that videos can be good babysitters. She also saw that her children were fascinated by watching older children at play, hence her series concept: *Babies At Play*. The fact that this concept was so simple was both a plus and a minus. Could it be too simple to find an audience?

Williams went to her local video store and quickly learned that although there's a great many tapes for children, there's very few for toddlers and preschoolers. Bingo! She had identified her target market. Parents of young toddlers would be the purchasers; the toddlers would be the "end users."

From their initial concept of *Babies At Play*, we recognized that the project had these strengths:

- high concept
- unique product offering
- no competition
- niche market opportunity
- very low production cost
- no major star necessary
- addresses the need for a video babysitter

We also discussed weaknesses in the concept. These included:

- the theme is weak (how can you differentiate the individual programs?)
- is babysitting too narrow?
- do the programs need to provide education and learning as well?
- no child development experts are endorsing the product
- no appeal in the video rental store (or is there?)
- no sponsorship

This was one of those "pet rock" kind of projects. Either it's going to work very well or it's going to fall on its face. Success will be a function of how well video production technique is applied to make the shows fascinating for young children. That, along with the project's timing, marketing strategy, sponsorship support, and just plain good luck. I'd love to impart some great production secrets here, but other than some very talented shooters using Betacams mounted on SteadiCam rigs to literally capture babies at play, that's about all there was to it. Post-production wasn't exactly daunting, either.

Because production costs were so low and the concept so simple, we encouraged the producers to find ways to bring additional value to the project. We felt there was little or no downside to this. We saved them money right away by persuading them not to produce a demo tape. Why produce a pilot or write a detailed script when the concept is so simple and easy to pitch? We felt it was better, in this case, to sell the "dream," rather than deliver something that may not meet the expectations of the video distributor/buyer.

We also felt that only one premium sale to a sponsor would give them more than enough to make the project profitable. We liked Gennette and Williams's "never say no" attitude, and although the concept was initially so simple, it resulted in a six-figure advance from a major studio to produce three short videos. They'll net a six-figure fee plus have a shot at some big-time royalties.

We sought permission from Gennette and Williams to tell the *Babies At Play* story because it exemplifies so many of the fundamental principles required to create a home video hit.

• Create a fresh concept. Their concept to videotape older children at play formed the basis of their "high concept." The idea is very easy to understand (and pitch).

• Identify a need in the marketplace. As stated, Gennette and Williams noticed that there were very few tapes for very young children. They saw a niche and had an idea to fill it.

• Produce the project on as low a budget as possible. The concept allowed for this; financiers like that situation.

•   Price the product appropriately for the marketplace. The tapes could be marketed at a low retail price point, thereby gaining access to mass distribution through mass merchants. Distributors like this too.

•   Identify distribution channels. Most distributors are aware of the burgeoning children's market and are looking to create and acquire product. Many companies already have a children's video line. Everyone is looking for new product. Gennette and Williams are selling something that had a clear distribution channel and could be readily marketed.

•   Go in with a "can do" attitude. Although they'd never pro-duced consumer home videos, the concept was not so difficult that a buyer would have qualms about letting them produce their own show. Had they wanted to create licensed characters, do a music video, a dance video, or an animation, the buyer may have required other pro-ducers to make the program. Gennette and Williams's "go get 'em" attitude gave the distributors the confidence to sign them up.

•   Ask the right questions. What we particularly liked about Gennette and Williams is that they asked each and every question, from concept and program development to budgeting, production and distribution. They wanted to be sure they understood every nuance and possibility for their concept. They acknowledged that they were new at the video game and were open-minded and flexible. They willingly learned and employed many new twists to their original concept.

•   Identify potential sponsors. The concept had excellent spon-sorship potential. What manufacturer of children's products (diapers, clothes, food, magazines, etc.) would not want to be associated with and support this project through cross-merchandising, couponing, or some other means? To a distributor, sponsorship means a nationwide merchandising partner that will help defray marketing costs. The sponsorship potential made this project even more valuable to a distributor.

It's not every day that first-time producers can strike a deal with a major studio, but by following clear and simple, time-tested principles for home videos, Gennette and Williams demonstrated that their dreams can become real.

What idea do you have on the backburner? What are you waiting for? Go get 'em!

SEX, LAWS & VIDEOTAPE MARKETING

A well-thought-out marketing plan is the key to financial reward. Too frequently producers get caught up in financing and production issues and overlook how their program will be brought to the market.

The case study that follows is a magnificent example of how three sets of entrepreneurs joined resources to create–not a single video–but a successful business delivering high value information about sexual harassment in the workplace to a targeted market.

The Program Objective

Sexual harassment is one of the serious issues facing today's workplace. It is complex and often misunderstood. It is crucial that employer and employees have a clear understanding of what constitutes sexual harassment and how to resolve situations if they occur.

The Players

Trisha Brinkman and Barry Chersky (Brinkman & Associates, 1300 12th Avenue, San Francisco, CA 94122, [415] 661-4040) are among the country's leading trainers and consultants on issues related to sexual harassment. Brinkman and Chersky have been the leading corporate trainers for the last 10 years and have conducted seminars for hundreds of businesses, corporations and educational institutions throughout the country. They are superb "camera ready" communicators with a strong commitment to clarifying the issues. They provided the "content" for the programs, and a dedicated client list for marketing purposes.

Paragon Productions (218 Ninth Street, San Francisco, CA 94103, [415] 626-7004, President, Kevin Comora) originated the project and secured the rights to the Brinkman talent and material. Paragon had 50 percent of the financing and had been working on the project for about a year before meeting the next partner whose vision made it all work.

Freeze Frame: This is the point where most producers run out of steam and projects fall apart. They've identified a hot topic, they've licensed the talent/material, they've completed a treatment or script and maybe even found some of the money, but then they get stuck.

Steve Michelson (Steve Michelson Productions, 280 Utah Street, San Francisco, CA 94103, [415] 626-3080) specializes in video publishing and is Executive Producer for the Beverly Hills Publishing Company. Founder of One Pass and former President of Scanline Communications, he is well-versed in publishing video programs for targeted audiences.

Michelson's vision for something beyond a "single video" and ability to bring all the players into a united effort (CB Associates) is an unusual achievement and hence the reason for being highlighted here.

The Product & Pricing

Changing Boundaries: Recognizing, Preventing, Resolving Sexual Harassment is an integrated, interactive set of products: an hour-long management video, an hour-long employee video, five employee guides, five management guides and one 100-page trainer guide.

The price is $1295. Or a single management or employee tape with guide are $795 each. Extra guides are an additional $2 to $5 each, depending on the quantity ordered. It is clear that there is a secondary back-end sale item here. One corporation might purchase the tape and then order 5000 guides!!

Price Justification

Did you get the price point? It's not a typo! *This product costs over twelve hundred dollars.* How in the world can you justify a $1295 price point?

First, if you think you are selling someone a videotape, you can't justify it. However, if what is being sold–and it's very important to fully understand this–is value-added courseware that allows the buyer to really solve their problem then the price might be right. In addition, if your courseware elucidates recent compliance sexual harassment laws then an even stronger argument can be made. If a corporation has sexual harassment charges brought against them, it may cost tens of thousands of dollars in legal expenses. From this perspective, $1295 is cheap.

Secondly, for several thousand dollars, you could hire Brinkman and Chersky to speak to your managers and employees for one day. But then they are gone. A video training course enables employees to benefit all year round.

Thirdly, Brinkman Associates' calendar is full most days of the year. Clients can either wait in line until they are available, or purchase the training tools and use it tomorrow. The corporation must provide someone to take on a leadership role–like a committed manager or human resources person–and adapt the training tapes for the company's needs. The training manual that accompanies the videos provides clear assistance in this regard.

Target Audience

There are several levels of targeted audiences for the programs. The first is the built-in audience of over 500 Brinkman client companies. While this may not seem like many, early marketing efforts have resulted in a 50 percent response rate to this group alone. If the numbers hold up, 250 sales would gross over $300,000. Not only does this help cover production and marketing costs, but these buyers provide downside protection for initial financial risk.

Other buyers are the 70,000 human resource directors throughout the country.

Competition

The producers did their homework. They scoured the earth for all other similar products. The competition consisted of a successful tape from BNA, a direct mail distributor. The BNA tape was several years old and priced slightly higher. The producers felt that *Changing Boundaries* would serve the needs of a wider range of companies than BNA's tape and that–done in a style that would be more interactive–could be more useful to purchasers.

Program Concept

The goal was to create modular training courses, all of which use the same body of knowledge for a one-hour course, a two-hour course, or a half-day seminar. The buyer receives videos and course books which help him or her use this body of information. Michelson says, "By carefully looking at the publishing requirements and consulting with Brinkman & Associates' own clients, we were able to determine that one tape would be insufficient. We needed to divide the content so that the managers received different content than the employees."

Rebecca Locke, an instructional design writer, was brought in to work on the content and to make the script more interactive. About the design, Michelson explains, "It's all part of understanding the market-place and determining how the product is going to solve the problem. How does it work? It is small bits of information that are reinforced by personal and interpersonal communication. That's where the value-added comes from. This is not a conventional TV viewing experience but a real life experience where the television is the catalyst. Once you use video in this capacity, it has enormous power. It empowers the individual to solve their problems with flexible modules."

Production Elements

There are three production elements with interactive linkage between the video and printed manuals.

1.   The scenarios: about a dozen "slice of life" vignettes of sexual harassment in the workplace. Some harassments are obvious and others aren't. These little windows into sexual harassment situations are about 90-seconds long. They are deliberately designed to combine more than one aspect of sexual harassment just like real life. They also reflect the cultural diversity of today's workplace.

2.   The trainers conduct a simulated training session with a diverse group of people in an imaginary corporation. As a viewer, you may identify with and share some of the perspectives of a shop manager, sales manager, an operations person, etc. "Your support group is worked into the video as they discuss the issues. Seeing the training session group on video kind of 'kick-starts' your own discussion," explains Michelson.

3.   There is the information, the content, the facts. There are the legal definitions of sexual harassment and supportive printed documents.

These elements facilitate the interactivity and discussion of the real-life viewing audience. The real learning and understanding takes place during the discussion, not the video viewing.

Packaging

A handsome leatherette binder that commands respect contains all videos and printed materials.

Distribution Channels

Level One. A small preferred group of existing clients (approx. 500) already aware of Brinkman's work. From the first 150 calls to this elite, highly motivated buying group, 20 programs were sold. A 13 percent response rate!

Not only are these people buyers, but they will tell others. Sometimes they are distributors or buyers themselves and will generate referred sales. Naturally you want to launch a product to the class of trade that will generate the most and buffer your cash outlay.

Level Two. The 70,000 human resource managers. This list will be tested before a mass rollout. It is expected that a sale will be made to one to two percent of that population generating between $906,500 and $1,813,000 in gross revenues.

This answers the burning question all producers should be able to answer: *"Is there a market for the product and how can you reach it?"*

Impressions for Success

The marketers feel that you need to have five impressions before a sale is made. Production is the easy fun part and is over relatively soon. Marketing requires a sustained and focused effort to succeed.

Impression #1 is telemarketing to the priority Brinkman client list; #2 is a review or publicity (such as this article); #3 is a direct mail piece which goes out 60 to 90 days after the telemarketing. (The direct mail piece is a four-color brochure which costs a little more than $1. A one percent response rate costs about $100 per order per mailing which is still only an eight percent marketing cost (e.g., $1295/100). Three mailings would cost 23 percent of the gross revenues, which by direct mailing standards is still quite low. This model works because the product is high-priced and can support these margins.

Free Trial

To further stimulate sales, the program is sent out on a free trial basis for 30 days. If, after 30 days, it isn't returned then it becomes a purchase. The marketers are relying on the buyer's desire to have the product, and their ability to understand that its value is that it can be used again and again by employees. It's not just a one shot video program.

Telemarketing Video?

An article in *Time* magazine demonstrated how large the telemarketing industry really is. In 1983, $56 billion dollars of goods and services were sold over phone lines and last year the number reached $300 billion. With the price of postage rising faster than telephone rates, marketers can reach people by phone for about one-third of the cost by mail. In telemarketing you only need a one percent to two percent response rate for success. The higher the price point, the better. Over 80 percent of telemarketing revenues come from sales to business.

There is no reason why these marketing techniques cannot be applied to selling video programs. Of course, the economic model must work. In this case, study the telemarketers' cost of about $10-15 per hour. They can make 75 calls per hour. Many are, of course, hang-ups, busy signals, or no answers. The average sales call takes about two to three minutes. This means they may talk to 10 or 15 people per hour, or 80 to 120 people per day, resulting in one or more sales per day. In this model, the cost of one sale is about $120 for the salesperson, plus the cost of the calls and overhead. Marketing costs are about 15-20 percent.

CB Associates will start with a few telemarketers and build as they gain experience.

Follow-Up & Line Extensions

As sales are made, follow-up calls can analyze the end user's result and collect testimonials for future marketing efforts. The marketers will learn what content is the most successful and can focus sales efforts on those newly discovered marketing elements.

Line Extension

It is very valuable for producers to determine if there are line extensions or series of related products that can be created in the event the first is successful. Why create only one product and walk away from a market you've penetrated?

With *Changing Boundaries*, the producers reformat the content for lower priced markets. Or they may reformat "customized versions" for companies that like the program but want their own version. For

$10,000, the producers can shoot customized footage incorporating the company logo, their buildings and employees into the existing programs.

Catalogs

The marketers also expect to use third-party distributors who send exclusive catalogs to specific markets. Other English-speaking territories like Australia, Canada and the UK are potential markets. Third-party distributors take a 10 percent to 20 percent fee ($129 to $258) for marketing.

Splintering Markets & Strategy

It is to the producer's advantage to determine as many markets as possible for his or her product. However care must be taken not to create confusion in the marketplace by having too many people offer the same product to the same market. The various distribution strategies must interlock and there must be coordination between sequential marketing to various markets. Naturally you will want to sell to the higher-paying customers first and work your way down to the lower price markets after first selling into the priority markets.

Decision-Making Process

Normally a distributor acquires the rights for distribution from a producer. End of story.

Not CB Associates which has developed a model that includes all the partners. Michelson says, "Ultimately what makes for good partnerships is running things like a business. All of us meet together like a board of directors to make decisions. Producers and distributors alike fail because they don't understand relationships between people. It's not 'thank you for the content, good-bye!' Everyone approves the copy, the deals and other aspects of marketing. We have minutes and voting procedures. When one party is making a deal with the partnership, the other parties negotiate with them. It's unusual, and it takes time, but it keeps us all heading in the same direction, and harnesses everyone's brain power. It works."

Harnessing the power of the team allows the different players (who may be closer to the market) to participate in the decision-making process. This reiterates the point that it's not the easy sells that make a business but dedicated, cooperative marketing efforts that succeed.

Marketing Environment

Producers need to pay attention to the mood, atmosphere and intellectual mindset of the market they are selling into. This bundle of products is a prime example of a "compliance video." The video connects to the compliance needs of a corporation which makes this product a *must have* tape for corporations. The law is very simple. If your company doesn't train your employees about correct behavior then, in the event of a sexual harassment suit, your company could be liable to the full extent of the damages.

Having a training program that covers all the issues helps to protect the corporation from negligence. Do you start to see how a $1295 price point is cheap? Savvy producers might think about other topics that might call for "compliance videos."

If you can deliver high-value information to a targeted audience for a high price point, you've got a real business on your hands. Now go get 'em.

CREATING A HIT RIGHT OUT OF THE BOX

I continue to be amazed how productions come about. Just when I think I've got the formula down, unexpected things happen. This is an account of a project we started about a year ago that both breaks and creates "the rules" of video marketing and distribution.

THE MAKING OF. . .
Kids on the Internet

Normally when I create a new video title I double-check to make sure the project has the following seven elements.

Formula for Success

- Addresses a need
- Is first (or second) in the market
- Carries or establishes a brand name and identity, name host
- Plays off a trend or social concern
- Is created as a series or line extension of the program
- Has outstanding packaging
- A number of distribution channels exist

I think I was pretty successful in establishing the first six items. The last item is another story altogether, which we'll get to. Here are the things we learned in the development of this program.

Address a Need

The Internet has hit the media like nothing before. Everyone I know is talking about it. The problem is that once you get on line, what do you do? Where do you go? The learning curve is quite steep. You can waste lots of time on-line. I thought to myself, "Wouldn't it be great if you could sit down with a master cyberspace pioneer who'd show you not only 'how-to' but 'why to'?"

217

Well-Known Host

I called my long-time friend Howard Rheingold, who wrote the best-selling books *Virtual Reality* and *Virtual Communities*. He is also a founder of *Hotwired* and forward thinking when it comes to the Internet. We were pals in San Francisco in the late '60s. In a few minutes I'd decided that Howard was that cyberspace master who could host a series of programs about the Internet. The first would be called *Livin on the Net*. It would be a rundown of the basics but also contain some big "aha's" and empower people with how to use the Internet to further their personal and professional lives.

Surf or Counter a Trend

Another program that we would produce would address what kids are doing on the Internet. There was so much bad press about the Internet, about censorship, and about the dangers on the Internet for kids that there were two things we could do–(1) agree with it, and play to parent's fears, or (2) show the great, positive things that kids are doing, thereby alleviating some of their fears. We chose the later.

We also chose to have kids teach how to use the Internet. They were funny, they were bright, they really held your attention while they told stories about e-mail, building web pages, reading dolphin newsgroups, adopting whales, saving the comic-book life of Superman, and doing their homework. The kids were clearly empowered by the Internet. Surprisingly the parents and educators that saw the show loved it. Many did not know much about the Internet and learned from the kids! A teaching strategy we intend to use again in the future as we extend the line.

Always Check Out the Competition–Don't Put Your Head in the Sand

At the time we developed the idea for an Internet series, there were only four tapes in the marketplace (and only one–from Canada–which in our estimation was any good). Today there are at least three dozen tapes and probably more by the time you read this. If you think this is a good idea folks—it was, it's over. The market is saturated. Clearly the Internet video genre is jammed with competitors. You must check out your competition for two important reasons. One, you must determine if there is any room in the marketplace for the type of videos your are producing. Second, you need to make sure you can differentiate your product from the competition's. The dozens of producers we consult with each year continue to overlook this important step. They are so attached to doing their project that they don't want to look, or hear about, anything similar. And that's a very dangerous way to begin.

Detailed Distribution Plans Should Come Before Financing

The financial projections for the video included the following markets:

- consumer video
- educational/institutional video
- direct marketing
- broadcast television
- premium sales

Initially we believed that the tapes could be priced high ($49.95), much like the MacAcademy instructional videos. By the time we got to market, prices had fallen (our tapes were not purely instructional), and if we wanted to get into the retail video market, we'd have to price them at $9.95! This, of course, changes the numbers and projections drastically. We expected the majority of sales to come from consumer video, then educational, then direct marketing. In actuality, I didn't even include the premium (where tapes are sold in volume to corporate buyers as a gift or promotional giveaway) market in my financial projections because you can't count on premium sales for revenue. Either they happen or they don't. It's a function of the buyer's needs. But as you'll see, this turned out to the leading source of revenue in the roll-out phase.

Make the Best Deal You Can–For Everyone!

When you've established the viability of the marketplace and how your video can be marketed then it's time to raise the money. I wrote a proposal which included industry trends and Internet information, budgets, and financial projections. Our lawyer drew up a Limited Partnership Agreement. We would create a series by first producing four videos, and if they were successful, roll the money back into new production and marketing. The investors' original equity would carry over into the entire line, thereby increasing their potential profit participation.

(I had an offer from an investor to sell most of the Partnership's shares but I felt the terms of double recoupment and a 70/30 percent split, instead of a 50/50 split were too tough so I turned down the deal.)

Because of a breakthrough (next paragraph) I decided to only sell a small portion of the shares in the Partnership. We immediately began production on the first two videos. Ken Lee (long-time Michael Wiese Production Vice President and staff producer) produced the shows. I directed and executive produced. (Ken was also responsible for making numerous marketing deals.)

Network With Everyone–Sometimes Your On-Talent Expert Has Great Contacts!

Through Howard Rheingold, we made a contact at Compuserve who got very excited about bundling Howard's *Livin' On The Net* video with their successful Internet in a Box (software that immediately connects you to "safe" Internet sites through Compuserve). However they didn't, at the time have a product manager, and said that it would have to wait a few months. During the conversation I mentioned that we were also doing a show called *Kids On The Internet*. The show had been shot at a FUTUREKIDS facility, the nation's largest computer learning centers for kids. It featured a dozen computer whiz kids showing you all the great things they do online (homework, games, e-mail, chat groups, web pages, etc.) Compuserve jumped on this idea and we made a deal to bundle our video with their Internet in a Box for Kids .

Although we had already started editing Howard's show, we immediately switched to the kids show to finish it by October, the deadline to get it out into the retail market by Christmas. The video was cut on an Avid by Chris Wayne at Crest National in Hollywood. It was posted digitally, and duplicated at the facility as well.

By the end of Christmas, Compuserve had ordered 50,000 units of the *Kids on the Internet* which we sold at a few dollars above cost. This income enabled us to finish Howard's video and do some marketing. (Compuserve later decided against bundling Howard's tape with their browser software–prices had fallen, and there was way too much competition now in the marketplace. See, in a fast-moving marketplace, the ground literally moves under your feet.)

FUTUREKIDS also bought 1000 units of the video (at wholesale) to distribute to their 400+ franchisees throughout the world. The video was to be used to promote the computer centers but also would be used as a giveaway promotional item if you signed up for a computer course. (FUTUREKIDS also wrote a six-week curriculum to accompany the video which we are marketing to educational institutions for $250.)

FUTUREKIDS also help us cast the kids, trained them for several weeks before filming, provided a free facility and computers, and were terrific throughout production in anticipating our needs. (David Ullendorff, a principal in FUTUREKIDS, formerly worked with me in New York producing political campaign television spots.) David and his colleagues at FUTUREKIDS were very deserving of their "associate producers" credits.

At the first of the year we found ourselves with three 30-minute videos (Howard's video had a Part I and Part II). And some in-kind marketing.

Every Deal Should Have A Marketing Component

Besides the sales of units to both Compuserve and FUTUREKIDS, the deals also included marketing. Compuserve would include us in all national press releases and press conference events, plus they gave us $45,000 in on-line advertising so we could advertise on their home page. FUTUREKIDS included us in their house newsletter mailings, press announcements, and several consumer magazine ads. As I always tell the producers I consult with, "You can never have enough marketing. When you make a deal, be sure it includes marketing. Money is not enough."

Television

We screened *Kids on the Internet* for PBS who, as of this writing, are showing it as part of their pledge campaign. Some 45 stations picked it up. We receive a license fee in direct proportion to how much money is raised. In addition, through our fulfillment center, we sell pledge products to the PBS stations and keep the profits. (We solicited many of our strategic marketing partners such as magazines, software manufacturers, publishers, computer learning centers, and others. We told them that we would feature their products during the pledge break in return for "free goods" which we in turn could sell to the stations. Everyone was delighted with this arrangement.) As of this writing the jury is still out and we don't know how much products we've sold. A PBS station will normally mark up the pledge premium that you sell them 5 to 10 times. So a video that you sell them for $5 is marked up to $25 or $50. "Pledge $50 dollars and become a PBS station member and we'll give you the video you've just seen. Pledge $100 and we'll give you this video, magazine, software, book and a coupon for a computer class."

Internet Marketing

One of the magazines whose product was included during the pledge breaks also gave us some free ad space in their magazine. Together we did a promotion on the World Wide Web where they gave away our videos and provided a link to our page resulting in thousands of hits to our page (http://websites.earthlink.net/~mwp) which featured an order form for the videos.

We are constantly coming up with new things to do on the Internet to promote the videos. Far too many things to go into in this article. It is part of our ongoing marketing plan.

It's Not Enough to be A Producer These Days

I think by now you are beginning to get the picture. It's not enough these days to just be a producer, to just make something. You have to think creatively about how to sell it and get it to your marketplace.

Unless your video has a well-known superstar attached, it will be very hard to get wide-spread attention for the program without innovative marketing.

Packaging

Readers of my columns know how strongly I care about great packaging. We go to extra lengths to make sure that our packaging is the best possible because it must stand out in a very crowded marketplace.

Forget the Majors

Unless you are producing a movie with a big star, forget about the major home video companies. They are too big and their overheads are too great to help you sell your videos. Most have to sell at least 100,000 units of a special interest video before they will go to the trouble of using their marketing machine for your video. That reduces the number of special interest titles that will be distributed a year to very few.

Plus the major's distribution machines will never get to the nooks and crannies and special markets where the bulk of your sales will come from. They never would have found the Compuserve deal, the PBS deal, or be able to sell into computer stores.

Instead what you want to do is employ as many video wholesalers, direct marketing partners, and catalogers for your video as possible. You want to get into those tiny niches with your line of products. (It is not cost-effective to market a single title in this manner.) Toward that end we are working with a handful of smaller companies who know how to sell Internet-related products.

As our sales increase and marketing expands, we will produce additional videos from a long list that we've already developed employing the same principles we've discussed above.

Pre-Production

Producer Ken Lee and I knew immediately that we would have to find bright, communicative, funny kids who had experience on the Internet. Not only that, they would have to be kids who could really communicate their excitement about the Internet to other kids. Not an easy assignment.

My first attempt was to log onto a kid's chat group on America On-Line saying that I was a producer looking for kids to be in a video about the Internet. Wrong! Silly me. The Webmaster immediately told me to get out of the chat group. When I responded, he pulled the plug and I was immediately disconnected. (I then went back and read the chat room rules–I had clearly made a big netiquette error!)

Then I found some kid's home pages and started writing them and their parents but there were just too many hurdles. The parents were suspicious and I had no way of interviewing the kids.

How was I going to find bright kids already on-line? I called David Ullendorff, one of the principals in FUTUREKIDS, the international computer learning facility for kids. I explained our interest in developing a video featuring their students as "kid experts" on the Internet. They were very enthusiastic about the video and put the entire support of the organization behind the project. They found the kids and brought in Craig Bach, Ph.D., a FUTUREKIDS instructional designer as a consultant.

David offered not only to help us find the brightest kids that attended many of their Los Angeles-area schools but also to train the kids with supplemental classes. He also introduced us to the Don Liebson, owner of the FUTUREKIDS facility in Manhattan Beach, CA who was kind enough to let us shoot for two days.

In exchange, we offered to include FUTUREKIDS signage in the show so that they could derive some promotional value in exchange for their services and to sell them some videos of the show for promotional purposes. We put FUTUREKIDS logos on some of the monitors, shot a few FUTUREKIDS web pages, and had signage on one of the walls of the facility. We never went out of our way to shoot the signs. They are there and are very unobtrusive. (At least we thought so. When the show was aired on PBS, they made us cut out, or ADO-up, any images where you could read "FUTUREKIDS." It took us a day and about $3,000 to cut this out.)

Casting

We wanted to find about a dozen kids, girls and boys, ages 9-14, with diverse ethnic backgrounds. About 30 or 40 kids came for an evening of quick 10-minute interviews. It was a kind of open house where we set up a high-band 8mm camera in the corner and interviewed the kids.

The criteria we used in selecting the kids was simple: energy, personality, and the ability to communicate stories about the Internet that other kids would relate to. If we found an appropriate candidate, we stopped taping, notes were taken, and contact numbers exchanged. Sometimes it would take a while to draw out the child and learn what his or her hobbies and interests and level of skill in the Internet were. By the end of the evening, we had about 15 kids that we thought we could use.

Ken Lee (who also wrote the show) matched up the kid's interest to the subject outline that I'd written. He did some additional interviews with the kids and their parents. We also discussed the content with Craig and David who designed a four-week prep course that would further get the kids up to speed on the Internet using their individual interests and our subject matter.

The notion was that by the time we started shooting the kids would be enthusiastic, and able to demonstrate and articulate various aspects of the Internet. The prep paid off!

Their interests included *Star Wars*, Superman, MUDs and games, dolphins, whales, alternative music, the Civil War, and aliens. Ken easily found a way to have them explore their interests and use the Internet to do so. The result were numerous stories of enthusiastic kids telling us about what they did on the Internet.

The stories surpassed our expectations! Kids were saying that the Internet was better than TV, that they used the Internet for home-work, and that they were making friends all over the world.

These individual segments would be held together by intros (and extros) of two kids hosts. We cast two more "Futurekids": a very bright girl–Rachel Valente–with a comedic, expressive boy–Brian Ballsun-Stanton. The "straight man/ comedian" combination worked very well.

In conceiving a show I frequently list all the elements that I think the show will have. This way, whenever I get into coverage trouble or want to pick up the pace I can look down the list and see the "ele-ments" I have in my card deck.

KIDS ON THE INTERNET was conceived to have these produc-tion elements:

• kid hosts
• kids on camera doing topics
• screen shots
• title graphics/chapter headings
• B-roll footage
• music found on the Internet
• adult instructor (evolved during the shoot)

We originally felt that we wanted the show to talk directly to kids and wanted to only use kids in the show. "No one over five feet tall" was our motto.

Early on in casting and in the follow-ups we endeavored to keep the whole process fun, never intimidating, so that the kids would know us, their material, and what to expect. The shoot would take place in the same environment as the casting session so there wouldn't be too many surprises. We wanted it too look fun so we keep the entire process fun by joking with them, encouraging them to cut up, and letting their real personalities come through.

Going in we also knew that we wanted to use music that we (or the kids) found on the Internet. For this we went to IUMA (http://www.iuma.com/IUMA), the Internet Underground Music Archives, which lists and has samples of over 800 bands. They helped us find the bands with whom we negotiated a very small fee and a credit (and home page address) in the show. IUMA's logo was placed on the video packaging in exchange for their help.

Production

The production was very simple. I directed and did not want or need a large crew. The crew consisted of director, producer, a lighting cameraman, sound mixer, and production assistants. We shot with a Betacam SP (with clearscan so we could shoot directly off the monitors without flicker), a small lighting kit, and a few props. Only when we had two kids on camera at one time did we need to mix two audio sources.

Cameramen Chip Goebert (a frequent shooter for CNN) and Danny Dimitroff put in a day each, and Marco Bird did sound.

If the host got too close to a computer (like leaning on it), we picked up some hum. We also discovered that we couldn't do any long shots of all the computers in the room. They all had different monitors and the clearscan could only correct for one screen at a time. (We had tested the camera on several monitors before the shoot but never on all the monitors in one scene. So we just avoided having all the other computers on. No problem.) Otherwise the production and shoot went very smoothly.

Ken had blocked out up to six hours for the hosts because we needed specific content to be covered. We also spent more time lighting and staging the hosts since they were the most integral part of the show.

The other kids came for about one to two hours each. Rarely did we need more time since Ken and Craig had so well prepared the kids in advance.

The script segments were all marked into individual lines or paragraphs. The kids learned the lines on camera and did as much material as they could. It worked very well. The material was fresh and did not have a teleprompter look to it. I felt the kids would do much better doing little pieces at a time. We'd written the show so that no one had to do many long takes.

I got the kids to improvise, to goof off, to shout things in unison—whatever I could to keep them loose and having fun. We only had one kid who got so nervous that his material wasn't usable, but we had double booked "content" with some of the other kids so we were covered.

Sometimes something funny would happen on the set so we would rewrite the material or use what the kids came up with.

We hadn't planned to shoot any "adults" but when we saw what a great relationship Craig had with his students we couldn't help ourselves. We shot Craig bantering with the kids and had him cover all the various "chapter" material that we intended to use. It didn't matter if it duplicated the "content" that we had already covered with the kids. Rather, we found that since it was done in such a different style and free-flowing manner that it reinforced the content. So we thread the large group shots throughout the show as "setups" for the hosts. It turned out to be a lifesaver because the kids material was shorter than we expected and we needed a way to lengthen the show.

Stock Footage/"B" Roll Elements

It's always great to draw from stock footage, but how can you get it inexpensively? I made a deal with San Francisco cameraman Michael Anderson (National Geographic) for B-roll stock footage that we needed. The deal was that I would pay his day rate, give him a shot list, and have a non-exclusive right to use the material in our show. I would provide him with a dupe master which he could sell through a stock footage house. Everybody won and I got a lot of B-roll material for far less than if I had to buy individual shots, plus it was customized for our show.

Ken also asked the kids to bring home video footage and still shots of themselves which helped develop their characters, background, and give us a better sense of who they are outside the computer school.

To further punch up the visuals of the show we added some footage from my feature documentary *Dolphin Adventure* and short film *Hardware Wars* as little "breathers" between the dolphin and *Star Wars* newsgroup segments. I made a deal with myself and that was that!

Post Production

The material was transcribed by Vic Caplan. The best shots were selected; time code numbers were written next to the dialogue. Then we did a paper-cut edit of the entire show.

We then organized the show within the chapter structure that was originally written. The chapter title graphics are:

> *E-MAIL IS EASY*
> *WANNA CHAT?*
> *I HEARD IT ON A NEWSGROUP*
> *THE WORLD WIDE WEB*
> *THERE'S NO PLACE LIKE HOME*
> *PLAYING IN THE M.U.D.*
> *WHY DO THESE KIDS LOVE HOMEWORK?*
> *ALIENS IN CYBERSPACE?*
> *SAFETY ON THE NET*
> *SURF TOOLS*
> *THAT'S NOT ALL FOLKS!*

The actual subject matter included segments on e-mail, chat groups, newsgroups, the World Wide Web, home pages, multi-user dimension games, homework, safety on the Net, and the equipment you need to get started.

We digitized the "in selects" from the paper cut and edited from a rough cut to fine cut on an AVID at Crest National in Hollywood with editor Chris Wayne.

We originally expected to do a one-hour show but the material didn't play at that length. A 45-minute version was still too long. So since this was a home video tape program (intended also for PBS), we edited a 28:30-minute version. In order to pad the show even more, we added a minute or so of "bloopers" and outtakes after end titles. It turned out to be very funny. The audience response to "kids being kids" was delightful.

We went back to the camera originals and on-lined the show in Crest's digital room. Chris and fellow editor Mike Fusco were the editors. We colorized some of the B-roll, did deliberate jump cuts and some flips and effects, but really keep the whiz-bang stuff to a minimum, since the kids are the stars.

Duplication

Chris Whorf and Wade Lageose of The Art Hotel in Los Angeles did the video packaging from a still I shot of the kids and the hosts. Crest National did the duplication.

Summary

What would I have done differently? Perhaps made sure that the kids knew enough about each topic so that we weren't caught short later. But in retrospect, an hour show for kids (or anybody) on the Internet is far too much. Too much material, too many new ideas. You really do get Internet overload if you haven't experienced it before.

Had we had more money for the shoot I might have animated some introductory sequences explaining what the Internet is, but once the kids get behind the computers you get it very quickly.

It was really an ideal short sweet shoot that yielded a lot of fun footage. The production was very simple and the results among kids, broadcasters and educators has been very rewarding. We are already getting e-mail from Australia, Argentina, Greece and other far corners of the world from fans of the show. And a few complaints from parents who asked why their kids weren't included in the show!! Maybe next time.

Now go get 'em. (But stay off the kids' chat lines, okay?)

I hope that this "case study" has inspired you and given you ideas for financing, marketing and distributing your own special interest videos. Remember, whenever you make a decision about what's in your show, you are also making a marketing decision. (Cut out this one sentence and paste it to your computer. It's the one most important principle about our business that I've learned in the last decade.)

Now quit reading and go get 'em.

NEW MEDIA

WATCH ANY GOOD BOOKS LATELY?

About 12 years ago, I was thrust into the business of developing, acquiring and producing non-theatrical, original programs for home video. The non-theatrical video, roughly defined as "non-feature film" programming, included documentaries, how-to's, exercise and more. Today we take these special types of productions for granted as we work out with Jane, build houses with Bob Vila, and generally use videos as an alternate form of education and enrichment.

Because I'm a book publisher myself and have a strong interest in publishing trends, I started my search for subjects in bookstores. My task was to determine which titles might "translate" into video productions for the direct-to-home market. It turned out that my initial hunch was correct; the publishing industry is an excellent source of subjects, authors and material for home video.

A Program for Stress Reduction and Relaxation Through Meditation.

Since then I've produced and developed television programs and home video hits based on such books as Shirley MacLaine's *Inner Workout* (based on Bantam's *Going Within*), Arnold Palmer's *Play Great Golf* (produced concurrently with the Doubleday book), *Diet for a*

New America (Stillpoint), *Non-Impact Aerobics* (Villard), and some 300 others.

I also looked to well-known franchises such as National Geographic and launched–through my employer at the time, Vestron Video–National Geographic's home-video series, which has sold millions of videocassettes. I consulted on the introduction of the Joseph Campbell *Hero's Journey* videos (based, of course, on his books) as well as series from the Smithsonian Institute, Nova, Audubon, and PBS Home Video.

There continues to be a great opportunity for video producers. Book publishers have identified and nurtured a "body of knowledge," be it the work of a doctor, philosopher, or financial consultant. These publishers have put in a lot of hard work developing their titles, so why not extend their franchise through video? If publishers are sincere about their new media status then they must start producing visual (and audio) materials as well.

Videotape distribution becomes a perfect "interim" media that will generate revenues through its own markets. If you are a video producer or a video publisher you have an added advantage because you are actually collecting material for your "database" libraries, which will be utilized in years to come on CD-ROM, interactive television, and other new media sure to come along. MPEG video publishing is already turning into a sizable production opportunity; FutureTel–a maker of MPEG encoders–is currently conducting seminars around the country to educate producers in this area.

Not only are the books and authors currently controlled by book publishers a boon to the video producer looking for material, these same producers–if they have the capital–can become publishers themselves and control all the rights. Recently our production company signed celebrity pediatrician/nutritionist Dr. Jay Gordon, and we created multiple products around the concept *"Good Food Today, Great Kids Tomorrow."* The books, audios and videos were promoted first through an infomercial and are now being sold in bookstores. When you work in the video realm, you have a body of material you can then use to market through video press kits and television, thereby expanding your marketing opportunities.

Many of the PBS lines I was involved in sold books and videos through 800 numbers. Why leave this up to chance? Why not take the initiative and create your own book and video products, and market them through television?

The infomercial that we produced for Dr. John McDougall's *The McDougall Program* cost about $150,000, but generated gross revenues in excess of $6 million, and who knows how many additional sales of all his books at the retail level.

We work as consultants with many video producers, and with broadcasters, and we help them identify those properties that would sell well in the video format. Here are some of the elements for success that we've identified:

- The subject matter needs to be visual.
- A well-known book title and/or author's name
- An immediately identifiable genre (exercise, comedy, nature documentary)
- A hot topic (new age, the environment, alternative medicine, children's health or education, spirituality)

Video producers should prepare themselves with video-distribution knowledge because they will have to address a book publisher's greatest fear–lack of knowledge about home-video distribution. Producers will have to understand video wholesalers, cataloguers, institutional distributors, as well as foreign television agents able to exploit multiple revenues streams for newly produced video products. This understanding will build confidence in video publishers, especially if the producer is looking for some marketing or financial support from them.

Video producers will need to get into the publishers' heads and convince publishers that the video buyer will love an "up-close-and-personal" experience with an author, presenter or expert. You must show publishers when, why and how the video format really shines. People loved reading Shirley MacLaine's and John Robbins's books. This experience was greatly enhanced when they had the opportunity to "be with them" through video. You already know this; publishers do not. They think in another reality called "print," where images appear spontaneously in the readers' minds.

Video producers also must bust the myth that video is costly. Yes, it's expensive, but not that expensive when you consider the upside returns. Home-video budgets are commonly $100,000 and up, which is not expensive when you consider that you can sell your program to television (domestic and international), through video and mass-merchant outlets, through specialty, educational and institutional markets, and through direct marketing.

For example, in US retail video alone, Shirley MacLaine's *Inner Workout* video sold more than 200,000 units at a retail price of $29.95 (wholesale gross of $3 million), and *Diet for a New America* sold 52,000 units at $19.95. The budgets were $450,000 and $168,000, respectively. Additionally, because of various cross-marketing between the book and the video, the increased awareness of these video titles helped sell more books.

To gain even greater economies of scale, two or more titles can be shot simultaneously. For about 30 percent more, we shot two Arnold Palmer *Play Great Golf* videos. The second video also sold more than 200,000 units!

Let publishers know that they don't have to pony up to all costs themselves (most won't, anyway). If the video producer can come in with some of the financing arranged through production houses, author and producer deferrals, or video distributors, they will have an excellent chance to get their hands around a pre-promoted book or author. Everyone wins: the book publisher, the video publisher, the book and video retailer, and the consumer (who has more choices of how to access the information or experience).

As video producers and book publishers move into CD-ROM and other new media that can combine text, video and audio, doesn't it make sense for both to join resources to create more products for these new media consumers? Of course it does! Call a publisher right now! Go get 'em!

THE INTERNET

Here I've compiled pieces from many articles that I've written about the Internet sites that interested me. Some sites may be inactive or may have moved since the piece was written, but never mind, because some of these sites will have links to numerous other sites.

For more than 600 sites on the Internet that relate to film and video, come visit our home page (http://websites.earthlink.net/~mwp).

The trouble with the Internet–and also its seduction–is that it is not organized. One can wander endlessly through both the mud and the heavens.

Money On the Internet

Since most of our video projects begin with financing, and because this is also the first question asked by many of our consulting clients, I thought we would use the Internet (actually, the World Wide Web [WWW]) to search for sources that may be interested in funding our video company, our start-up multimedia company, or television or video projects.

The search was quite simple and I only looked to one source. (The great thing about the World Wide Web is that many home pages provide links to other home pages. Sometimes hundreds of other resources will be attached to one page. What I'll provide in this column will be just enough to get you into trouble and to introduce you to some sources of financing.)

From my Web navigator (Netscape), I clicked on "Net Search" and then typed in "venture capital." This immediately gave very quick access to some of the following resources. Need a couple million dollars to launch your new CD-ROM company? Read on.

Yahoo: Business: Corporations: Financial Services: Financing: Venture Capital http://www.yahoo.com /Business/ Corporations /Financial_Services/Financing/Venture_Capital/

Yahoo is generally one of the first stops for whatever you are trying to search. Yahoo's creators are some of the first to begin to index and categorize the material on the Internet and to provide links to what you are looking for.

Venture Capital
http://www.netview.com/svg/vc/

This page is currently in development but plans to list other venture capital organizations. The one listed (and the creator of this home page) is Accel Partners in San Francisco.

They are a private venture-capital firm which invests in entrepreneurial companies that they believe can be leaders of selected technology-driven markets. They have a capital base of over $350 million and will consider virtually any size project.

This firm is right up our alley. Their page lists the specific new companies in which they have recently invested and these include companies who create interactive home improvement software, object-oriented databases for multimedia, educational interactive TV applications, higher education curriculum software, CD-ROM databases, multimedia tools and information delivery, multi-platform authoring software for multimedia, on-line entertainment software, and more. Obviously they have a great interest in the new media software.

Adams Capital Management
http://acm.com/acm/index.html

This is a private venture-capital firm that invests in telecommunications, information technology, healthcare and manufacturing businesses. Companies that are part of their investment portfolios include desktop conferencing, digital video development tools, video compression technologies, and more.

240

Connexx International
http://www.gc.net/connexx/vca.html

They offer computerized databases of private financing sources throughout the world. They will provide seed money, start-up capital, and expansion funding.

Fostin Capital Partners
http://tig.com/Fostin/index.html

Here is private venture-capital firm that invests in information technology.

IBC: Venture Capital Firms on the Net
http://tig.com/IBC/NetStats/Names.html

This home page lists the capital firms who own domain names on the net. This list was generated by cross-referencing an independent list of 850 active venture capital firms.

Venture Law Group
http://www.venlaw.com/

Venture Law Group is law firm with 25 attorneys. It specializes in representing deal-intensive technology companies, both public and private, and the venture capital fund sources and investment banking firms that finance them.

Here are two resources that I found on the Web that will take you deeper in locating more venture capital companies.

Infon Venture Capital Directory On CD-ROM
http://www.halcyon.com/bhammer/infonvc.html

This is a CD-ROM for Windows 3.1 and Windows 95 which allows you to search venture capital firms by fund size, investment size, location, and industry preference. Plus you can search 2000 investors by education, directorships and past employment.

The addresses of search "hits" are automatically exportable to your wordprocessor for merging into form letters. It also includes the full text of A. David Silver's #1-selling *Venture Capital Sourcebook* and has an interactive video of a venture capitalist and an attorney discussing the financing process.

Given that you often will pay a large fee and/or give away equity in your project for a "money finder" that will search for venture capital firms for you, this product is a steal at $99.00 if it, in fact, will do everything they claim it will.

Business Press On-Line
http://www.maestro.com/mall/buspress

This is a publisher of some reference guides for locating financing, and their publications include *Venture Capital: Seed and Early-Stage Financing*, an informative guide listing over 200 venture capital firms.

They also publish *Venture Capital: Clubs and Additional Resources* which points you to the venture capital clubs which have emerged all over the country during the past decade. These clubs are a new approach to bringing together the entrepreneur and small business owner with the providers of capital. This concept cuts out the traditional venture capitalist and puts you in touch with the people providing the actual funds! The book has over 250 listings.

While it only took me about five minutes to locate these resources and companies, I must now follow up with these companies to see if they are, in fact, interested in the new media projects that my clients and I create. I am not recommending any of these companies but I certainly will explore them further. With your visionary business plan in hand, I suggest you do the same.

Crewing Up

We have surfed the Net and financed our project. (That was quick, wasn't it?) Now we have new tasks before us. We need to shoot all over the United States, and we have to get the show written, hire the crew, find facilities, and go into production. No problem.

The World Wide Web (WWW) is absolutely loaded with production-oriented information from facilities and crews to film commissions and stock footage throughout the whole world.

Yahoo - Business:Products and Services: Entertainment: Video: Production Services
http://www.yahoo.com/Business/Products_and_Services/Entertainm ent/Video/Production_Services/

Again Yahoo is always one of the first places to start. You go to "search" and type in "video production" and you will find lots of listings. Visit other production companies and facilities. Even if it's not someone you might ever work with, you can get a good education in how people are marketing their products and services. Learn from your competition!

Mandy's Film and TV Production Directory has a new address.
http://www.mandy.com

Here you can search by states, major cities, or foreign countries. The big cities have tons of information while, as is to be expected, the smaller geographical areas have fewer resources. Everything from actors, art directors, and assistant directors to voice-overs and writers can be found at Mandy's.

Let's see if we can find a local writer in Minnesota who knows the area and can write a segment for us. Bingo! I found Leigh Pomeroy Productions and while he doesn't have a home page, he does have an e-mail address: eighp@ic.mankato.mn.us. (Everyone write to Leigh today and make him feel famous! Leigh baby, I get 10 percent!)

From his listing, I see that he writes for film, video and radio and has over a dozen credits. He writes a wine column and teaches.

Also in Minnesota is Reynard Film, ward0038@maroon.tc.um n.edu, an indie feature production group that also produces commercials, industrials, music videos, and shorts. *We're funny too*, they add.

Stock Footage

Chicago Moving Image Scene
http://www.rtvf.nwu.edu/Omnibus/Chicagoindex.html

For those segments we want to do in Chicago, there is a site maintained at Northwestern University's Department of Radio/TV/Film. If you are a service provider, production company, or media-related organization and would like your information listed here, you can e-mail CWebbYoung@nwu.edu.

(In fact, everyone reading this who offers their services should post themselves on as many appropriate sites as possible. What I do is once I find a site where there is some reason for cross-marketing, I drop them a note saying that I am linking them to my site and ask if they'll do the same. When it comes to directories, give them a listing. (Let's hear from any readers who've actually been hired via the Internet.)

The Chicago site provides other video and multimedia sites, phone numbers to know, a list of Chicago production resources, post and production companies, information about Chicago, service providers, crew, talent and a listing board for jobs, plus links to other sites.

New York's Film & Video Web
http://haven.ios.com/~nyfilm/

For New York City, this site promises all of the up-to-date local unions' wages, benefits and work conditions as well as an extensive array of production support companies.

Desktop Video
http://ciinext.inre.asu.edu/~guy/Video1.html

This web site has begun to present the basic concepts of Desktop Video Production. There is information on preproduction, production, post, duplication, distribution, formats, editing, etc. I looked under "lighting" and there were only two not-too-impressive tips. Remember that the Internet is still very new and constructing a home page, especially one that wants to be as comprehensive as this one, takes time. Drop them a note and help out!

Newsgroups

Newsgroups are both the best and worse sources of information on the Internet.

Let's say that you've got a question about some gear you are thinking about purchasing, or you want to visit some town and you don't know the video scene. Whatever your question, you are sure to find an answer by posting your question to the appropriate (emphasis on appropriate) newsgroup.

A newsgroup is a "virtual community" of folks who share the same special interest. You can subscribe to these groups for free and then (daily) read all the postings in the newsgroup. You might ask about the new digital Betacam camera. Title your posting "Help Digital Betacam" and you'll get many replies ("re: Digital Betacam") from people all over the world who own (or want to sell) the gear.

Some newsgroups such as rec.arts.cinema are very chatty and have hundreds of postings which rave on about the newest movies (boring), while others, like ucb.digital-video, are generally downright quiet. One of my favorites is rec.video.prodcution and worth a frequent visit. The more involved you get in helping others, the more help you will receive. Here's a list of newsgroups that you may want to check out.

Media-Oriented Newsgroups

alt.animation.warner-bros
alt.cable-tv.re-regulate
alt.dcom.catv
alt.education.distance
alt.graphics
alt.politics.media
alt.satellite.tv.europe
alt.tv.animaniacs
alt.tv.babylon-5
alt.tv.commercials
alt.tv.infomercials
alt.tv.liquid-tv
alt.video.laserdisc
aus.films
clari.biz.industry.broadcasting
clari.canada.newscast
clari.nb.broadcast
clari.news.movies
clari.news.tv
comp.graphics
comp.graphics.animation
comp.graphics.raytracing
comp.multimedia
comp.publish.cdrom.multimedia
comp.publish.cdrom.software
comp.sys.amiga
comp.sys.amiga.graphics
comp.sys.mac
comp.sys.mac.graphics
comp.sys.sgi
comp.sys.sgi.graphics
misc.writing
misc.writing.screenplays
rec.arts.animation
rec.arts.cinema
rec.arts.disney

rec.arts.movies.production
rec.arts.tv
rec.music.video
rec.photo
rec.photo.advanced
rec.radio.broadcasting
rec.video
rec.video.cable-tv
rec.video.desktop
rec.video.prodcution
rec.video.releases
ucb.digital-video
uk.media

Music Business on the Internet

We are producing a series of videos on the Internet. What we needed was music from around the world to convey the feel and expansive nature of the Internet. The first stop on our search was Yahoo (http://www.yahoo.com) where we searched for "music." We got lots of music sources but what was most impressive was the site for IUMA.

IUMA or the Internet Underground Music Archive (http://www.iuma.com) has been getting a lot of media attention lately and producers should know about it.

IUMA was created in late 1993 by a group of young entrepreneurs interested in computers and music. What started as a two-person hobby has turned into a thriving organization with a large office and staff. The site receives over 300,000 "hits" per day.

The interface has very cool '50s style radio graphics that you can click on which let you visit and sample music from over 800 bands from all over the world. There are some 30 different musical genres including A Cappella, Ambient, Blues, Children's, Classical, College, Indie, Country, Dance, House, Techno, Rave, Easy Listening, Electronic, Experimental, Folk, Funk, Hard Rock, Hard-Core, Industrial, Heavy Metal, Hip Hop, Rap, Humor, Instrumental, Jazz, New Age, Pop,

Progressive Rock, Punk, Reggae-Ska, Rhythm & Blues, Rock, Spoken Word, Surf, Thrash Soul, Weird, and World Beat.

Many of the bands are "unsigned." Some bands have been discovered and signed by larger labels by appearing on IUMA.

Bands pay about $100 which gets their picture, a text description, and a sample of their music on IUMA. Web surfers can download a short excerpt of their music or a whole three-to-five minute song. It's a great way to sample music!

With our 28.8 modem, it took about a minute to download a sample. We also downloaded a music reader from IUMA which allowed us to listen to the sample. We quickly found what we liked and didn't like.

We interviewed, Ahin Savara, Executive Vice President of IUMA, for one of our video programs. *"The Net is actually the complete secret power tool that allows for music to connect with other people. Without the Internet, none of this would have happened. And I look at it as yet another extension of computer science... because it's really changing how we're going to go about listening to music. IUMA has hundreds of independent bands from all over the world. And not all of them want to become huge stars, even though that's the sole focus of the whole music industry–to make stars."*

IUMA's goal is to bring the music lover as close as possible to the music by providing a venue for artists to have potentially global exposure via the World Wide Web.

IUMA's graphic interface has a place for "new arrivals" and you can search for bands "by location" and by "genre."

To give you an idea of what you'll find, I checked the genre "ambient" and was given these choices of bands, their tune, the genre, location, date uploaded, and quotes about them:

7kings
"Perception Is Reality"
Ambient, Electronic
New York, New York, USA
Date Uploaded: 1994-08-09

7kings is the ambient–or is that iambent?–project put together by producer David Barratt slicing ambient grooves with vocal samples that help make the world make less sense.

Anomie
"Never Again"
Ambient, College/Indie/Lo-Fi
Santa Cruz, California, USA
Date Uploaded: 1994-07-20

A humongous wall of sound that moves and sings with life of its own. Rebecca Chenitz's vocals are other-worldly. -russ

Aramian, Marc, "Darwin"
New Age, Ambient, Classical
Marietta, Georgia, USA
Date Uploaded: 1995-07-03

Reviewer Joe Torre puts it this way: "Aramian stops at nothing to create visual musical scenery. He does whatever it takes to wrap the audience in a gripping ambience as it propels along evoking one emotion after another... a picture gallery of sound." Some orchestral, some pop, Marc Aramian's music style is eclectic.

Besides being an excellent musical database that's fun and useful, IUMA points to the future of music sampling. With full-motion, downloadable video coming on-line very soon, IUMA is the kind of site videographers should think about emulating to distribute and market their own "video samples" and "video movies" in the not-too-distant future. License some music on-line!

Mixed Bag of Recommendations

Here are some of sites that were recommended to me by *Videography* readers. Some good, some great. The main thing is–get your home page up on the World Wide Web as soon as possible. Experiment. Cross link with your colleagues.

These sites will give you some ideas on how to begin or improve your existing sites. Just remember, the little independents frequently do a much better job at employing the Internet to market their wares than the multi-national corporations!

Here's a mixed bag of sites:

The Music Bakery
http://www.computek.net/musicbakery/

Music, image, and sound effects libraries that let you download sample clips or even license off the Net will be the wave of the future as downloading becomes faster. Here's what you can do today.

I was the 106th viewer to this new site which specializes in providing royalty-free, buy-out music. You can download and listen to samples from their sound library which includes Bebop Jazz, Rock, New Age, Dramatic, Patriotic, High Energy and Sports, Corporate Industrial, Latin, Big Band, Contemporary Jazz, Classical, World Music, Country, Dixieland, and Orchestral genres. It takes a minute or so to download a 15-second clip which sounds pretty good when played on an audio reader.

Earlier I mentioned IUMA (Internet Underground Music Archive (http://www.iuma.com) which is one of the best music databases around with over 800 bands from around the world.

Video Schmideo
http://www.intac.com/~frelancr

Mike Sime is a freelancer who pops up everywhere on the Internet marketing his production services. His home page features a lighting catalog, his resume, his service and rate card, a client list, and seven ways to reach him. He says he's landed quite a few jobs marketing through the Internet. So it can be done!
The Information Bank: Documentary Researchers
http://soho.ios.com/~davewade/infobank/

The Information Bank helps you locate moving images for your documentary or news production by searching electronic databases. They can also locate still images and find relevant people for on-air interviews.

For a recent documentary, a client needed a statement from Senator Kennedy that they had read in an article. Using an electronic database, the Information Bank located where he had made the comment, and then tracked down the tape to a Miami archive.

For a documentary on Imperial China, they found Underwood & Underwood photographs of the Boxer Rebellion in a book and then located the collector who had the original stereographs stored in an Arkansas shoe box.

Located in Washington, DC, they work with commercial stock houses, the United States National Archives, the US Library of Congress, and Washington's libraries, government agencies, lobbying groups, and foreign embassies. Their simple home page is a billboard which refers you to a phone number.

Media Merchant Online
http://www.bn1.com/mmweb.html

These guys are doing it right. Here you can sample then purchase sound effects, music photos, and clip art. They have over 20,000 sound effects, 5000 music clips, 30,000 clip art pieces, and 20,000 photographs all available for immediate search and download (all royalty-free). Prices per file range between $1.95 to $9.95.

They claim their sound effects libraries have been endorsed by Oliver Stone and Martin Scorsese. Their music comes from a variety of production libraries in the world with works in every imaginable style. They feature the works of over 200 independent professional composers from around the world whose works can be heard on national television in productions such as *Baywatch* and *Seinfeld*. They also have broadcast licenses available for radio, television and film. Check it out!

Production Weekly
http://users.aol.com/prodwekly/pw/pw.htm

I was the 136th visitor when I was invited to this new site. Production Weekly is a weekly breakdown of projects in pre-production, preparation and development for film, television, music videos, commercials, et cetera.... It covers all of the major markets from Los Angeles to New York and all points in between (as well as Canada).

New listings are received on a daily basis, directly from production companies, so be sure to e-mail them and tell them what you are doing.

Each listing will have the title and company information including the phone and fax numbers as well as the above-the-line crew (i.e., Producer, Director, UPM...), location and calendar details.

Production Weekly also provides other useful information on "the call sheet," such as upcoming events and industry news.

media z
http://www.zpub.com/mediaz

A new San Francisco-based web site which features local production and talent contacts, updated news of interest to media folks, and links to other sites. It's worth a visit no matter where you live.

Leo Films, Home Video
http://www.next-exit.com/leo.html

Leo Films is a distributor of direct-to-video titles such as *Bad Trip*, *Power Slide* and *Good Girls*. They offer their exploitation-genre films to chains and mom-and-pop video stores. Stop here to see how videos are being marketed on the Internet.

The Crew Net
http://crew-net.com/

Created by free-lance professionals for free-lance professionals, the Crew Net is designed to provide instant, up-to-date information on crew personnel and production-related companies throughout the world. Set up as a kind of industry co-op, the Crew Net offers both film and video professionals the ability to post their resumes on-line for producers worldwide to see.

They charge a low membership fee which allows them to promote the Crew Net in a variety of trade publications.

Cinemedia
http://www.gu.edu.au/gwis/cinemedia/CineMedia.home.html
http://www.afionline.org/Cinemedia/CineMedia.home.html (USA mirror site)

The granddaddy of them all, Cinemedia claims to be the Internet's largest film and media directory with over 9000 site links (at last count).

This site has been completely redesigned and is frequently updated. Its creator, Dan Harries, is really on top of things making this the premiere site for media. You can't do without this link!

The main button categories are Radio, Cinema, New Media and Television. If you click on Television, you can further search TV Programs, Networks and Stations, Media Regulation, History/Research, Actors, Schools, Organizations and Flix/ Pix/ Sounds, TV, etc.

The Cinema page takes you to Films, Actors, Theaters, Production, History/Research, Studios, Festivals, Schools, Organizations, Pix and Sounds. The Reference Room has book and copyright information, various web browsers, and graphic viewers, and a hot "what's new page to find the latest new media offerings.

The AFI (The American Film Institute) mirrors this site in the US and you can find information about the AFI film festival, their professional workshops, calendar, awards and film-preservation programs on their home page.

I was so impressed by Dan's work that I asked him (along with his collaborator, Bert Deivert, in Sweden) to write the book *Film & Video on the Internet: The Top 500 Sites* for my publishing company.

Create a home page and write a book! Go get 'em.

NEW MEDIA: NEW SPOUSE?

I am already spending too much time in front of monitors. And I don't mean television. With a new baby in the house it is clear to me that there are other priorities. Besides shouldn't we ask ourselves some big questions about all this technology before we so quickly embrace it?

They wanted me to speak. In two days I was to be on panel entitled "Studios, Independents, Networks and New Media" at a conference held locally. I didn't know what to say.

The moderator asked me to consider what the future relationships between independent producers and the studios will be with the new media. He asked, "With the new media, will there be a different relationship than currently exists between producers and studios, between recording artists and labels, between authors and publishers?" My answer: "I don't think so." It's going to be a very short panel.

Let's look to history to understand my answer. When cable television, and later home video, began to develop, the studios didn't pay much attention until they began to see an erosion of their audiences. Then they moved in. It was time for vertical integration. Today, the lion's share of home video revenues go to the majors. Yes, there are some independents who have been able to hang on, but the majors are the ones who control distribution.

With the new media there will initially be a plethora of players trying to create new standards, proprietary hardware, and software, but this will ultimately shake down to large conglomerates that will acquire the smaller companies whose services and products prove worthy. There may be some surprises as the phone companies enter the playing field, but ultimately the winners will be absorbed by the multinationals.

Why should we expect that new media should bring about any profound changes in the way Hollywood does business? The president of the conference I planned to speak at talked about the day when "a JFK interactive might be able to bring in $40 million to a studio." Industry speculators expect interactive media to build new divisions within the film and music industries. I'm sure that will happen. The media formats may change, but will the relationship between the video producer and the financier/distributor change? There is no reason to assume it will.

I think somewhere along the line, however, we missed asking the first question–way before what profits we will see, way before how much money the studios will make, and way before who the new players will be. We missed the most basic question: "Is new media such a great thing and why? Or why not?" Is anyone asking this question?

What's So Great About the New Media?

It's fun. You can do more. We all know what's great about the new media because every ad or review or brochure we read tells us the upside. Each month this magazine reports on desktop video, but that's just part of the larger "multimedia" scene. Each month I rush to open *Videography* and my stack of computer magazines to see the latest and the greatest.

But in this rush I fear we do not ask ourselves some important questions. After all, we are in the courtship phase of a new relationship with technology, which results in us bringing the new media into our homes and our lives. From all accounts, we are going to be spending a lot of time with it. You could even think of the new media as a "new spouse." (Now there's a concept!) For our kids, a multimedia PC with reference works, interactive instruction, and games can become an "imaginary friend." Shouldn't we be concerned about choosing a spouse for ourselves and a friend for our children? Of course. But where is the new media watchdog? Can we at least see a medical and psychological history of the new spouse?

Consider: Video data terminals emit a range of electromagnetic radiation. Long-term users can experience health problems. People on average already watch television nearly eight hours a day, more time than they spend on any other activity. People relate to the events and people of television as if they were real. Reality and fantasy are blending. We have lost touch with one another. The high-speed ability of the new media, information gathering, processing and communication has sped up the world. There is tremendous stress in our lives as a result of new media's pace. We have lost touch with natural rhythms.

Yes, the new media offers great financial opportunities. Yes, you may have more new toys on your desktop than you ever imagined. And yes, like the automobile, there may be psychological, communal and environmental fallout that we should think about now before rushing head-over-heels toward the new technology. Technology isn't good just because it is new. Yet somehow we forget this and find ourselves on a kind of Divine Mission. Let's really look at who benefits (and who doesn't) from the proliferation of new media.

Don't get me wrong. I don't plan to stop producing television, videos or other media. But I do plan to examine the long-term effects of what I am doing. I do care about the end result. I want to leave something behind of value. I have personally seen enormous changes throughout the world as a result of our technology. Thinking about the effects of our actions seven generations ahead has great merit. It's worth applying. With technology exploding, with multinationals getting larger and larger, where do we fit in?

What Does the Video Producer Bring to the Party?

The second question we can be asking ourselves is "What can the creative individual bring to the new media party that the large corporations and studios cannot?" And the answer is an old one, which bears repeating: Ideas. The corporations will always need ideas. And because business people are trapped in a corporate-culture fish tank, there will always be individuals outside the corporation that can out-think and out-create them. But ideas themselves are not enough, because ideas are not copyrightable.

You need to put your idea into a form (whether it's a video, a CD-I, a software program, or a movie) that can be copyrighted. Then it is yours, and you have the property which (presumably) cannot be stolen. You are then in the catbird seat, and can go to the studio or multimedia conglomerate with something that you own. If they want it, they have to deal with you. This is one of the ways that an independent producer can establish a meaningful relationship with a larger entity. The independent producer is dependent on the studio for financing and distribution, and the studio is dependent on the producer for the property rights.

Add to your property a new way of telling a story or sharing information (through a multimedia format), and the independent producer can leverage an even greater position. You may have created an authoring system or a special effect. You may bring particular graphic style or sensibility to the property. All these elements will enhance the value of your position with the studios and corporations. Keep asking yourself, "What can I provide that the studios cannot?" You'll find plenty. It's easy to get intimidated when you walk through Paramount's gates until you look down at the property under your arm that bears your copyright. Remember you can always "just say no."

Hey, maybe I had something to say to this panel after all. And I did. In the meantime, go get 'em.

AFI/APPLE LAB: VIDEO BAUHAUS

This is one of the first articles written in 1991 about the AFI Computer Center, now a hot digital video showcase in Los Angeles. You can take classes there with masters of production. You can also attend media salons, and see the latest demos. The vision for the center as discussed in this article was surpassed shortly after its first anniversary!

If you live in or visit L.A., you can't afford not to stop at the AFI. (Read the Digital Jam Session article to get a feel for what goes on there.)

The two voices in my head chatter something like this:

"Hey, I could use my Mac for editing and for creating an animated title sequence. I'd save bucks, and I could do it all at home!"

"Yeah, but if you foul it up and it doesn't work, you'll just have to do it over again."

"But it might look cooler than the Harry and certainly cheaper, and no one would have seen this look before.."

"Go ahead if you want, but you're on a real tight deadline. This is a real important job, and if you screw it up....."

And so what happens is that fear rises and keeps us from trying new things. But production is exactly the time to quit dreaming about new technology and really use it. You've got a production budget!

But where do you go to learn? Who else has worked with computers and video? How can you improve your learning curve? The answer is to go to the AFI/Apple Center in Los Angeles.

Jean Firstenberg and James Hindman of the American Film Institute (AFI) and John Sculley, chairman/CEO of Apple Computer Inc., are creating the AFI/Apple Center though a collaborative effort. Apple donated the computer hardware and the AFI contributed space, staff and expertise. (The Sony Institute of Applied Video Technology is also housed at the AFI.)

I recently met with 50 film and video professionals at the AFI, and we collectively shared a vision for the Center. We all have varying degrees of experience with computers and a passion to learn more. Members of the AFI/Apple Center Steering Committee include fellow columnist Scott Billups, motion-picture consultant Michael Backes, Robert Greenberg of R/Greenberg Associates, Post Group VP Linda Carol Rheinstein, storyboard consultant Van Ling, and software developer David Sosnawe. Our job is to dream a little to come up with what this facility can be, and then put it together. We'll need to raise funds, solicit hardware and software, and gain other support from the professional community. The AFI and Apple have gotten things off to a good start. Now it's up to the rest of us (and perhaps you too) to figure out what to do with this opportunity.

I, like many of the others on the committee, see this as a kind of "Bauhaus of the Nineties." But instead of fine and applied arts converging, now it's computer and film/video technologies. It is apparent that these two worlds depend heavily on one another.

As video futurist, Eric Martin said earlier in the year:

"We're really on the lip of an abyss. We're in for some profound changes. The computer is replacing all tools because it increasingly is all tools. In the digital universe, a sound-is-a-tool-is-an-image-is-a-word-is-a-movement. Since it is all one language, the boundaries between media begin to blur. We're becoming one technology, one medium, and indeed, one decentralizing, interconnecting world culture, and a lot of that is because of this technology."

Just as the technology is converging, so are the interests of a wide range of film, television and video industry heavyweights who make up the AFI/Apple Center advisory committee. They include Michael

Crichton, George Spiro Dibie, John Dykstra, Richard Edland, Herbie Hancock, Bob Stein, Michael Nesmith and 40 others.

On the day of our meeting, the large group broke down into smaller groups and brainstormed ideas for the Center.

Feature film director John Badham said: "We're very much in a time of transition, like going from horse-and-buggy to automobile. One key role for the Center is to help guide the transition into computerization for the film and television community. There are those who are actively participating in the change. There are others who know it's happening and want a better understanding. There are others, most people in fact, who don't even know that blacksmiths are on the way out."

Central notions that came out of these sessions were that the AFI/Apple Center can hold public seminars, symposia, conferences and other educational activities that can help expose the new technology and its applications to the creative film/video community. The groups also emphasized that training activities were necessary for both entry-level practitioners and the more intense high-end users. Working professionals can also meet to share ideas and explore state-of-the-art solutions. New groups will be formed to help define the new activities in future meetings.

There were also a number of companies and organizations that wanted to co-sponsor educational activities with the Center, either for their own members and employees to improve their skills, or as a way to increase the overall trained pool of professionals familiar with emerging technologies. A primary need that was identified was that there are simply not enough trained individuals who know how to use the emerging technologies in film and video production.

In a poll of the advisory committee, it was learned that computers are already being used for financial budgeting and reporting, project organization, presentations, music composition, publishing, storyboarding, pre-producing, production, post production, training, multimedia production, sound production, membership database, motion control of cameras, book publishing, electronic intermediate manipulation of image, scriptwriting, image creation, and integrated computer networks tied to design, animation, motion control, (CAD-CAM), modelmaking, editorial, image processing, illustration, live-action, video and options.

One major goal of the Center will be to create liaisons between developers (of hardware and software) and (film/video) producers. An immediate goal is to get the hardware and software companies to move toward integration. The group agreed that there are many terrific programs and systems, but they cannot be linked or fully integrated at present.

It is a most exciting time to be involved with all these imaginative thinkers and doers. Everyone was stimulated, and many ideas were floated. People who knew one another only by reputation were able to meet, and, in some cases, new collaborations were formed. It felt like the Sixties; you had the feeling anything was possible.

The dream is to create "the production facility of the future." (Download, produce and upload your next feature!) With the high intentioned brain power assembled, and the support from the AFI and Apple, there's no reason why this can't happen. Film and videomakers are among the first to recognize that if you can dream it, then you can do it. Now go get 'em.

(AFI/Apple Center (213) 856-7600)

THE MAC AND I:
SOMETHING FROM NOTHING

My Mac and I wait for the Muse. As she arrives, electro-chemical impulses bolt through my brain, speed through the ends of my fingers, and rest as charged bits on Mac's hard disk. To inspire and move our audience, we gather, access and process volumes of information.

Long ago I gave up the limiting title of videomaker for the much more expansive moniker of communicator. And wonderful things happened. I began to express myself in a variety of forms–not just video!

And as a communicator, I owe a lot to the Mac and how it has empowered me to organize and process information. And that's what this column is about–the communication process. A metaphysical happening, because when you really think about it, we are really making something out of nothing.

Stage One

We choose to create something. If we have a "vision," then having already seen the outcomes we can proceed in a very focused manner. Perhaps it's just a notion. We conceive.

Stage Two

We gather information, images and sound. The Mac is the warehouse for all notes, ideas, text and images. All relevant names and phone numbers are logged onto a database.

Stage Three

We access this information. We know who to talk to and where to go to get information. I may use the Mac's modem to research online data bases, to send and receive graphics, scripts and treatments. The modem, phone and fax have replaced many in-person meetings. Many people who work with me do so from their Macs in their own homes. We meet in a "virtual office" on the computer screen!

Stage Four

At some point we have to stop accessing and begin to process the voluminous text, images and sounds we've collected. Depending on the medium, this stage may include writing, rewriting, polishing, recording, editing, mixing, animating, mastering and duplicating.

Stage Five

We communicate through the fruit of our labor–a communication piece– usually a product through which we can share our knowledge. It could be a video, a book or a CD. Or a phone call, a modem transmission, a seminar. To communicate, we may also market, promote and distribute the product.

Throughout the entire process, there are also a myriad of other Mac-produced "communication pieces" such as photographs, pitches, presentations, proposals, drawings, illustrations, budgets, deal memos, contracts, scripts, resource guides, typography, titles, sales sheets, covers, advertisements, packaging, press releases, reports, memos, letters, faxes and phone calls.

It's incredible. The central tool for organizing, processing and sharing information is the computer. Yet I don't consider myself in the computer business. In 1976 P.M. (pre Mac), this process was far more cumbersome. I needed lots of time and assistants to gather and process information. Today–thanks to my Mac IIci with its peripherals and programs–I can do more with less. And it's fun. When I turn on my computer, the first file that is displayed is labeled play. I am programming my unconscious and conscious mind to enjoy whatever I am doing.

I am always learning new uses for the Mac. It's tremendously exciting. If you haven't already taken the plunge, do so. Start using computers.

Learn as much as you can. If you already use them, expand your abilities. Find out how other communicators are using computers to create. Take classes at such places as the Los Angeles-based American Film Institute's Apple Media Lab or sit at the feet of other Mac buffs. You'll find your power to communicate will expand exponentially. Now go get 'em.

CD-I 4 ME?

New formats like CD-I made me feel insecure. Should I think about producing CD-I's? To answer that question, I reviewed many CD-I's and wrote this article. However, since "Videography" doesn't review software, they passed on the article. Still I think you'll find it to be a good overview of the possibilities of this medium.

I had to find out. It was long overdue. After all, it's been a year since I attended a CD-I conference. Just how far have CD-I's come since then?

I did participate in the last three big waves of video production: pay cable, home video, and infomercials. Am I missing a new bandwagon? Will people actually buy CD-I's and if so, why? Or, why not? What does the current crop of CD-I programs actually look like? In short–do they work? Is CD 4 me?

I decided that the best way to find out would be to spend a day looking at as many CD-I's as I could. A friend experienced with Philips' software who knows the best aspects of their CD-I's would be my guide, boosting me higher on the learning curve. I would evaluate what I saw as a consumer (does it interest me?), and as a marketer (but how do you sell it?), and, lastly, as a producer (is there an opportunity here?).

We used what looks like an ordinary CD player–a Philips CD-I player and a remote control device which you point at the screen and then a cursor appears. You can "click" the on-screen buttons to interact with the CD-I and get it to do things.

The flagship of the Philips CD-I collection is the impressive Compton's Interactive Encyclopedia. This monster disk has the 26 encyclopedia volumes condensed into 5200 articles which include slides and motion image clips, plus 32,000 short articles, and 130 picture montages with CD quality music and narration.

We started with a pathway called "title finder" and typed in–"airplane"–our subject. A text-filled screen appeared. (The articles are primarily text with some photos.) We clicked on the first photo in the article which started a narrated slide show of aviation history spanning from the early Wright Brothers' plane to the recent Stealth aircraft. Most clips run about a minute or less. Related articles–fuselage, wings, engine mounts, landing gear–also appear under "title finder."

In the encyclopedia, there are 19 subject areas–art, earth, economics, geography, literature, religion, science, technology, etc.–providing other pathways to access your area of interest.

Text scrolling was slow compared to my Macintosh computer. The text is very big and easy to read, but the page layouts lack inspiration. It really needs the touch of an art director or typographic designer.

CD-I's do not yet present acceptable full-frame motion video, so whatever video appeared was displayed in a frame about 1/6th of the screen size. This small video image is displayed in a graphic of an "entertainment room wall console" so that you feel like you are sitting in a room (the light dims) and watching television. Matting the small video into an environment is a clever way to get around the technical problem and takes the viewers' awareness off the fact they aren't seeing a full screen video picture. Nevertheless, the small frame video is not very involving. You are looking at something, rather than feeling like you are in the picture. For interactivity to really work, you have to feel like a part of it (e.g. virtual reality). CD-I's like Escape from CyberCity and Lords of the Rising Sun do an excellent job of involving the viewer in action. I am told that by the end of 1993 there will be full frame video.

There is a built-in Webster's International Dictionary. You can put your cursor on any word in the text, click on it, and a definition will appear. You can even click on words in the dictionary itself for definitions.

It's a shame that you can't print out your own reports (or download to your PC or Mac) from the CD-I player. This missing function hampers the CD-I players' usefulness.

There is also a world map. Click on your destination, and it zooms in. Click on the text for a country or city, and you get more articles, photos and facts.

I got a little impatient. Compared to clicking around the channels on my television, this program feels slow. I want to scan the information at a much faster rate. However, I can easily imagine viewers–adults and children– wandering for hours through text and mini-videos learning and exploring at their own pace. I like it.

Philips was smart to feature this ambitious CD-I. It must have cost a bundle–millions?–to produce which will not be recouped through sales of the CD-I alone. Instead the program drives sales of the hardware. In one promotion, Philips offers a gift certificate for software: you have your choice of the encyclopedia (which retails for around $299) or several other lower priced CD-I titles.

Another personal favorite is Gardening by Choice: Flowers and Foliage in association with Ortho Books. (There is a second CD-I in production in association with Better Home and Gardens which provides much better name recognition for marketing.)

The basic menu is a United States map. You pick where you live, and the "climate zone" is instantly set. A house appears with six different types of flowers to choose from: bulbs, perennials, house plants, container plants, annuals and roses. Pick one. You are then asked to pick either "sunshine" or "shade," and you are shown a list of flowers which prefer sun or shade. You continue making selections such as color and height, and you end up with flowers that meet your specific criteria.

There are 600 index cards with descriptions of each flower: name, type, light, height, space, when to plant, bloom, colors. There is a personal "index box" where you can save the selection of your favorite flowers. There are also photos of every flower. Flowers are listed by both the common name and the botanical name.

There is a video demonstration on how to plant flowers in rows that is displayed on 6 panels within the full screen. This is another clever way to avert attention away from the smaller video image, and, in this case, it works very well.

Gardening is a terrific CD-I. It's very useful and engaging because you are customizing your own gardening needs. The potential of CD-I is clearly seen in this program.

Zombie Dinos From Planet Zeltoid ($39.98) is one of those games that sends dexterous users 12 years into pixel heaven. For the rest of us, well, it's a tough game to win. You travel back in time to locate and rescue dinosaurs before they are destroyed. It's a race against the Brain Blobs to save the planet. There are 14 scientifically accurate dinosaurs displayed in 3-D stop-motion. Very cool. There is live action footage (of dino character hosts) set in graphic environments. (Producers check these segments out!) This is a game designed to teach kids all about dinosaurs. Good choice of genres, Philips! Kids can't get enough of dinosaurs.

Beauty and the Beast: An Interactive Storybook Adventure ($19.98) has an interesting twist. Parents can set their child's age level at "4 and younger" or "5 and older." Parents can also turn audio prompts on and off; they can run the 28 minute show with or without subtitle story text. Besides the basic story, there are 75 "games" for each age level.

The beautifully produced, limited animation has rich effects, music and voice. The "games" teach recall, comprehension and creative thinking (they are really animated "multiple choice test questions." Here, I agree with the marketers–please, it's better to call them "games"). A voice responds to each choice. ("Try again").

The CD-I's slow interactivity works well with the kid's programming. Since the show's pacing is slow, you don't notice that the program is also slow. The technology matches the user's needs in this case.

More Dark Fables from Aesop, narrated by Danny Glover, is well written and uses quality limited animation. The CD-I has 12 stories. There are 36 puzzles based on each story. The morals of each story are explained, which is a nice programming touch.

Jazz Giants ($19.98) has 19 great classic legendary audio performances and a combination of slide show/paint box effects and text notes. The performances are outstanding and include the biggest names in jazz. (Great for the marketing marquee.) However, the title is ultimately disappointing, because there are no live action shots of the performers–only stills, many black and white. The quality of the surrounding graphics are poor, and this CD-I will certainly not age well. Well-written biographical and text notes are excellent and loaded with fascinating information on the recording session, the personnel, and music technique. But most buyers will only read this once. You have two choices: you can listen to the music alone, or listen with biographical notes.

What you are essentially buying is an audio CD packaged like a CD-I. The only reason a jazz aficionado would be buy the CD-I is that it doesn't cost any more than a CD and you get the linear notes. Buyers may feel burned here thinking they are getting something new. It's simply not sophisticated enough. Marketers know that when introducing new products–and especially something as important as a new line of AV programs–you have to keep the quality up or your customers won't be back for more. Bad choice here.

Rock Guitar ($69.98) gives you a choice of musical pieces that you can learn at your own pace. (We chose Hendrix' Purple Haze.) You can choose to hear: lead, rhythm, lead and rhythm, lead and band, or metronome, and you can choose to see: lead, rhythm, or lead and rhythm . You have great control over how you'd like to learn. You see the music score (each note illuminates when it is plucked–cool!), plus a small live action video picture of fingers playing the guitar. You can set the tempo, so that you can start slow and then move up to performing speed as you learn. The only place Philips missed here was that they should have included some name host (Eric Clapton?) to give the CD some marketing heat.

The Great Art Series: Art of the Czars ($39.98). Here you visit Russia's St. Petersburg and stroll through the city, stopping by the palaces and churches. You get a good feel for the city. Then you come to the Hermitage Museum, learn how it's laid out and where each school of painting (Dutch Masters, Impressionists) resides. You explore each collection and select the paintings you want to study. A voice over tells you the interesting features of your selection. You can also view (pre-selected) close-ups of each painting. The reproduction of the paintings is only fair compared to the high resolution of an art book. The CD-I also includes the history of the tsars showing you what each built and what paintings each purchased for the collection. Fascinating stuff.

The high quality original music by Tchaikovsky, Grieg, Corelli and Rachmaninov is well placed for each painting school period.

Escape from CyberCity ($39.98) has full cel-animation and throws you into an action-packed movie as one of the characters. It's a shoot-em up where you try to infiltrate the city and escape. Very involving. Call in the 12 years olds with lots of arcade shoot-em-up experience or suffer a thousand grotesque deaths.

Lords of the Rising Sun ($39.98) is a fantasy samurai adventure set in 12th century Japan with armies, ninjas, swordsmen and archers. It combines the arcade-style "chop-em-up" ninja warriors with history, and war strategy as it utilizes actual Japanese castles and monastery locations. (Does the history and learning aspect help parents justify the purchase of what is essentially a violent program?) The graphics are terrific and make you feel you are there. A Japanese princess (live action video) in a fantasy graphic setting implores us to save her. Machos that we are, off to war we go. Moments later we are face to face with a ninja warrior who throws star-like weapons at us which progressively wounds us. We hear the realistic impact of the weapon cutting into our flesh and see our blood spatter against the shoji walls. Whoa! I'm dying! Awesome dude. No doubt this will be a big seller.

Producers should go to school on this one for the mix of live actors in pure graphic settings. The potential of computer blending of media and interactivity is just beginning.

The Best of Draw 50 is based on best selling books by Lee Ames. There are 50 illustrations that you can learn to draw one stroke at a time. Categories include: monsters, vehicles, dinosaurs, buildings, athletes, animals, horses and Christmas. We picked Frankenstein from the monster bin. You determine your own pace, erase or start over. You learn art tips along the way. There is a timer which lets you know how far into an illustration you are. Great for kids. Production is okay.

I've heard about, but haven't seen, what's touted to be the most popular new kids' CD-I, an "electronic coloring book." Kids pick characters and paint them, and the CD-I will play a cartoon utilizing the characters the kids have colored. (Is this a plot by the Harry paintbox manufacturer to train the next generation of video artists?)

Interactive Guide to the Colleges of Your Choice: The ACT College Search '92. Your survey to over 3200 colleges. (I tried to find the best party schools, but it doesn't have it.) This CD-I, however, has everything else you want to know including student ethnic and religious mix. You can search for what you want by certain curriculum criteria to narrow your choice down to 12 colleges. The CD-I them provides the addresses for the admissions office.

Summary

The jury is still out. It's too early to say whether this format will actually make it. Sources tell me there are 20,000 CD-I players in the marketplace. Prices are still high and exceed $1000 per player. Many CD-I's are co-productions between PIMA (Philips Interactive Media of America) and independent producers.

They've used some high profile promotable elements in the CD-I's, but perhaps not as well as they could. They've probably spent as much as they can on production, which is enormously expensive. However, those consumers versed in higher quality film, video, graphics and print will find that the production quality just isn't quite there.

I'm not ready to jump in until the installed base of buyers is much greater because 1) if I go to all the trouble to produce a CD-I, I want a large audience, and 2) the economics of production require it.

On the production side, what appears to be lacking most are skilled graphic designers, typographers (where are the typographers!!), and art directors. These are relatively inexpensive production elements that can bring added value to the user's experience. Most of the CD-I's reviewed here are weak on text design.

Philips is clearly trying to communicate that "CD-I's are for everyone," and I feel they've made a very powerful opening statement with this round of program offerings. Yet I still have the feeling that we are seeing the early Model-T's coming off the assembly lines, and vast improvements will be made in the months and years to come. We've got to start somewhere, and it will take an enormous amount of energy and persistence (kudos to Philips) on the part of the manufacturers, the marketers and the new media producers to move CD-I's forward. I'm rooting for you all.

So, are CD-I's for me? Not yet. I'll sit on the sidelines for now. As for producing, my strategy is to create proprietary properties that can be translated into CD-I's when my time comes. So, on my next shoot, I'll bank some extra footage for my first CD-I (or CD-ROM or...?)

Until then, go get 'em.

DIGITAL JAM SESSION

The premiere is at hand. At least 70 or 80 people are packed into one of the demo rooms at The American Film Institute (AFI) Apple Computer Center for Film and Videomakers in Hollywood. Two huge monitors stand at the front of the room. Between them are several laserdisc players, linked to a Mac Quadra 950 with 6MB of RAM, RasterOps' MoviePak, and various hard drives and other peripherals.

The Challenge

It all started early this year when Nick DeMartino, Director of the Center, called and asked if I'd participate in an upcoming two-day workshop at the AFI's Twelfth National Video Festival, February 4-7. The workshop was part of the Festival's Desktop Computer Media Division, a new event sponsored by this magazine and its quarterly supplement, Videography's QuickTime Professional.

Nick had invited half a dozen film-, video-, and other electronic moving-imagemakers to work together to create finished QuickTime "movies" in two days. On the third day this material would be transferred to laserdisc players and programmed. On the fourth, it would be premiered for the Interactive Media Salon, an ongoing evening event.

Step One: See Atchley's Performance

The first step was to see an interactive multimedia performance by video performance artist Dana Atchley. We would use his authoring system, which employs Macromedia's MacroMind Director (developed by Patrick Milligan, Atchley's collaborator and programmer). Atchley would guide us through the process, and at the end we'd have a collection of one and two-minute personal QuickTime stories to premiere on Atchley's interface.

274

The AFI's theater was packed; several hundred people had to be turned away. Atchley–a practitioner of the "Spalding Gray stage monologue tradition"–was inspiring. He squats down next to a monitor displaying a "video fireplace" and begins spinning stories. They are illustrated here and there with very short clips of artifacts, interviews, music, and text, which is projected on a large screen behind him. He interacts with these visual pieces and is able to stop or advance them with a remote control mouse. Atchley has prebuilt dozens of sequences. As his show starts, Atchley feels out the mood of the audience, selects some of the icons displayed on the large screen, and drags them down onto a "road" that is the linear path the performance will take. This way, the audience is aware of the structure of the performance–even if they don't know exactly what will be called up with each icon.

Dramatically this builds expectations and drama. Atchley tells a little story, moves around the stage, and confronts the audience. He selects an icon, and clicks on it; and something happens–often a video clip. He may let it play out while talking over it or singing along with it, or he may stop it and start it or skip it altogether.

It's his show, and he's not about to let the technology tell him what to do. That's the best part of what he's put together. He controls everything. His performance is not driven by the technology; rather he employs it, effortlessly, like a high-tech shaman.

Atchley has documented everything that ever happened to him on something like a dozen different visual formats. And at last, (Eureka!) along comes a technology that can finally put it all together! He can store it, access it, share it, and perform it.

Step Two: Decide What to Do

I was instantly inspired. Like many of us, I too have saved almost any visual element of my family's history. I wanted to put my life story into QuickTime as well. In 1974 I did that–sort of. After traveling for two years alone throughout Japan, Bali, India and East Africa, I made a one-hour autobiographical documentary called *Silver Box*. Then I toured art museums throughout the country, answering questions.

When I got to Seattle the local film reviewer bashed Silver Box. "How could anyone be so egotistical to make a film about themselves?" the reviewer asked. Excuse me, I thought. Painters, writers, sculptors and other artists use the material most readily available (themselves)–why can't filmmakers? But I didn't say that then. I was simply crushed, and never showed the film publicly again. Fast forward to the present, and I find myself inspired that Atchley was so courageous in using the material from his own life.

For me, it took several years to optically print everything (slides, photos, Super-8 and 16mm film) onto one medium: 16mm film. The collage effect actually worked quite well, as does Atchley's synthesis to the digital realm.

Our assignment for the workshop was to prepare a one or two minute piece–something we could complete in two days using QuickTime with PhotoShop and whatever else we could get our hands on. I have tons of material from various films and videos I've made (Dolphin, Hardware Wars, Bucky Fuller, Diet For a New America), that I could easily throw together. I'd have great images, high production values, and could make an impressive piece–but that was too easy. Atchley had challenged something in me, and I knew it was time to get back to my Silver Box idea. My piece would be very personal.

Other Influences On My Decision

I should also mentioned that I was equally motivated by a work that screened at the AFI following Atchley's performance. It was a QuickTime movie called Big Warm Bear Arms, by Greg Roach of Hyperbole in Houston, Texas. It had been named Best of Show just weeks earlier by MultiFacet Communications' Second QuickTime Festival, held during San Francisco's MacWorld Expo.

Roach, also the creator of the much-acclaimed Madness of Roland, had fashioned a QuickTime movie in which the images were hardly there: children running through a forest; special-effect fireflies;

wonderful music and poetry by Roach. It was extremely evocative, and the audience was stunned into silence by its beauty.

What I loved about this piece was that he used QuickTime, with all its current funky-chunkiness; and it worked great. He didn't try to make it do something it couldn't. He used the inherent image quality to his advantage –something I've seen few others do. The images were almost shadows, and so the audience really had to participate and fill in. And to fill in they drew from their own childhood memories. And it really, really worked.

That's the kind of piece I wanted to make.

Step Two: Writing and Previsualization

First I looked at the emotional quality of my life over the last few years. I traveled to Bali; got married. We met a birth mother and father, and adopted a child. My mother died. Could I cover all of this in one or two minutes?

The night before the workshop I wrote a 45-minute script. Too long. Looking for the essence and evocative language, I ended up with one phrase and a few words for the graphics. The act of writing a long script got my creative juices flowing, and gave me a chance to review all the potential material I might use.

Step Three: Sharing Ideas

On the first day of the workshop, Atchley got the group of us talking about ourselves and what we thought we might want to do–digital therapy. It was a delicate matter.

I was looking for structure, so I'd know where my work would fit into the whole. But since the presentation was nonlinear, there is no beginning, middle, or end. Curiously enough, we each found we were working with similar elements–weddings, Bali, adoption and fire. There was already some connection between what each of us was doing.

We all worked quietly on our own pieces. And from time to time, we'd help one another on a technique or a program. There wasn't much time. We had a show to put on!

Step Four: Finding Meaning in the Digitized Image

I digitized about 5 minutes of Hi-8 footage using Screenplay and Adobe Premiere. I started to cut a traditional kind of movie, but it wasn't looking right. As I worked with the postage-stamp size images, I realized that what I really was looking for were "open ended" icons and symbols that, to an audience, would be loaded with emotion and meaning. (Whether or not they got all the content that was there or that I intended was really a secondary issue.)

An underlying theme I worked with is the transitory nature of existence. Since I love Balinese shadow plays, I selected a single image–a "tree of life" leaf-like shadow puppet that fluttered like a huge moth against the flame from an oil lamp. It became my motif that opens the piece and at various times it acts as a transition. Even if you don't realize it's a shadow puppet, it feels magical, ritualistic, shamanic. I used it like it was some great paint brush passing over life events–changing, blessing, forming life itself.

It's tough to express all of this; it's clear how much more powerful images are than words. But paradoxically, it's only in the articulation of this that it seems clear what I was doing. Working with the images was an intuitive –almost unconscious–process, and I felt everyone was going through something similar. Experimenting, changing, trying again. With digital editing the changes are fast, the feedback immediate. With QuickTime, we are clearly dealing with an entirely new process. It's akin to video and film, but very different because it instantly combines so many elements and because the image quality is primitive and elemental.

Step Five: Editing

My shot list is rather short. The tree of life shadow puppet is my motif and transition element.

I tried to bring out the extraordinary in the ordinary, to find those transcendent moments in our lives that others would recognize, merge with, and make their own.

A very evocative cello solo bonded my images together. Occasionally, I would let an "ordinary reality" sound bleed through and then return to the transcendent world called forth by the music.

The tree of life and shaman at the beginning suggested mysticism, spirituality and ritual. From there I just played with the dynamics of the image and music and kept condensing the content in the images to just the essential. I did learn that the image has to be quite graphic to be easily read. I continued to boil my "alchemical pixels" down to a no-frills shot list:

Bali Shaman reads Geraldine's palm
("You'll have two children...");

MS silver wedding cup and our faces
("This cup represents union...");

MS Geraldine at reception, in wedding dress
 ("I've waited a long time for this...");

tree of life shadow puppet;
silhouette of couple playing in surf;
title: birth parents;

birth mother's face smiling, wind blowing her hair;

delivery room, man strokes pregnant women's head;

doctor lifts newborn in air;

newborn's fingers in my hand; portrait of baby;

baby and Geraldine look into mirror
("What a pretty baby...");
tree of life/cello diminuendo on audio track....

Impressions

I am very inspired by what you can do in QuickTime with Adobe Premiere. It's all there on one Mac screen: two video tracks, three audio tracks, a track for special effects (dissolves and wipes), and a graphics track. It's a poor man's Avid nonlinear editing system (which I have used). Digitizing is slow, previewing your piece is slow, and when it's time to have the computer "make your movie," you're better off going to lunch (my two-minute movie took about 12 minutes to process).

The Gear

Some of the hardware we used included a Kodak DCS 200 camera, several Sony and Canon Hi-8 cameras, SuperMac's Video Spigot, and a HP Scanjet Scanner. On the software side we used SoundEdit Pro, Adobe Premiere, Macromedia's MacroMind Director, Adobe Photoshop, Fractal's Painter, and Screenplay. Most of the computers were Quadra 700s or Mac IIci's. Harry Mott is the AFI's facilitator and assisted everyone in the workshop, but he still found time to create his own wonderful QuickTime movie on a Quadra 950.

Other Explorations

Most of my colleagues' pieces were very personal stories. Some were in the traditional documentary style. They worked fine. I think we need to explore what these QuickTime movies are really all about. Atchley and Roach certainly have their arms around it, and are doing the most innovative and free stuff I've seen yet.

The rest of what I've seen—not that much, really—consists of established media conventions and techniques wrapping. People are trying to do what they have done in other media, except now it's QuickTime. It's like the Burns and Allen television show from the early Fifties. Even though it was shot on film, they began and ended it with conventions that mimicked vaudeville and radio. A comedy skit was delivered on a stage complete with curtain and canned applause and laughter on the soundtrack. But Burns and the other early television pioneers figured it out. So can we. Let's allow the medium of QuickTime to show us what it wants us to do with it.

I'm convinced that those who take these new tools and use them like artists will find a whole new market for their work. New Age music grew out of a new tool (the synthesizer), and a new genre was created. If you create a killer QuickTime movie on CD-ROM, people will buy it.

Start working with this stuff. Take a class; read the quarterly Videography's QuickTime Professional. Go to a workshop, and buy a system. Get yourself on the learning curve and explore, and then teach others.

Step Six: Fame and Fortune

So there we were at the "Interactive Media Salon" premiere. Atchley showed some of his pieces. Then we each spoke briefly about the experience of the workshop and what we were trying to do. Then we showed our pieces.

I was nervous. I'd been working in video and film for the last 22 years, but have rarely been in the same room as my audience. Now my little movie was about to be shown to a packed room. Anticipation. My wife and daughter sat next to me, stars of QuickTime/my life. I hoped everyone would like it.

They did. The audience, which included all of the workshop partici-pants, was fascinated, enthralled and even moved by our little movies. I sense that everyone had the feeling they were in on something–at the very beginning.

Now it's your turn. Go get 'em.

DESKTOP VIDEO:
VISION AND APPLICATIONS

I couldn't resist adding this retro-article which is kind of a digital polaroid of the past. At the "Desktop Video" Conference, I first met editor Brian McKernan who asked me to write for "Videography" magazine. (This article did not appear, nor was it edited by McKernan.)

The event itself was the first I am aware of on the subject of desktop video. I pitched the "desktop video" conference concept to UCLA Extension (the sponsors). They didn't quite understand it, but were pleased when the auditorium was packed. The people who spoke continue to be luminaries of the new technologies.

Technically, the article is out of date, which shows just how very fast things are moving in digital video.

Desktop video! You've seen this catchword everywhere, but what does it really mean? A Desktop Video Conference sponsored by UCLA Extension tried to answer this question.

There were as many definitions of "desktop video" as there were speakers. Most agreed on these characteristics: 1) it's cheap and affordable; 2) it uses a computer platform; 3) it fits on a desk top; 4) video can be brought in and out from the platform; 5) it is multimedia and a hybridization of forms and formats; 6) it is an evolving and very fast changing format; 7) it is a coming together of film, video, television, graphics, text, animation, painting, storytelling, audio and music; 8) it's easy to use; and 9) it does everything you can do now with traditional video systems and gives you more control.

Sounds great to me. Where do you get one? Well, that's the crux of the problem. The vision is there, but there is no one, high quality integrated system. There is no one-stop solution for desktop video.

Once a low-cost, broadcast quality system comes into being, there will be a rush of creators from many disciplines scurrying into production. There were previous explosions of production in home music recording studios (thanks to MIDI-ed synthesizers) and in desktop published books, magazines and newsletters (thanks to the laser printer).

The conference was an information-packed day with participation from hardware and software companies, from video visionaries looking two to five years into the future, and from video producers who couldn't wait for the revolution to begin so they could put together their own desktop video systems. What follows is a kind of "frame grab" of the most interesting bits and bites.

"The boundaries begin to blur between media."

Eric Martin, former Dean of the School of Arts at the California Institute of the Arts, used a Macintosh to create images for a corporate presentation for IBM! Eric sees the congruence of all media coming into one digitized form. The producer's job is to somehow grab hold of this new and very powerful technology and to use it in ways that do not imitate earlier forms.

"Today's new format becomes tomorrow dim memory," cautioned Martin. "We have to struggle within us to become fluent and meaningful in our ability to manipulate these new tools and come up with new ideas." At the same time, there is a conservative bias to not see the meaning of what this evolving meta-medium is. Martin said, "All interesting new tools tend to first be used in the spirit of the tools they appear to replace." From what Martin has seen of many current paintbox operators, he thinks they must be asking themselves "how many highlights can dance on the head of a pin?" He said, "We can invent something subtle and powerful, but we don't know how to use it. We seem to have a genius for trivializing our tools–Porches get driven to supermarkets, Nikons get used for snapshots, and computers get used as glorified typewriters."

Reflecting back, he said, "Memory costs about 1/40th of what it cost in 1980. Ten years from now, a desktop computer will be 500 times more powerful than it is today. It's going to do different things. We have to realize that we're in just a moment, in a blur, and we're headed for something considerably more profound. Which is the ultimate digital collapse into a single box, into a single working environment, that's easy to use.

"This change is accelerating more at the desktop end when compared to the high-end. Desktop video is at the very start of a period of hybridization. We're really on the lip of an abyss. We're in for some profound changes. The computer is replacing all tools, because it increasingly is all tools. In the digital universe, a sound-is-a-tool-is-an-image-is-a-word-is-a-movement. Since it is all one language, the boundaries between media begin to blur. We're becoming one technology, one medium, and indeed, one decentralizing, interconnecting world culture. A lot of that is because of this technology."

"The new Hi-Band 8mm camera features a built-in time code."

The first piece in the desktop video puzzle begins with the camera, a primary tool for generating imagery. Conrad Coffield, Director of Marketing for SONY Professional Products, demonstrated several cameras and editing decks. The Sony EVO-9100 features high-resolution images of more than 400 TV lines. It uses two kinds of videocassettes, the Hi8ME (metal evaporated) and Hi8MP (metal powder) tape to deliver the high quality image. Most important, the new Hi-Band 8mm camera features a built-in time code generator to record time code on the videocassette while it is recording images. This simplifies the editing process enormously. (No longer do you have to transfer 8mm to Beta, or 3/4", or 1" with time code in order to edit. Consequently, you do not lose one generation of picture quality as you previously did by bumping across to another editing format.) The 2 lb. camera also comes with a range of other accessories including rechargeable batteries, which makes it a unique low cost but high quality component to a desktop video system.

Nevertheless, SONY does market two new Hi8 recorder players. One is the EVO-9800. The other is a dual deck machine, the Video8 Video Memo Writer VCR, EVO-720, which includes two decks in a single housing with the ability to do quick edits, program edits, inserts and audio dubbing and some title recording. It comes with a jog dial and shuttle ring.

SONY's cameras are cheap and easy to use. However, Coffield made the point that the Hi-Band 8 was not designed to replace other existing SONY formats like Beta or 3/4". Each has its place. For example, the editing system is only accurate to a few frames.

Coffield was clear in pointing out that although many producers are looking to Hi-Band 8mm and producing some spectacular results, SONY does not as yet provide a complete Hi-Band 8mm production system as they do with the Beta format. Nevertheless, producers will undoubtedly experiment with Hi-Band 8mm, pushing the technical limitations as far as they can, and, in some cases, creating programs that are acceptable for broadcast.

Coffield spoke about work being done at SONY. "Clearly our future is an all-digital domain. 100 MB/sec really isn't enough to get the same kind of quality you get in analog. If memory was free, it would be no problem. So now analog is still the best compression format going for the professional market. We can't go backwards, we have to go forward. Digital is probably 4 or 5 years down the road that will offer the quality and performance this group will demand.

"New tools bring 'a new language' to the videomaker's repertoire."

An innovative device, which videomakers will flock to purchase for their Hi-Band 8 and S-VHS videocameras, is the Steadicam JR. Surprise guest, Jac Holzman, former chairman of Panavision and currently chairman of Cinema Products (which manufacturers the Steadicam JR) premiered this production tool to the public for the first time. He demonstrated how this new tool brings "a new language" to the videomaker's repertoire to eliminate bumps and jitters in hand-held camerawork.

Commodore Business Machines Graphics Marketing Manager Christopher Kohler demonstrated the AMIGA, a very low-cost integrated desktop video system. There are some limitations, such as resolution, which restrict it for many professional applications. It is being used in an "off-line" capacity, for example, in creating 3D frame models, which can then be further processed on other systems.

Combining video with graphics requires that the video image be loaded into the computer. Karen Mills demonstrated Mass Microsystem's new ColorSpace IIi board which is installed into a Macintosh II computer and allows for titles, graphics, animations and special effects to be laid over video. The video image can be digitized and combined with other images. Mass Microsystem's boards are used mostly for corporate television, business and institutional sales promotions, presentations and training.

> *"Two or three people still have to do the same work,*
> *which is possible with desktop video."*

John Rice, former editor of Videography, felt the first opportunities for desktop video are in the corporate market to be used for "sales and marketing, training, employee communications, in presentations, as internal memo communications, corporate public relations, motivation, special events and as video news releases."

Rice said, "There are videotape productions which cost $1000, and others which cost $1 million. Desktop video is bringing more people into video, and the computer is key. Where else do you have a large base of computer users than in corporate life? They are the first to see the applications. We are seeing a creativity of applications, all from the corporate market. As some corporations are reducing their video departments from 25 or 30 people to 2 or 3 people, they still have to do the same work–which is possible with desktop video."

Steve Sanz, David Watkinson and Scott Billups are creative producers, and each produces corporate videos, logos and commercials. Steve Sanz, showed examples of logos created, using Macromind Director, an animation program.

David Watkinson, who produced three 1-hour videos for a law firm, responded to audience concerns that much of the desktop animations they saw were "chunky." "Better broadcast stuff takes a lot of time to render, and the image you get on the screen can't refresh fast enough to be able to dump it out onto videotape in real time. So you have to send it out one frame at a time, which takes more time and effort. There is a whole market that doesn't care if things are chunky. And it's affordable for a whole new type of producer who before couldn't afford to do it. But with camcorders, they can shoot it, do animation and spice it up. They can do a 'Jane Fonda' workout tape or whatever they feel they are an expert in. And they can sell it mail order."

Watkinson talked about the competition. "With my Macintosh, I can almost compete with companies that have paintboxes for lower end industrials. Everything is 8 bit video dumped from a Macintosh real time. I use Macromind Director for animated titles. Macintosh and PC's hooked up to a laser disk is the platform of choice for interactive video, and that's coming on strong in education, in-house corporate training and kiosk presentations. In the interactive area, we are not trying to compete with the big guys, we are the big guys."

Scott Billups may have produced more desktop video hybrids than anyone. He gave us a walking tour through his "desktop video system." His system is configured for 3/4" U-Matic because "it's the standard format throughout the world. You can show it anywhere–agency, broadcast or cable. It doesn't have the best resolution; nor is it cost effective. But there are 2.5 million machines throughout the world. Hi-Band Pro 8mm is good for field gathering, but the tape doesn't stand up to editing."

Besides desktop video, Scott uses his system for scripting, storyboarding, budgeting and schedule breakdowns. "For industrials videos, I can make ancillary income because it is very easy to grab a frame off of a video, digitize it, and throw it into some desktop publishing software. The next thing you know, it's in your client's brochure."

"The Macintosh is sort of an all-terrain vehicle of computers."

Billups is waiting for engineers to design low cost desktop edit control systems. "In edit control, Macintosh is not going to be the leader. If you put it head to head with other equipment, it's going to lose miserably. Conversely, there is no other computer except the Macintosh that lends itself to all the various applications in desktop media. It's sort of an all-terrain vehicle of computers."

Billups's system consists of a video editing system, an audio sweetener and mixer, cinch generator, wave form editor, time base corrector and other more traditional pieces of equipment. He uses a Massmicro Color Space II ("which is very versatile") and Truvision's New Vista ("with 32 bit color, capable of very high resolution"). "For general industrial use, it's quite sufficient. But if you want to do something for broadcast, you'll want to use a real broadcast encoder/decoder. Purchasing one costs $6000, so you might want to rent it."

He uses a monitor that's capable of displaying both the computer non-interlace mode and the NTSC interlace mode. This gives him the capability of previewing graphics before they are laid down on video. The programs he uses are MacroMind Director, LetraSet Color Studio (paintbox), Photo Shop, and Strata System–photo realistic rendering–all of which have similar applications to the high priced, professional Waveform or Personal Iris systems. He uses the Amiga as a pre-production tool. He says "the cost on Waveform for a short sequence will be $5000-10,000. On the Amiga, you can cut 60% off the budget. "

"The learning and investment curve is enormous in desktop video," said Billups. Scott recommended that "you go to seminars, manufacturers, and SIG's (special interest groups), and subscribe to Mac Week, Videography and Film & Video Magazine to keep up on the latest developments." His system costs between $180,000 and $250,000. Hardly "desktop" by our definition, but Billups's set-up successfully competes with systems costing 5 to 10 times as much.

"Audio is much further along than video."

Audio production requires less computer memory than video, which makes desktop audio production practical. Peter Gotcher, president of Digidesign, said, "Don't treat audio as an afterthought. Desktop audio systems can be operated by a non-technical person with a personal computer. Audio is much further along than video. You can do all elements of audio production with the exception of multi-track. Que-Sheet is our interface with video editing and creates editing lists for doing audio production.

Sound Tools is a professional system with 1300 systems installed worldwide. It costs $3200, and requires a Mac II (or SE) and a large hard disk. Sound Tools locks to time-code, and is a 2 channel, digital audio recording and processing system. It is software with a board that plugs into the Macintosh, which records CD quality sound to a standard Mac hard disk for editing and processing. Random access editing is 10 times faster, because you can immediately jump in real time between different audio elements. Gotcher said, "It's a lot more creative because you are willing to experiment. We're trying to put editing in the hands of creative people and remove the engineer or middleman which has been very time consuming and inhibiting to the creative process."

Audio Media is very similar and has all the audio circuitry on one Mac II card. It doesn't support time code but it will work with Macromind Director and Hypercard. This is designed for people who are working in a self-contained Macintosh environment with animation and hi-fidelity 16 bit sound and are not working with external image sources.

The choice between Sound Tools and Audio Media comes down to whether you are working with other image sources (like video which requires time-code) or just within the Mac.

Michael Backes is a visualization consultant to the Advanced Technology group at Apple and was a consultant on the special graphic effects for the film, The Abyss.

> *"The great thing about scanned art
> is that it makes Rembrandts out of mental midgets."*

"We called up our storyboards very quickly from a 160MB hard disk. We scanned them at 256 grey levels, which was 2 files of 75MB each. When they say multimedia eats hard disks, it's really true. I'm waiting for optical disks to mature because they will have 600MB on a cartridge and cost $50-100. Now I am using a drive from Mass Micro that holds 45MB on a removable hard disk cartridge that you can carry around.

"We used a Tectronics color printer with a grey scale ribbon to print out original copies of the storyboards to give to special effects for The Abyss. We used Pixel Paint, an 8-bit color paint program. We can take a storyboard and flip it, resize it, move it, and paint it. The great thing about scanned art is that it makes Rembrandts out of mental midgets."

Normally, in feature film production, you do drawings, painting and blueprints for the sets. Rarely does a director really know how the set will work until it's built. Backes has a novel computer solution. "On The Abyss, we drew a blueprint on a computer screen and had the computer turn it into a three dimensional drawing. We could use the mouse and literally walk around the set in real time. It was a wire-frame drawing without any major detail, but it did give you a sense of 3-D. The programmer is now doing a program called Walk-Thru that will be out later this year which will include light sources and shading. You can walk around the set and see if the camera will fit or whether the set will have to be enlarged."

When Apple introduced the Mac IIci in Los Angeles, John Sculley played a 4 minute animation in real time from a Mac on the screen. How'd they do that? Backes said, "It was coming directly off the hard disk. This was a technique called 'triple buffering' which is throwing three images from the disk up into the video RAM one at a time and doing a juggling act. It works great. We can get real time playback with 16 bit animation. The sound was played off a CD player, and we synced them. The computer had nothing to do with the sound."

There are also desktop solutions for creating commercials and on-air graphics said Backes. "Desktop video gives you the ability to capture video images from a videographics board like TruVisions Nu-Vista card (generates sync and is $7000), the Rastar Ops card ($1500), or the MassMicro card ($3000-4000). You can take a 3-D object and stick an animation on it. You can grab 15 seconds of Casablanca and mask it to a 3-D object, then move that object around and Casablanca plays back on it. It looks really great. Desktop video is expensive right now, because there are not a lot of one-board solutions. The Amiga is interesting, but I view it as a low-end solution."

Al Alcorn is a member of Apple's Advanced Technology Group, and the inventor of Pong–the first interactive video game. He let us peek behind the doors at Apple.

> *"You will initiate the action in an artificial reality*
> *where the graphics will be fast enough*
> *to interact with human beings."*

Apple is busy working on "speaker recognition." Alcorn said, "The keyboard is not the best way to enter information–talking is the best way. We are building a software and hardware model on how the human ear works so the computer will recognize your voice."

Apple is also working with an animation-like in-betweening technology. Alcorn said, "We use constraint-based animation and modeling where we create an environment with laws of physics with mass, gravity and elasticity. You can deal with an object just like you would a real thing." He showed snippets of video research, such as an animation of a string which has no mass or gravity. Extending those principles to the 3-D world, he showed a Luxo desk lamp that had various base weights. The desk lamp was animated to jump. "We put in constraints, minimized muscle power, gave it a starting point and an end point. We made the Luxo lamp jump with various gravities, by just dialing up the base weight and making it heavier." The lamp leapt gracefully from one side of the frame to the other, until the weight was so heavy it seemed hard pressed to move only a few inches. The gravity built into the program gave an extraordinarily realistic look to the movement, which was done without conventional animation in-betweening.

Alcorn gave us a sense of an interactive media in an artificial reality space. He said, "Instead of someone scripting the action, you will initiate the action in an artificial reality where the graphics will be fast enough to interact with human beings."

Jim Fancher is a producer and system designer at Pacific Ocean Post. Having worked with most of the new technologies, he was able to give an overview on what's missing in desktop video.

"This year what we'll see is a 3rd wave of video boards
with a compression algorithm working at real time video rates."

"There are two types of editing systems. Linear editing plays back tapes in sequence. Non-linear creates a huge data base from which you can random access your material. No more tape searching. The non-linear system creates a play list where you create pointers to information, and when you ask it to play it back it sequences it back out. There are a number of professional non-linear editing systems, Montage, EditDroid and a few others. All have found niches in video post production. Most are very expensive and aren't desktop video.

"In desktop video, there is the AVID, which uses non-linear editing, and a linear editing system from Larry Seehorn. There is also a HyperCard editing system that has not been released, and another from Julian Systems. All are geared to 1/2" or 3/4" tape for analog acquisition and editing. Except for AVID, they all emulate linear editing systems. AVID costs $80,000, if you want it to work.

"I haven't seen any Mac-based editing systems that I would want to live with. There are many editors in IBM that do a good job of machine control working through the VLAND type of interface. ASC, CASE System, is $7000 including the computer. It won't do graphics. The IBM PC is a very cheap solution as a platform for linear editing."

In addressing the "chunky" graphics question, Fancher said, "The issue is software. So far on Mac we haven't seen good software. The reason that the animation you see is so chunky is because it's calculated on a frame basis. Even where you get Macromind Director to move a circle, it still looks chunky because it is frame-by-frame at 30 frames per second. Higher end systems are all doing it at 60 fields per second.

"Mac just can't display 30 frame video, so when you get very complicated objects in Macromind Director it slows down. You might get 2 or 3 frames per second updated on the Mac, which isn't fast enough. So the only solution to that is to put things out non-real time, just like I do it in a 3-D graphics program–a frame at a time."

Fancher's work at Pacific Ocean Post has taken him into the digital desktop video realm. He said, "We're getting out pictures in the digital domain. D1 is an agreed upon, international standard for digital television and is the closest to a computer type picture. The bus speed just isn't there to get pictures out of the Macintosh in real time. For example, moving 25 MB/sec fills up your 40 meg hard disk in 2 seconds. We were looking for something that would store a whole lot of data, and we came up with 8mm tape. We work with a company that manufactures a tape drive that utilizes the same tape transport that goes into the Hi8 machines. They modify that tape transport into a data stream to back up systems, which allows you to record data on the tape. So we're not doing an analog recording on the tape, we are doing digital recording which holds 2.2 gigabits of information and gives us the storage capacity for digital television. The drives run about $5000. I can store about 50 seconds of real time broadcast television on a tape. The bad news is that it takes 2 hours to get it on video, off frame by frame."

Fancher creates full broadcast quality 3-D animations on the Swivel 3-D program and puts them out onto 8mm tape. "It's $5000 and is the equivalent of a $140,000 broadcast recorder. It takes 20 seconds a frame to output it to an 8mm tape."

Fancher sees data storage as the main problem now. However, image compression becomes one solution. "The walls we were up against with recording real time motion pictures on the Macintosh were bus speeds and data storage. At several megabytes per picture or 25 MB/sec of data, storage would rapidly exceed data storage. But if you begin to get significant amounts of compression, you can store significant amounts of pictures on standard hard disks. Compression programs like Stuffit give you a 2:1 compression. You can compress 6 megs to 3 megs. This year what we'll see is a 3rd wave of video boards with a compression algorithm working at real time video rates which will let you to store broadcast quality images on reasonably sized hard disks hooked to your computer."

Michael Nesmith was one of the first music video pioneers. He was the first to start a videotape distribution company (Pacific Arts Video) over a decade ago, and he was the first to publish a videomagazine. His eloquent luncheon speech gave the conference attendees a lot to chew on.

> *"This ability has uncovered another world–*
> *another place that only exists*
> *in the world of the computer."*

"As computers made their evolutionary journey, they went from huge clunky machines standing alone barely reachable by man to small portable devices that could communicate with each other. This ability to communicate was a powerful and under-appreciated force in the life of a computer. This ability has uncovered another world, another place that only exists in the world of the computer. Even though this world has no fixed boundaries, it is very, very real. It is cyberspace. It is the world of virtual reality. It has an incredible importance to you, and me, and the world as we know it.

"Everything you've been hearing about in today's conference is coming together to give us a look at this new virtual world. We have in our hands the tools to discover more and more of the virtual world and to define it in some degree. The computer has helped us discover a new world, and now we have a window through which we can look at it. We don't have to sit typing into the computer to retrieve the ideas. With desktop video, we can see it.

"We've got a lot of growing to do. The language of film, which has been created for a two-dimensional, single point-of-view, now has to expand to include the multi-dimensional multi point-of-view. The present techniques of filmmaking now become just a point of departure rather than a mature skill. The power of the video camera, coupled with the computer and the power it has to see the virtual world, gives us a new opportunity to define this world and make it beautiful just for beauty's sake."

While the vision of desktop video hasn't perhaps been invented yet, there are numerous indications that companies and producers are working fast and furious to bring it into reality. It will be at least another year before we see desktop publishing systems that will allow producers to take in analog video, digitize it, store it their computers, use non-linear, random access systems to edit sound and picture, and then lay the images out of the computer onto high quality tape. If we can't do all of it today (at personally affordable prices), we can certainly do pieces of it. The conference indicated to many that there's every reason to start experimenting now with some of the tools that exist for your current projects.

Now tool up, and go get 'em.

WHAT'S THAT SOUND?
EVERYBODY LOOK WHAT'S GOING DOWN.

Sometimes, frequently actually, our blatant jump into accepting technological artifacts troubles me. This was written during one of those moods.

We'll see and hear some great new things about video technology as we walk the floor at NAB (National Association of Broadcasters convention) this year but we might also think about what is happening to our Nation as a result of television.

Seems like every time we turn around we learn we're doing something bad for our own health and the health of the planet. We want to do the right thing so we rid the house of fluorocarbons; we eat fruits, vegetables and legumes; we start a compost heap; we recycle; we reduce our water and energy consumption; we use rechargeable batteries. This week I took an electric car for a test drive. I want one. Even so I keep feeling that I'm not doing enough. Something's still wrong. These are just Band-Aids. Deep down the congenital qualities of my lifestyle will be unable to restore the great losses to the planet and other human beings. It's a sobering thought.

Just when I'm feeling this vulnerability and sense my own shortcomings about being a responsible human being along comes Jerry Mander's new book, *In the Absence of the Sacred* (Sierra Club Books)–a powerful work that pounds the final nail into the coffin of self-doubt. I think a hard look at one's values are fine from time to time. Self-critique sharpens the mind and prepares the course of action in one's life. *But, geez, Jerry. . . does this mean I have to stop producing television?*

Mander's book is an examination of technology–television and computers–and its failure to deliver on the promise of making life better as it destroys other cultures whose people and knowledge may provide answers where our technology fails. A chilling premise. Mander made me sit up and listen. I highly recommend you get your hands on this book today.

It's easy to point to the smokestack industries and ask, *"How can they pollute like that?"* As television and video producers, we may congratulate ourselves about our "clean industry." At least we don't create acid rain. But is television so benign? Mander thinks not. He has hit on some truths about television that responsible human beings should not ignore.

Ten years ago he wrote the powerful book, *Four Arguments for the Elimination of Television*. With *In the Absence of the Sacred* (Sierra Club Books), Mander—a kind of visionary "Billy Jack"—swings his bat at our reality about television and hits a homer.

He prepares the ground with statistics:

•   Almost 99.5 percent of homes in the US with electricity have televisions. Information from a single source in the country can be sent to virtually everyone.

•   Marshall McLuhan spoke about a "global village." He said we'll be speaking to each other through television but he forgot that the poor don't talk back. It's the One speaking to the many. Closer to the nightmare Huxley or Orwell envisioned. It's like 1984 has come true and no one noticed.

•   Every day 95 percent of the US population gets a "hit" of television. The medium is addicting. The tube is on for nearly eight hours a day in the average home. Adults watch five hours, kids watch three and a half hours, and older Americans watch nearly six hours. This means that <u>the average adult spends more time watching television than doing anything else</u> except sleeping, working or going to school! Television has replaced the activities that our ancestors pursued only a generation ago. Community events, cultural pursuits and family life are a rarity.

Then Mander drives home the effect of the pervasiveness of television:

•   We now live *inside* the media. We are physically and psychically

297

immersed with a machine. TV enters people's minds and leaves images within that they carry with them forever. Television, an external environment, becomes internalized. It is science fiction and it is real.

• When humans watch television, their eyes don't move. Their brains go into an "alpha" state, a non-cognitive, passive-receptive mode. Humans become *receivers*.

• There is a blurring of reality. Humans buy products seen on television; talk to their friends about television shows (as if the people and events were real and part of their lives); dress, act and speak like television people; and even elect their leaders from what they've seen on television.

• This is not only true about the United States. As television spreads around the globe, it is becoming true of Africa, South America, Indonesia and places where there are not even roads. People in mud or grass huts are watching satellite broadcasts of *Dallas* and *Kojak*. Over 50 percent of television watched outside the US is reruns of popular American programs.

• Television is not democratic. It is one-way. It is the transmission of American values and lifestyle with the end result being a worldwide monoculture. Anyone who has traveled anywhere has seen the tangible and pervasive American cultural cancer throughout the world. Kentucky Fried Chicken in Bali!

• Seventy-five percent of commercial network television time has been paid for by the largest 100 of the 450,000 American corporations. When a little guy does buy television time, any effect will be lost within a sea of commercial messages.

• The average American sees 21,000 commercials a year which say the same thing: *"Buy something–now!"*

• It's a scary thought. Our entire population is sitting night after night in a passive state receiving information from faraway places: imagery placed in their brains telling them how to live their lives. If this were science fiction, you'd say they were being brainwashed. But since it's real, you would say they are being "entertained." What's wrong with this picture?

With other media, such as radio and books, the viewer is a much more active participant. There is eye movement, thinking and interaction. The imagination is being used. Thoughts and images can be examined to a much greater extent than with television and its constant onslaught of images–sometimes real, sometimes fiction, sometimes special effects, but always moving at a quick pace. Drug-like. Mood-altering. The net result, fears Mander, is a generation of young people who are less able to act on their own, or to be creative. Educators already confirm this. This new drugged generation feel they can't experience life without technological and chemical props.

• The speed of television has accelerated our nervous systems. Life is much faster than it has ever been. When ordinary life seems slow, the TV junkie pushes the "on" button. If you don't want to think, you reach for the remote control and start "clicking" to increase television's speed.

• The visual hyperactivity is staggering, seductive, captivating. All form, no content. When you turn off the set, life is very slow, quiet, ordinary. TV seems better, and so "click" back on it goes. The natural world really *is* slower and subtle. To feel Nature, human perceptions must be slowed down.

Televisions, computers, cars encourage just the opposite–constant change. Attention spans have shrunk. Our children cannot maintain attention. They cannot learn, they cannot read, and they cannot think for themselves. We have synchronized our minds and bodies with television. We have become incompatible with Nature. We are living within the rhythms of our television and it's no wonder we cannot seem to do anything to reverse our assault on the environment when our very tools and our entire consciousness is tuned to technology rather than the winds and rains, or the rising and setting of the sun.

Mander's premise is that what's happened isn't so much a result of a conspiracy by the military or corporations as it is from a *de facto* conspiracy of technical factors. We've simply unquestionably assumed that technology, for its own sake, its own evolution, is good and haven't examined the far-reaching implications of the technology that you and I employ day in and day out–in our work and recreation.

Television reaches into every home in our country, and someday maybe will reach into every home in the world. Combined with powerful imagery, television encourages passivity, isolation, confusion, addiction and alienation; and homogenizes our values and shuts out alternative visions.

Television implants and continuously reinforces dominant ideologies. It accelerates our nervous systems to match the television rhythms and makes us into a new kind of human being–less creative, less able to make subtle distinctions, speedier, and more interested in *things*. We have to ask ourselves is this the kind of world we wish to create? Live in? *Does this mean I have to stop producing TV?*

Maybe I should produce more "good TV." So I called Jerry Mander, who I knew from my San Francisco days a decade ago. I told him I thought his book was great and that I'd like to make a PBS television special based on *In The Absence of the Sacred.* I told him I didn't know where I'd get the money but like last year's PBS special, *Diet for a New America*, which I produced and was also unsponsorable, I'd find a way. He asked me how I'd structure it. I said I really didn't know but like *Diet*, maybe I would structure it around Mander's own personal quest for knowledge and asked if he would be the host of the special. He said "no." Here is a man who walks his walk, talks his talk. Jokingly I asked if I could <u>read</u> the book on television. He didn't have a problem with that. Anyway, I like him very much. His book makes you think. At least I hope so. (Having just made the final installment on your new chip camera, maybe you are not ready to read this.)

We've accepted the view that technology is neutral or "value free" when in fact every technology has inherent social, political and environmental consequences. Technology is sold to us with great positivism. We've come to believe in a better future through technology but if you look at the track record (oil spills, Gulf War, ozone destruction, rain forest loss, longer work weeks, the poor getting poorer, etc.) you could argue just the reverse. Mander suggests that we should assume all technology is "guilty until proven innocent." Furthermore, he proposes that we shouldn't judge a technology by the way it benefits us personally but rather ask what is the holistic view of technology's impact. The real question is who benefits most? And to what end? And at what price?

I'm on the steering committee of the American Film Institute and the Apple Computer Center. Our goal is to incorporate computers into all phases of television and motion picture production. In addition to Mander's conscientious assault on television, here are his very valid negative points about computers.

He says that computer (and television) technology has sprung us headlong into an entirely new existence, one that will permanently affect our lives and the lives of our children and grandchildren. It will speed up profound changes on the planet, yet <u>there is no meaningful debate about it, no ferment, no critical analysis of the consequences</u>. As usual, the major beneficiaries are permitted to define the parameters of our understanding.

While we all believe (or have been sold) on the notion that if we don't have a personal computer we'll be left behind, here's what is lacking in the small print according to Mander:

• Health and environmental problems occur in the communities in which the machines are built, among the workers who build them, and among the people who use them. High concentrations of trichloroethylene, a carcinogenic solvent, have seeped into drinking water near manufacturing plants. There have been high incidents of miscarriages, reproductive disorders, hair loss, and chronic asthma resulting from exposure to toxins during manufacturing. From computer users, there have been reports of fatigue, eye strain, migraines, cataracts, miscarriages, birth defects, premature births, and infant death. Video display terminals emit a range of electromagnetic radiation. The idea that computers are cleaner than other industrial products is wrong.

301

•   Computers have not eliminated toil and allowed us to pursue higher goals. The benefits go to those who own the computers. Managers benefit because they can monitor workers' output precisely while blue-collar workers lose their jobs to robots. Computer operators are the coal miners of the '90s.

•   Computers bring about conceptual change. Forests are now talked about as "management units" containing "habitat capacity" with "maximum sustainable yield," all of which reduce the needs of natural life and our understanding of them. American Indians, the stewards of the land, have decided through spiritual and intuitive means how game populations should be hunted. When Indians and other native groups are given computers, will they too begin to conceptualize nature in objective terms, while the more mythical, sensory and spiritual outlooks are sacrificed?

•   What about computers in schools? "Computer literacy" is already required in many colleges and high schools. Computers are praised for allowing students to work at their own pace and because they give the students one-on-one attention. But what kind of person does this educational process produce? As Marian Kester in the *Toronto Globe* wrote: "If children are separated from their parents by hours of TV, from their playmates by video games, and from their teachers by teaching machines, where are they supposed to learn to be human?"

•   Surveillance may be the greatest danger of computers. Already TRW has credit records of 120 million Americans. The Medical Information Bureau has files on 20 million people. The federal government has collected 4 billion separate records on the population, about 17 records per person. With the ability to interlock these database records about your health, how you spend your money, where you live and work, your corporate performance, and market research information, there isn't much left to the imagination. Be assured that the FBI, and the CIA, and local police already have the ability to know a hell of a lot about you. And I do mean you, dear reader!

• The largest institutions–the military, corporations, governments and banks–can only be as large and as globally far-reaching as they are able to quickly communicate mind-boggling amounts of data among their diverse branches. With satellites, an institution can encompass the entire planet. National boundaries no longer exist. With this speed up of economic activity, funds may be moved instantly, increasing the speed of human and corporate activity and the rate of change on the planet. Is this good? It is for those who benefit most–the large institutions. For the rest of the world, the acceleration is harmful. For indigenous peoples, who operate in small-scale economic communities, computerization threatens the survival of their traditional collective institutions.

• I like my computer. It's *friendly*. (Great marketing word.) It allows me to do a lot of work, much faster. Computers are empowering. But who benefits most from computers? The largest institutions that have the ability to expand globally. The accelerated pace at which forests are felled in Indonesia and Borneo, oceans are mined in the Pacific, and dams are built throughout the world reflects the increased ability of corporations to operate from central managements and still influence daily activities throughout the world. The computer is hardly neutral.

• The invention of the computer instantly changed the speed at which war could be waged, the scale of its destruction. Computer technology has already produced an unprecedented degree of military centralization. Generals sitting in an underground war room can fire missiles and track their progress not unlike those depicted in the film *War Games*. Managing war like this separates humans from the consequences of their actions. We at home have already experienced this detachment during The Gulf Television War.

These notions have stirred me up considerably. The genie is out of the box and how do you get it back in? It's very easy to get caught up working with computers to edit video, create computer graphics, and prepare budgets, but when do we look up, like Mander has done, and ask ourselves what is really going on beyond our own work platforms?

303

What Mander says is true about computers: there are health problems, they have created a new level of stress with the acceleration of life and work, they do force us to conceptualize in dehumanizing ways, they are creating a new breed of kids, they have invaded our privacy, the larger institutions do benefit the most, and they are a terrifying weapon of war.

I trust it's not too late to take our head out of the pixels and see what the widespread use of computers is doing to our lives and the lives of others. We automatically assume we are on some kind of great Crusade or Divine Mission with our technology. Did the corporate marketers give us this notion which we've failed to examine? But perhaps the greatest loss of all, as a result of our technology, will be the native cultures of the world who for millennia have prospered without our technology. It took Jerry Mander 10 years to write *In The Absence of the Sacred*. Getting through our own biases to understand our own use of this technology is the assignment for the month. Now go get a copy of Mander's book and start reading.

THE FUTURE

WHERE ARE WE COMING FROM?
WHERE ARE WE GOING?

This is an essay for the book, "The Age of Videography," to which I was asked to contribute. Like many contributors, I looked at the changes in the our industry through my own autobiography. This is the entire text of the essay (the actual chapter that appeared was shorter).

Growing up as a child of television and now being a producer of video programming, I have seen the medium move forward, sideways, and into the new emerging, converging forms. My own fascination with video was evident 30 years ago in 1966 when I first fooled around with a television camera at KQED in San Francisco. My subject was an elaborately costumed Chinese opera character called "Monkey" who we set flying across a Mylar background. I aimed the camera into a video monitor creating a feedback loop. Wow! I was hooked. But my fascination with video and television began much earlier.

At 11, in a darkroom, illuminated only by a red light bulb, and gazing into a tray of photo chemicals, I saw an image magically appear. I knew instantly the visual photographic arts were for me. During a series of summer jobs at a newspaper and with a commercial photographer, I held a 3 1/4 x 4 1/4 Speed Graphix camera with flashbulb one year and a 35mm camera with a zoom lens and electronic strobe the next. Things were moving fast.

But once the pictures stopped "fading in" on the photographic paper, it was a frozen still image. I wanted to see it move. The next summer I was a production assistant working on documentaries: eventually shooting, editing, and negative cutting. But the biggest single life-changing event again happened in a darkened room.

At a tiny hometown cinema–The Art Theater in Champaign, Illinois–I saw my first "art film." Then another, and another, and pretty soon I was going almost every night. It was incredible. The on-screen characters' behaviors, attitudes, concerns and even the way they moved and talked were entirely different. The bubble popped. The world view of Champaign was too small and I wanted more. (The same thing happened in the same theater to film critic Roger Ebert at about the same time!)

I saw that there were so many different ways for humans to live, and different things to experience. I saw that I had been encased in a cultural glass bubble away from life's multitude of possibilities.

A few years later, in film school at The San Francisco Art Institute, I pushed the possibilities of the visual envelope as far as I could. In addition to my first television class project on "Monkey," I took archetypal subjects (I loved Jung's book *Man and His Symbols*) and made experimental films. Sets were made entirely from one roll of white butcher paper but nevertheless *the images transcended its material limitations.* Film and video had the ability to create new surfaces and textures. What the camera pointed at was no longer "real." I loved guiding an audience through a dream-like state: terribly exciting for a 19-year-old to feel 2000 people mesmerized by his cinematic dream. I felt like a puppeteer whose medium was light. (The film was premiered by Salvador Dali and invited to Director's Fortnight at Cannes.)

Six years later, I experienced what I had only come to view in the Art Theater in Champaign. For two years, I traveled around the world, mostly alone, from Japan, throughout Southeast Asia, India, East Africa, Egypt and Greece. I explored ancient cultures and religions, digging for the source of ideas and knowledge. In Indonesia, I first discovered and then studied the shadow play, Bali's archetypal precursor to radio and television. Quite a leap from a darkened movie theater in Illinois into the jungles of Java.

During those years the only place I found I could make money was Japan. I showed my films and videos in museums, universities and art theaters. I produced a five-day live multimedia event called "Nocturnal Dream Show." The intent of the show was to demonstrate that we all live in "the same electronic pipeline." (At the sub-atomic level, we are all interconnected energy fields. I was hoping to create an experiential version of this in the audience.) Multimedia, in those days was not CD-ROMs, but film projections, light shows, live bands, dancers and audience participation theater. If you lived through the '60s, you know what I'm talking about. If you didn't... never mind.

In Japan I borrowed a Sony Portapak–a 1/2 reel-to-reel videotape recorder. What an invention! No film processing, you could playback what you shot. A kind of motion picture version of the Polaroid. Projection was a problem and so was editing. It was not as easy to edit as film. But nevertheless, I was excited about traveling in a caravan around Japan with musicians and dancers and videotaping them and the audiences, then playing back the interaction and videotaping that. I wanted to blend actual, visual and virtual realities into a kind of electronic feedback loop soup where time and space disappeared. Got it? (If not, lick the tiny dot at the bottom of this page.)

There is something very organic about the video image. When you videotape the human body and duplicate the image many times, the image of the body starts to look like an energy field, which is what it is. I became very excited about the possibilities of using video to record the human body in new ways. I flipped out when I first saw sonographic images of a fetus which I immediately incorporated into one of my short films. Incredible potential this video stuff!

When I returned from traveling, I made independent films and videos. But the life of the independent then (as it is now) is fraught with economic ups and downs. I wanted the kind of accelerated learning that I had while traveling. So I threw myself into something really crazy. Commercial television.

That did it. My art friends turned their backs on me. The art houses and museums canceled showings of my new films. Wiese had gone "commercial." (Not really, I just wanted some new experiences, a paycheck, and use of equipment that I did not have to pay for!)

I became a segment producer for a live, nightly, talk-variety style show. My job was to come up with guests and stunts for one to three seven-minute segments per night. Five nights a week. The other segment producers seemed discouraged; their segments never came out as written. The host was often the wild card frequently deviating from the cue cards. Live television it was, unpredictable and danger-ous. "I can work with that," I told them.

One night I staged a segment called "Robot Wars" (the title was stolen from my short film, *Hardware Wars*, as was the concept). It was to be a large fight between two huge robots made from junkyard parts. It was staged in the local Cadillac dealer's car lot next to the studio. (Thank goodness he moved his cars!)

We took the audience out of the studio and into the car lot during a commercial. It was already packed with pink-haired punk fans of the creator of the robots. Their creator, an avant-garde sculptor, gave a very Bob Dylan-esque interview, simultaneously setting off explosives in the robots. The host was terrified and ducked for cover, losing con-trol for the first time in his career.

Unfortunately this was the same night that Bob Hope canceled his appearance on our show but no one told the station manager who packed his family into the station wagon and brought them down to meet Mr. Hope. When he saw my segment running amok (with the huge Cadillac signs in the background), and these 15-foot-tall rusty robots catapulting huge flaming spears above the heads of the terrified host, audience and tattooed punks, he looked for the nearest produc-er. He felt I was making an anti-materialist statement that would alienate his sponsors, and let me know that my talents might better be employed elsewhere. Like out of state. The rest is history.

So I moved to New York and produced political campaign TV spots. We shot in film and posted in video. These 30- and 60-second zingers were powerful in their ability to influence voters' decisions. But bot-tom line, they were dishonest. The politicians cared about the votes and would say anything to get them. (Big surprise.) But I saw that the power of television, even when tapped for a few seconds, was enor-mous. I couldn't understand why no one was using this powerful medium to convey truthful, life-enhancing information. My job was a close-up study in media manipulation. (We won 17 of 18 campaigns.)

I quit after less than a year after have produced over 200 TV and 60 radio spots. I never got a full night's sleep and I don't think the only reason was that I was editing many nights. I didn't feel right about what we were doing.

Pay cable had just hit and things were hot. I got a job as director of on-air promotion and production for The Movie Channel. The channel needed programming, so my department created on air graphics, IDs, promos, star profiles, and contests. Mostly promotional stuff. I had hoped that one day my writers and producers would produce real "original programming" but we were never given the opportunity. Our segments were purely promotional and self-serving.

One ongoing assignment from our boss, Bob Pittman (boy wonder and founder of MTV) was to create an on-air look to differentiate us from our main competitor, HBO, who was using slick, high-resolution, expensive 3-D animation. We let a couple of *Saturday Night Live* graphic artists loose on the new Quantel Paintbox and came up with a cool, hip, retro electronic look. We were the first to use the Quantel Paintbox for broadcast! When viewers channel surfed, they knew when they were watching The Movie Channel.

Around the time that I had produced over 1200 programs, The Movie Channel merged operations with Showtime and half of us were let go.

Unlike my father's career, which lasted 30 years at one place, I have gone from experience to experience. I was never very interested in having "a job" per se unless it included learning and making a contribution. Unfortunately, that's not what today's job market calls for and so many of my "jobs" were not soul-satisfying and only filled more video landfills with quickly forgettable programming. But I was able to spend millions of dollars of someone else's money to learn. A kind of high-priced "independent study program" if you will. I was learning, but was I making a difference? Not much.

I had traveled far from the late '60s when I created a few "save the world" films and documentaries. Now I was making thousands of "who cares about the world" television pieces. Maybe my friends were right to turn their backs on me when I entered the world of television.

If only the power of television could be employed for "good works." If only the two could come together somehow. They seemed miles apart.

Vestron was, at one time, the world's largest independent producer and distributor of videos. Next I won the catbird's seat as vice president of their original programming department. I was given a checkbook and the mandate to produce a lot of programming. I could do whatever I wanted as long as it would make money. Look out world, here I come.

Sports, kids, comedy, exercise, documentaries, music, direct-to-video movies were all genres that I acquired and produced. With a release schedule of over 110 titles a year, every other week I had to release six videos into the marketplace backed by a full-tilt publicity and marketing machine. It was heady. I had a list of 50 projects "in development" on my desk, and about a dozen projects in various stages of production every month with average budgets ranging between $150,000 to $250,000. It was a great time for experimentation, not only with production techniques and program formats, but with marketing as well.

Ninety-eight percent of what we released made money for the company, about 80 percent made money for the producers. We were young, we worked hard, we made other people lots of money. The company's founder added hundreds of millions of dollars to his personal bank account. It was not our genius, but the hungry marketplace that filled the coffers.

But in the heady atmosphere of "everything we touch turns to gold," Vestron started making movies just as the video store shelves were filling with product. The "B" and "C" titles (other than *Dirty Dancing*) that Vestron was producing found neither a home on these shelves nor in movie theaters. Plus a bank reneged on their $100 million line of credit, sending Vestron into bankruptcy; 12 international offices closed and over 500 people went home.

I had had such a terrific and creative time at Vestron and learned so much that "life after Vestron" at another video or television company did not appeal to me. The video business was on a down trend and no other company could provide that kind of action, fun and responsibility. I had learned what I needed to learn.

In addition, I had had enough "quantity" time. Now I wanted to go for "quality," producing only a handful of media piece each year instead of truckloads. I would take my video production and marketing experience and return to the world of the independent and make only videos or television that I felt had something worthwhile to contribute.

I developed and produced a series of *Lifeguides* for KCET in Los Angeles: TV special and videos which included *Diet for a New America* and *Healing Sexual Abuse*. I consulted on launching video labels and series: PBS Home Video Line, Joseph Campbell's *Hero's Journey*, and Children's Television Workshop (for Republic Pictures). I produced a best-selling video with Shirley MacLaine, and several health-oriented infomercials on vegetarian lifestyles.

Having been on the breaking wave during the "go-go" years of cable television and home video, I have kept my eyes open for the next big play in the new technologies. While many of my colleagues rushed into CD-ROMs, I didn't understand how it is yet a business: too expensive to produce, no clear distribution channels, multiple platforms, and few compelling titles. (Can you name three terrific CD-ROMs titles, really fast? Thought so.)

The Internet and World Wide Web did excite me because everyone could be a publisher worldwide. No one has to vote. You want to express something in text, sound or images? Just upload it. It is not censored by economic forces like just about every other medium I can think of–at least not yet.

An experience that I had that still raises the hair on the back of my neck 20 years later is an exercise that I did that allowed me to peek into the future. It was a simple visualization where you were to visualize your office of the future. Sounds fun. I saw a Japanese room with tatami mats and shoji screens (I was into that then) filled with monitors. Before me was a huge mixing console where I could synthesize visual and audio elements from anywhere in the world, and then broadcast whatever I made from these images back out into the world. This is pretty much what my office can do today given digital video editing, and the World Wide Web! Are you interested in what your office will look like in the year 2010? What the media world will look like in the future?

Technologies will continue to evolve so quickly that most people won't be looking at the effects and fallout of so much technology. It's a rush to the next new proprietary standard. It is staggering to me to look at all the cameras, editing systems, and release formats that I've used in my career–and I don't feel that old! It's been a constant learning process. If you snooze, you lose.

But there is some danger here. The great emphasis on the next wave of tools takes our attention away from the work itself. Are we really producing the kind of images that enhance and contribute to human life and sustaining the environment? Are we envisioning a positive future with world-wide cooperation or are we looking to expand our market share first? Or are we fueling a desire (by what we broadcast into third-world countries) to pursue and emulate what we already know are dead-end consumption-addicted lifestyles? Or are we enabling and empowering other cultures to find their own voices, images and icons that pop our own cultural bubbles and help <u>make us</u> more knowledgeable about the human condition?

Are we really being responsible for the harmful, violent and economic results produced in society by our programs or do we cop clichéd pleas such as "It's just entertainment" in the same way some argue that tobacco isn't addictive? Do we really want our population, and that of the world, to watch an average of nearly seven hours of television a day? Is that the best use of our lives?

When given the opportunity, do we "just say 'no'" when asked to participate in the production or distribution of another mindless sitcom, action-adventure or 30-second propaganda piece because we know its nutritional value is less than zero? If we aren't, why not?

Can anyone say that television or video has lived up to its potential? What is its potential? Instead of dumbing down our people with Beverly Hills and The Hamptons cultural values, might there not be other worthy sources and mindsets to inform, educate and inspire us? Where are the "bodies of knowledge"? Where are the world cultural treasures that will bring us greater appreciation of our place here? Where are the great teachers, who when brought to television, could enlighten our short journey here? Where are the daring programming executives who shout "Hell, no, we won't take it no more!" and find ways to convert their commercial swords to plowshares?

I'll tell you who they are. It's everyone reading this. It's the men and women who've walked the video path to this point. You've heard all this before. This is not new news. You know who you are. You've come into your own power in this business and developed the skills. I know that you know it's now time to make a difference. Leave a legacy. Teach the next generation. Each of us wants to find his or her own way to respond to these questions—that's the mandate for the next 20 years.

Now go get 'em.

HOME STUDIO:
DREAM OR NIGHTMARE?

Most people I talk to dream of the day when they can work from home. You've heard the rap by now: "With desktop video and all this other new technology (fax, cellular phones, computers), there's no reason why many of us can't be telecommuting."

Setting up a professional digital production studio at home is one thing, but what about the business aspects of that? Before you totally cut loose for those greener pastures of no commuting, consider a look at some of its potential rewards, benefits and responsibilities.

I know whereof I speak, having had it both ways. I hung my first pro-duction-office shingle in 1977, in San Anselmo, CA (across the street from George Lucas's office). In those days, I went from project to pro-ject, usually financed through limited partnerships. If we didn't have anything in production, we weren't eating. My strategy was to create films (and other products) that had a life of their own and could pro-vide annuities. There are only so many hours in the day that you can exchange for dollars. At some point I wanted to use those hours for what I really wanted to do, and not have to worry about whether they were bringing in bread and the rent money.

Unfortunately, after many years of financial highs and lows (mostly lows) making independent films, I realized that I needed more experi-ence. I needed to create more products and spend more (of someone else's) money, and climb higher up the learning curve.

I spent much of the '80s working for various corporate media compa-nies doing commercial television, political campaign spots, pay CATV, and home video. This gave me a salary I could depend on (until I quit or got laid off through mergers or cutbacks). The illusionary "one big happy family" concept quickly dissolves if quarterly projections aren't met.

After leaving Vestron Video, my last "inside" corporate job, I decided to go it alone even though I had several offers from other media companies. My sense was that I had gained a lot of knowledge about production, marketing and distribution that I could use to produce programs with some real social value. The corporate world's eye is always on profits, regardless of whether the product is contributing to society.

Fortunately I had also been writing a few books (during my spare time), which brought in a little income, plus there were several consulting jobs with National Geographic and the Smithsonian Institute, which helped buffer the first few months.

The Entrepreneur's Personality Profile

What you quickly learn when you start your own business is that it requires a personality that has some or all of the following qualities:

•	You must be highly organized; you can't spend too long at something that is nonproductive.

•	You must make good use of your time, have focused goals, be highly motivated, and be a self-starter.

•	You must also be confident, a good salesperson, be a "closer" (able to close the deal), and have a track record you can sell.

•	You might also try to be lucky; that's done by working like hell to "make your own luck."

•	You must be able to live with uncertainty about the future and still have a positive mental attitude that everything will turn out just fine. Those with weak constitutions need not apply.

A network of contacts and relationships in many areas of business is also a resource many fail to consider. You're going to have to find clients somewhere for your production and services.

I had the benefit (or curse) to understand that newly created products–whether they be videos, television programs, books, audios or games–all had to go through development, financing, production, marketing and distribution phases. Therefore I looked for ideas that could be formatted into as many different media forms as possible. This way, my energy would be maximized by increased revenue streams from not just one product, but–hopefully–many. Take the topic of children's health as an example: in product form, it's a book, video and an audio; it can be marketed via infomercial and retail.

An Exercise: Assessing the Pros & Cons

These are the principal things my company does: digital nonlinear off-line editing; pre- and postproduction wrap-ups; book design and layout; graphics scanning; book, treatment, proposal, budget, article and script writing; overseeing of video, film and book projects; advertising; direct-mail marketing; customer service; 800-number order-taking; consulting; and product and program development.

As we get into a discussion of the pluses and minuses of setting up a home studio, you might want to get out a yellow legal pad, draw a line down the middle, and compile your own list of pros and cons. This exercise will give you some objective way to assess whether this is the path for you. Three years ago, I built a separate structure on our property where I go every morning at dawn. My two full-time employees show up at 8:30 and 10:30. Here's what I like about it:

• 	I am available to my family any time (for some this could be a minus because of the distraction factor). Working only paces away from my home allows me to eat lunch with my two-year-old and be there when the normal child care routine is disrupted by special events, etc.

• 	Setting my own schedule, I can go to the gym, an early movie, or go on holiday.

• 	What I build is mine. No longer am I making the stockholders a bundle. When I have a hit, I reap the rewards. When I have a failure, well....

• I can make decisions over what projects we will do, what clients we will serve, and what jobs we will turn down. We tend to do projects we feel are worthy and contribute something to society.

• Today's technology allows us to compete with far larger organizations. Creative talent is always the key, but if you can access that, the computer and software tools available today can enable you to do more with less.

• No corporation can "downsize" me or retire me.

• There's great satisfaction in doing your own thing.

Now, here's what I don't like about an at-home studio/business:

• Loneliness. Maybe you won't like working alone or with just a few other folks. Maybe you like lots of people milling around. Corporations do provide a kind of surrogate family, although once you leave you'll see just how weak those bonds really are.

• You'll wear many hats. I personally like that, but others may find it very difficult.

• You must contend with business duties, such as payroll, paying taxes, unemployment, workmen's comp, insurance, etc. You must oversee accounting, legal, finance, banking, pension funds, business licenses, and permits. You may need to set up a corporation or Sub-S corporation. This type of stuff is usually invisible when you're working in a corporation; now you're the one who has to do it.

• You must operate lean and mean. Good-bye expense accounts. It's now your money, and you'll have to operate with a low overhead. I like it that way, but if you're accustomed to entertainment-industry standards you may miss the perks.

• You must handle your own negotiations. You must make the deals with third-party suppliers, employees and vendors whose services and products you will need.

• You must be a closer. I mentioned that earlier, but you really can't stress it enough. Not only will you have to close clients and project funders, investors and distributors, you may also have to invoice and collect. That can be a real drag.

• You'll need some start-up capital. Your own money? A second mortgage? Whose money? How much of your own company will you have to give away if you use outside money?

• You must have a stomach for risk-taking.

• You must oversee employees and deal with human-relations issues.

• You must figure out how to keep more cash flowing in than out.

• You'll need to market, promote and publicize your services and products.

Balancing Act

I knew that many of the projects I wanted to pursue may not be moneymakers. I knew that I'd need to have other work–but not full-time–so that I could pursue my own interests as well. So I set aside some time for spec projects, and the rest of the time for income-producing projects. This continues to be our model: Book and video publishing bring in a steady income that allows me to do other things that may or may not ever generate income.

In-House or Out?

What's wonderful about having your own home-based business is that there are many other such businesses that can provide the services you'll need so that you won't have to carry the overhead of a large staff. You can run very lean and mean, which is what's required to turn a profit and stay competitive. Wide-bandwidth networking is beginning to make possible "virtual facilities," collaborative video workgroups made up of individual project studios and post houses. These groups can be formed on an ad hoc basis according a given project's needs.

Some might argue that home-based digital project studios will take away business from existing video facilities. I believe just the opposite is true. The more people that are creating video content independently, the more they will rely on the large houses for the high-end gear, finishing and other "service bureau" functions.

As "video publishers," we go outside for production crews, line producers, camera equipment, postproduction editing, videographics, tape duplication, and many other services. Servicing small suppliers–such as ourselves–will continue to be an even bigger business for the traditional post house. In fact, I believe that post houses would be wise to provide help or outside consultants for the "front-end" (e.g., financing) needs of project studios; without that, small producers cannot afford the post house's services. A facility might also help–again, through a consultant–with back-end distribution; when the producer is successful (and stays in business) so does the facility he or she comes to for service-bureau functions.

Marketing

Clearly, a project studio operator has to intelligently decide what he or she is–and is not–going to provide. Will you do everything in the production arc, or just certain aspects of it? Maybe you'll only do production and leave the financing and distribution of it to someone else. Maybe you'll only provide graphics or editing. You will need to decide what your "ace" is, and then market your product or service, differentiating it from the many who may be doing the same thing.

We continually market our company with: book distribution; seminars; film, video and new media festivals; flyers, newsletters and catalogs; and–best of all–through the products we create. We have a publicist whose job it is to come up with several press releases about our company that can be placed in the media. When you're in the communication business, you must communicate.

The Key

The secret to making all this work is a belief in yourself. It's a belief that you're unique and have something special to contribute. Next you must communicate this to others who will want to work with you. You must maintain a professional attitude and treat people in a manner in which you'd like to be treated.

Understand what you're getting into. If the pluses outnumber the minuses, go to it. Now, what are you waiting for? Go get 'em!

APPENDIX

THE HIT LIST:
VIDEO DISTRIBUTORS

The Hit List

Got a program that deserves widespread distribution, but don't know where to go to make that happen? This column frequently deals with techniques for marketing your video. This time it features a list of companies that video producers might want to use to begin their search for a distributor for direct-to-home video programs as well as business, corporate or educational videos.

There are hundreds of distributors. The list that follows is only a place to begin–not a recommendation of any particular distributor. It's up to you to find the best match between your program and the abilities of the distributor. Take your time and be careful in your selection. A distribution deal is usually a long-term marriage, five to seven years. So do your homework, and get it right. Each distributor has a personality, a different market share, and a different marketing approach. Many distributors enter and leave the market quickly. By the time you use this list, many may have moved, gone out of business, or changed phone numbers. This list is comprised of two kinds of distributors: home video and institutional/educational.

"Home video" suppliers are those companies that acquire, and sometimes finance, videos intended for the direct-to-the-home market. The suppliers manufacture the tapes, develop marketing materials, and sell their tapes to retail outlets (which rent and/or sell tapes) to consumers. Most sell the videos through wholesalers and sell direct to the larger retail accounts. The core of the direct-to-the-home business continues to be movies. But many of these suppliers also distribute "special interest programs," which can include genres such as how-to, children's, exercise, music and other non-movie programs. Generally the retail selling price is in the $9.95 to $29.95 range to consumers. Depending on the price point, producers can expect a

10-20 percent royalty based on gross receipts. For a further explanation of how this all works, I recommend you read my book, *Film and Video Marketing.*

"Industrial, corporate, or educational" video refers to those distributors that acquire and sometimes finance videos for sale to institutions. Many corporate training videos are distributed by these companies. Price points range from $99 to $9,999. Sales of a few hundred to a few thousand tapes is considered good, depending on the production budget and marketing costs. The list contains some of names of people who can help you.

How to Use the "Hit List."

1.   Ascertain whether your program or proposed program is best suited for home video distribution or business/corporate use.

2.   See the appropriate list.

3.   Begin calling the distributors. Ask for their catalogs. Ask if their company handles your type of program (e.g., a computer training tape, a time management tape, etc.). If not, ask for the names of other distributors who do handle that kind of program.

4.   Review the catalogs of the companies who handle programs similar to yours. Assess whether you like their pricing, marketing style and the other aspects you see.

5.   Call the company's acquisitions or program development or marketing director. Explain what you've got. Make your pitch concise, to the point, and in the language and style of the catalog. By making sure you are pitching to a qualified buyer, you have a much better chance of finding distribution for your program. If they are interested, they will request that you send your proposal or finished tape for their review.

6.   All companies are different. Some will "review" your program for months, others–if they perceive it to be a highly marketable idea or tape–will get back to you immediately.

7.   If you've gotten this far, you very possibly will start negotiating to obtain the best possible deal you can. It may involve a cash advance against royalties, an ongoing royalty, a marketing commitment, or any number of other features.

You will probably get lot of "no's" along the way. Don't fret, because every "no" you get just might bring you closer to an eventual "yes." Now go get 'em!

ABC Video
Jon Peisinger, President
1200 High Ridge Road, 3rd Floor
Stamford CT 06905
(203) 968-9100

Aims Media
Jeff Sherman, President
9710 DeSoto Avenue
Chatsworth CA 91311
(818) 773-4300

Aims Media
Biff Sherman, Director of Marketing
9710 DeSoto Avenue
Chatsworth CA 91311
(818) 773-4300

Ambrose Video Publishing
Bill Ambrose
28 W. 44th St., Ste. 2100
New York NY 10036
(212) 265-7272

American Media Inc.
4900 University Avenue
W. Des Moines IA 50266

(800) 262-2557

Artist View Video
12500 Riverside Dr., Suite #201-B
No. Hollywood CA 91607

(818) 752-2480

Baker and Taylor
8140 No. Lehigh Avenue
Morton Grove IL 60053

(708) 965-8060

Barr Entertainment
Alex Bell, President
12801 Schabarum Avenue
Irwindale CA 91706
(818) 338-7878

Barr Entertainment
Jim Johnston, Director of Marketing
12801 Schabarum Avenue, PO Box 7878
Irwindale CA 91706
(818) 338-7878

Bennett Video Group
Ed Madison
8436 W. 3rd St., Ste. 740
Los Angeles CA 90048
(310) 821-3329

Best Film & Video Corp
Roy Winnick, President
242 No. Canon Drive
Beverly Hills CA 90210
(310) 274-9944

BFA Educational Media
2340 Chaffee Drive
St. Louis MO 63146

(314) 569-0211

BFS Limited
350 Newkirk Road North, Richmond Hill
Ontario, Canada L4C3G7

(905) 884-2323

BMG Distribution
Joe Schults, General Mgr BMG Kids &
1540 Broadway - 26th Floor
New York NY 10036
(212) 930-4607

BMG Distribution
Mindy Pickard, BMG Video
1540 Broadway - 26th Floor
New York NY 10036
(212) 930-4607

BMG Distribution
Strauss Zelnick, Head of North America
1540 Broadway - 26th Floor
New York NY 10036
(212) 930-4667

BMG Distribution
Bob Hinkle, BMG Video
1540 Broadway - 26th Floor
New York NY 10036
(212) 930-4667

BMG Distribution
Susan Rosenberg, Acquisition
1540 Broadway - 26th Floor
New York NY 10036
(212) 930-4667

BMG Kidz
1540 Broadway
New York NY 10036

(212) 930-4320

Broadway Video Entertainment
1619 Broadway, 9th Floor
New York NY 10019

(212) 265-7621

Buena Vista Home Video
Ann Daly, President
350 So. Buena Vista St.
Burbank CA 91521
(818) 562-3780

Buena Vista Picts. Distribution
Linda Palmer, VP, Non-Theatrical
3900 W. Alameda Ave., Twr Blvd., #2400
Burbank CA 91521
(818) 567-5016

Cabin Fever Entertainment
Tom Molito
1 Sound Shore Drive
Greenwich CT 06830
(203) 863-5200

Cabin Fever Entertainment
Jeff Lawanda, EVP
100 W. Putnam Avenue
Greenwich CT 06380
(203) 863-5200

Cambridge Career Products
PO Box 2153
Charleston WV 25328

(800) 468-4227

CBS/FOX Video
John Ruscin, President & CEO
1330 Avenue of the Americas, 6th Floor
New York NY 10019
(212) 373-4806

CBS/FOX Video
Joan Blanski, VP, Marketing
1330 Avenue of Americas, 6th Floor
New York NY 10019
(212) 373-4800

Central Park Media
John O'Donnell
250 West 57th St., Suite 317
New York NY 10107
(212) 977-7456

Churchill Films
4909 St. Louis Ct.
Culver City CA 90230

Coalition for Quality Children's Video
535 Cordova Rd., Suite 456
Santa Fe NM 87501

(505) 989-8076

Coliseum Video
430 West 54th Street, 2nd Flr.
New York NY 10019

(212) 489-8156

Columbia TriStar Home Video
Benjamin Feingold, President of Home
10202 W. Washington Blvd.
Culver City CA 90232
(310) 280-8000

Columbia TriStar Home Video
Paul J. Newman, Director of Non-Theatrical
10202 W. Washington Blvd.
Culver City CA 90232
(310) 280-6139

Columbia TriStar Home Video
Betsy Caffrey, VP, Special Markets
10202 W. Washington Blvd.
Culver City CA 90232
(310) 280-5513

Columbia TriStar Home Video
Lexine Wong, VP, International Sales
10202 W. Washington Blvd.
Culver City CA 90232
(310) 280-6139

Coronet/MTI Film & Video
4350 Equity Drive
Columbus OH 43228

(800) 777-8100

Dartnell Corp
4660 No. Ravenswood
Chicago IL 60640

(800) 621-5463

Direct Cinema Ltd
Mitchell Block, President
PO Box 10003
Santa Monica CA 90410
(310) 636-8200

Discovery Communications
7700 Wisconsin Avenue
Bethesda MD 20814

(301) 986-0444

Facets Multimedia
Milos Stehlik, President
1517 West Fullerton
Chicago IL 60614
(312) 281-9075

Fast Forward Marketing
Steve Wallace
3420 Ocean Park Blvd., Suite 3075
Santa Monica CA 90405
(310) 396-4434

Films for the Humanities and Sciences
PO Box 2053
Princeton NJ 08543

(609) 275-1400

Films Inc./PMI
Charles Benton, Chairman
5547 No. Ravenswood Avenue
Chicago IL 60640
(800) 323-4222

Films Inc./PMI
Christine Lundberg
5547 No. Ravenswood Avenue
Chicago IL 60640
(800) 323-4222

Films Inc./PMI
Joanne Greene, Acquisitions
5547 No. Ravenswood Avenue
Chicago IL 60640
(800) 323-4222

Fox Lorber Home Video
Richard Lorber, Pres
419 Park Avenue South, 20th Floor
New York NY 10016
(212) 686-6777

Goldenbooks
Eric Bogen, President
850 3rd Ave., 7th Flr
New York NY 10022
(212) 583-4400

Goldenbooks
Leigh Anne Brodsky, Director of Marketing
850 3rd Ave., 7th Flr
New York NY 10022
(212) 265-7621

Goodtimes Video
Joe Cayre, President
16 East 40th Street
New York NY 10016
(212) 951-3000

Hallmark Home Entertainment
Steve Beeks, Exec. V. President
6100 Wilshire Blvd., Suite 1400
Los Angeles CA 90048
(213) 634-3000 /

Hallmark Home Entertainment
Glenn Ross, Senior Vice President
6100 Wilshire Blvd., Suite 1400
Los Angeles CA 90048
(213) 634-3000

Hanna-Barbera
Fred Siebert, President
3400 Cahuenga Blvd. West
Los Angeles CA 90068
(213) 851-5000

HBO Home Video
Preston Lewis, Acquisitions
1100 6th Avenue
New York NY 10036
(212) 512-1405

Healing Arts
2434 Main Street
Santa Monica CA 90405

(310) 399-3700

Hemdale Home Video
7966 Beverly Blvd.
Los Angeles CA 90048

Image Entertainment
Martin Greenwald, President
9333 Oso Avenue
Chatsworth CA 91311
(818) 407-9100

Inscape
Michael Nash, CEO
1933 Pontius Avenue
Los Angeles CA 90025
(310) 312-5705

J2 Communications
Jim Jimirro, President
10850 Wilshire Blvd, Suite 1000
Los Angeles CA 90024
(310) 474-5252

King World Direct
Burl Hechtman
12400 Wilshire Blvd., Suite 800
Los Angeles CA 90025
(310) 826-1108

KQED
Pamela Byers
2601 Mariposa Street
San Francisco CA 94110

Kultur/White Star Video
Ronald Davis, President
195 Highway #36
West Long Branch NJ 07764
(908) 229-2343

Kultur/White Star Video
Dennis Headland, Marketing
195 Highway #36
West Long Branch NJ 07764
(908) 229-2343

Live Home Video
Roger Burlage, President
15400 Sherman Way, PO Box 10124
Van Nuys CA 91410
(818) 908-1363

Live Home Video
Ellen Pittleman, VP, Production &
15400 Sherman Way, PO Box 10124
Van Nuys CA 91410
(818) 988-5060

MCA VIDEO
Steve Galloway, Video Acquisitions
70 Universal City Plaza, Suite 508-3
Universal City CA 91608
(818) 777-4010

MCA/Universal Home Video
Andrew Cairey, SVP, Marketing & Sales
70 Universal City Plaza, Suite 435
Universal City CA 91608
(818) 777-4300

MCA/Universal Home Video
Suzie Peterson, Senior VP of Creative
70 Universal City Plaza, Suite 435
Universal City CA 91608
(818) 777-4300

MCA/Universal Home Video
Patti Jackson, Acquisitions
70 Universal City Plaza, Suite 435
Universal City CA 91608
(818) 777-4634

MCA/Universal Home Video
Bruce Resnikoff, Music Acquisitions
70 Universal City Plaza, 4th Floor
Universal City CA 91608
(818) 777-4090

Media West Home Video
PO Box 1563
Lake Grove OR 97035

(503) 624-8008

Mediatech East
216 W. 18th Street, 4th Floor
New York NY 10011

(212) 463-8300

Medical Electronic Education Service
1560 Sherman Avenue, Ste. 100
Evanston IL 60201

(800) 323-9084

329

MGM/UA Distribution Company
Madelyn Fenton Hammond, VP Distrib.
2500 Broadway St.
Santa Monica CA 90404
(310) 449-3000

MGM/UA Distribution Company
George Feltenstein, SVP, MGM Classics
2500 Broadway St.
Santa Monica CA 90404
(310) 449-3000

Miramar
Kipp Kilpatrick
200 2nd Avenue W.
Seattle WA 98119
(206) 284-4700

Morris Group
2707 Plaza Del Amo #601
Torrance CA 90503

(310) 533-4800

MPI
16101 So. 108th Avenue
Orland Park IL 60462

(708) 460-0555

Mystic Fire Video
Dave Fox, President
524 Broadway, 604
New York NY 10012
(212) 941-0999

Mystic Fire Video
Matt Kapp, Acquisitions Manager
524 Broadway, 604
New York NY 10012
(212) 941-0999

New Life Options
14431 Ventura Blvd. #312
Sherman Oaks CA 91423

(818) 990-5410

New Line Cinema
Stephen Einhorn, President of Home Video
888 7th Avenue, 19th Flr
New York NY 10106
(212) 649-4900

New Line Cinema
Michael Karaffa, Exec. VP Marketing
116 N. Robertson Blvd., #200
Los Angeles CA 90048
(310) 854-5811

New Line Cinema
Louise Alaimo, VP, Mktg & Non-Theatrical
116 N. Robertson Blvd., #200
Los Angeles CA 90048
(310) 854-5811 /

Nightingale-Conant Corp
7300 No, Lehigh Avenue
Niles IL 60714

(800) 572-2700

Oracle Film & Video
1820 14th Street, Suite 203
Santa Monica CA 90404

(310) 450-6637

Paramount Home Video
Eric Doctorow, President, Worldwide Video
5555 Melrose Avenue, Bludhorn #302
Hollywood CA 90038
(213) 956-5525

Paramount Home Video
Jonathon Bader, Acquisitions/Business
5555 Melrose Avenue, Bludhorn #302
Los Angeles CA 90038
(213) 956-5525

PBS Video
Dan Hamby
1320 Braddock Place
Alexandria VA 22314
(800) 424-7963

Perennial Education Inc.
1560 Sherman Avenue - Suite 100
Evanston IL 60201

(847) 328-6700

Pioneer Laserdisc Corp of America
Y. Kobayashi, President
2265 E. 220 St.
Long Beach CA 90810
(310) 835-6177

PM Home Video
Len Levy, President
9450 Chivers Avenue
Sun Valley CA 91352
(818) 504-6332

Polygram Video
Alain Levy, Chairman
825 8th Avenue, 25th Floor
New York NY 10019
(212) 333-8000

Polygram Video
Bill Sondheim, President and CEO
825 8th Avenue, 27th Floor
New York NY 10019
(212) 333-8000

Prism Entertainment Corporation
Barry Collier, President
1888 Century Park East, Suite 350
Los Angeles CA 90067
(310) 277-3270

Public Media
Adrianne Furniss
5547 No. Ravenswood Avenue
Chicago IL 60640
(312) 878-7300

Pyramid Film & Video
Randy Wright, Pres.
2801 Colorado Avenue
Santa Monica CA 90404
(310) 828-7577

Quality Video
7399 Bush Lake Road
Minneapolis MN 55439

(612) 893-0903

Questar Video, Inc.
680 No. Lake Shore Drive, Suite 900
Chicago IL 60611

(312) 266-9400

Random House Children's Media
201 East 50th Street
New York NY 10022

(212) 572-2600

Republic Entertainment
Bob Sigman, President
5700 Wilshire Blvd., Suite 525
Los Angeles CA 90036
(213) 965-6900

Rhino Home Video
Arny Schorr, VP, General Manager
10635 Santa Monica Blvd.
Los Angeles CA 90025
(310) 474-4778

Samuel Goldwyn Company
10203 Santa Monica Blvd.
Los Angeles CA 90067

(310) 552-2255

Shanachie
Jon Zeiderman, Sales and Marketing
421-1/2 So. Maple Drive
Beverly Hills CA 91212
(310) 278-8338

Shanachie Home Video
Sherwin Dunner, Head of Acquisition
13 Laight Street, 6th Flr.
New York NY 10013
Written

Showcase Entertainment
21800 Oxnard Street, Suite 150
Woodland Hills CA 91367

(818) 715-7005

Simitar Entertainment
3850 Annapolis Lane, Suite 140
Plymouth MN 55447

(612) 559-6000

SOFA ENT
9121 Sunset Blvd.
Los Angeles CA 90069

(310) 276-9522

Sony New Technologies Inc.
Steven Yee, Marketing
550 Madison Avenue, 5th Floor
New York NY 10022
(212) 833-6800

Sony New Technologies Inc.
Elizabeth Copinger, CD ROM, Acquisitions
550 Madison Avenue, 5th Floor
New York NY 10022
(212) 833-6800

Sony New Technologies Inc.
Mitchell Cannold, President
550 Madison Avenue, 5th Floor
New York NY 10022
(212) 833-6790

Sony Pictures Classics
Michael Barker, Co-President
550 Madison Avenue
New York NY 10022
(212) 833-8833 /

Sony Pictures Classics
Tom Bernard, Co-President
550 Madison Avenue, 8th Flr.
New York NY 10022
(212) 833-8833

Sony Wonder
Wendy Moss, Snr. VP Marketing
2100 Colorado Avenue
Santa Monica CA 90404
(310) 449-2090

Spinnaker Software
1 Athenaeum St.
Cambridge MA 02142

(617) 494-1200

Strand Releasing
1460 4th St., Ste. 302
Santa Monica CA 90401

(310) 395-5002

Superior Home Video
PO Box 249 / 687 Bent Ridge
Barri IL 60010

(217) (no listing)

Sybervision
Paul Eisele, President
One Sansom Street, Suite 810
San Francisco CA 94104
(415) 677-8616

Time Warner/WEA
John Scott, Sr. VP Sales & Distribution
111 N. Hollywood Way
Burbank CA 91505
(818) 840-6288

Turner Home Entertainment
Stuart Snyder, Exec. VP, General Manager
1050 Techwood Drive
Atlanta GA 30318
(404) 885-0505

Turner Home Entertainment
Danielle Silverman, Acquisitions
1050 Techwood Drive
Atlanta GA 30318
(404) 885-0505

Tyndale Family Video
351 Executive Drive
Carol Stream IL 60188

(708) 668-8300

U of CA Ext, Dept. Ctr. for Media & Indep.
2000 Center Street, 4th Floor
Berkeley CA 94704

(510) 642-0460

Video Learning Library
15838 North 62nd Street
Scottsdale AZ 85254

(602) 596-9970

Vidmark Entertainment
2644 30th St.
Santa Monica CA 90405

(310) 314-2000

View Video
Bob Karcy, President
34 E. 23rd Street
New York NY 10010
(212) 674-5550

Virgin Video
Amy Stanton, Senior Director
338 No. Foothill Road
Beverly Hills CA 90210
(310) 278-1181

Warner Bros. Home Video
Sergei Kuharsky, VP, Marketing
4000 Warner Blvd.
Burbank CA 91522
(818) 954-6000

Warner Vision
Stuart Hersch, President
75 Rockefeller Plaza
New York NY 10019
(212) 275-2900

Warner Vision
Dina Metzger, Director of Development
4000 W. Alameda Ave., Ste. 250
Burbank CA 91505
(818) 977-8550

Wellspring Video/Video Collection
Al Cattabiani, President
27 Summit Terrace
Dobbs Ferry NY 10522
(914) 693-2366

Western Publishing Company
1220 Mound Avenue
Racine WI 53404

(414) 631-5158

Wild Wing Productions
16161 Ventura Boulevard, Suite 532
Encino CA 91436

(818) 757-1293

Wood Knapp Communication
Betsy Knapp
5900 Wilshire Blvd.
Los Angeles CA 90036

Word Publishing
1501 LBJ Freeway, Suite 650
Dallas TX 75234

(214) 488-9673

CONSULTING
SERVICES

MICHAEL WIESE PRODUCTIONS can help you think bigger, create new programs, expand your markets, develop product lines, find co-production partners, locate distributors, design marketing plans, and develop your unique pathway to success.

We have provided our consulting services to clients large and small including: **National Geographic Television, The Smithsonian Institution, WNET, KCET, PBS Home Video, Hanna-Barbera, Mystic Fire Video, The Apollo Theater, The American Film Institute, Buckminster Fuller Institute, Republic Home Video, King World Television** and numerous independent producers. For more information, please call Ken Lee.

CALL TODAY
1-800-379-8808

*THE FIRST BOOK TO DIRECTLY ADDRESS FILM AND
TELEVISION DIRECTORS ABOUT WORKING
WITH ACTORS.*

DIRECTING ACTORS
CREATING MEMORABLE
PERFORMANCES
FOR FILM & TELEVISION
by Judith Weston

Directing Actors is a method for
establishing collaborative relationships with actors, getting the
most out of rehearsals, recognizing and fixing poor performances, and developing your
actors' creativity.

Ms. Weston discusses what constitutes a good performance,
what actors want from a director, what directors do wrong,
script analysis and preparation,
how actors work, and the direc-
tor/actor relationship.

This book, based on the author's
twenty years of professional acting and eight years of teaching
Acting for Directors, is the first
book to directly address film and
television directors about working with actors.

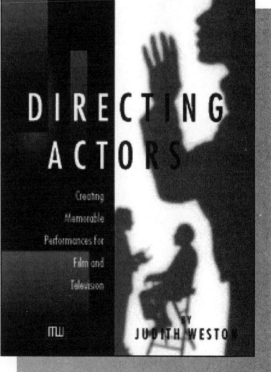

*"After living on movie sets for over fifteen years, Judith's class opened a door for
me to an aspect of that creative process about which I had never really been
aware—acting."*

Ron Judkins, Production Sound Mixer
Jurassic Park, Schindler's List

"Judy's class made me better able to judge actors' performances."

Arthur Coburn, Editor
The Mask, Dominick & Eugene, Beverly Hills Cop

$26.95, approx. 300 pages, 6 x 8 1/4
ISBN: 0-941188-24-8
Availabe June 1996

THE TRICKS OF NO-BUDGET FILMMAKING!

PERSISTENCE OF VISION
AN IMPRACTICAL GUIDE TO PRODUCING A FEATURE FILM FOR UNDER $30,000
by John Gaspard & Dale Newton

NEW !!

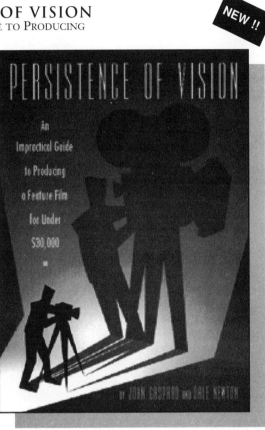

PERSISTENCE OF VISION reveals the treacherous and often humorous process of creating ultra-low-budget feature films for $30,000 or less. It includes practical information on writing the script, budgeting, raising financing, casting, putting together a crew, and dealing with distributors.

This step-by-step book is an invaluable tool for all ultra-low-budget and novice filmmakers and includes interviews with ultra-low-budget filmmakers and a large Appendix of essential forms and contracts.

When it comes to producing successful films on a shoestring, authors John Gaspard and Dale Newton know of what they speak. Together they created "Resident Alien" and "Beyond Bob," two critically-acclaimed ultra-low-budget features using the tactics and strategies outlined in this book.

$26.95, 450 pages, 40 illustrations & photos
ISBN: 0-941188-23-x

YOU'LL LEARN HOW TO:

- WRITE FOR A TINY BUDGET
- CREATE UNIQUE CHARACTERS
- MAKE PRACTICAL BUSINESS DECISIONS
- FIND INVESTORS
- BREAKDOWN A SCRIPT
- CAST
- CREATE LOW-BUDGET SPECIAL EFFECTS
- GET YOUR FILM OUT INTO THE WORLD

TO ORDER CALL 1-800-379-8808

LATEST INDUSTRY INFORMATION--INSTANTANEOUSLY!!

FILM & VIDEO ON THE INTERNET

NEW !!

THE TOP 500 SITES
by Bert Deivert and
Dan Harries

Love film but over-
whelmed by the Internet's
maze of terrific (and not
so terrific) information?
Want to get to the good
stuff fast and not spend
needless hours searching
for the treasures of film,
video, and new media?
Then this book is for
you!

FILM & VIDEO ON
THE INTERNET sep-
arates the wheat from
the chaff by identifying
and rating the top 500
film & video sites on the
Internet.

This is an excellent book
for film and videomak-
ers, students, teachers
and film buffs who are
looking for the Internet's
latest resources on film,
video, and new media.

Each site is identified by name, its location on the Internet, category (such
as "Directors" or "screenwriting"), a rating on its usefulness, and a brief
review.

FILM & VIDEO ON THE INTERNET also includes helpful information
about e-mail, newsgroups, the World Wide Web as well as a handy cross
reference index for quick access.

$26.95, 400 pages, illustrations, 0-941188-54-x, *available April ' 96*

This FILM & VIDEO ON THE INTERNET diskette lets you
point and click on your web browser so you can instantly go
to the top 500 sites reviewed in this book.   You'll have a
great database of resources available instantly. Only $29.

SAVE MONEY!! BOOK & DISKETTE BUNDLE: $49

TO ORDER CALL 1-800-379-8808

Film Directing
SHOT BY SHOT
by Steven D. Katz

The most sought after book in Hollywood by top directors is filled with visual techniques for filmmakers and screenwriters to expand their stylistic knowledge. Includes storyboards from Spielberg, Welles and Hitchcock.

$24.95, 376 pp., 7 x 10
750 illustrations and photos ISBN 0-941188-10-8

Read the Hottest Book in Hollywood!!!

THE WRITER'S JOURNEY
MYTHIC STRUCTURE FOR STORYTELLERS & SCREENWRITERS
by Christopher Vogler

Find out why this book has become an industry wide best-seller and is considered **"required reading"** by many of Hollywood's top studios! THE WRITER'S JOURNEY reveals how master storytellers from Hitchcock to Spielberg have used mythic structure to create powerful stories which tap into the mythological core which exists in us all.

Writer's will discover a set of useful myth-inspired storytelling paradigms (i.e. *The Hero's Journey*) and step-by-step guidelines for plotting and character development. Based on the work of **Joseph Campbell**, THE WRITER'S JOURNEY is a **must** for writers, producers, directors, film/video students, and Joseph Campbell devotees.

Vogler is a script consultant who has worked on scripts for "The Lion King," "Beauty and the Beast" and evaluated over 6000 others.

"This book should come with a warning: You're going to learn about more than just writing movies–you're going to learn about life! The Writer's Journey is the perfect manual for developing, pitching, and writing stories with universal human themes that will forever captivate a global audience. It's the secret weapon I hope every writer finds out about."

- Jeff Arch,

Screenwriter, *Sleepless in Seattle*

$22.95 paper, ISBN 0-941188-13-2, 200 pages, 6 x 8

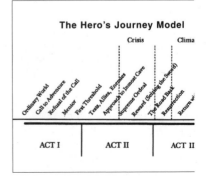

ORDER FORM

To order these products please call 1-800-833-5738 or fax (818) 986-3408 or mail this order form to:

MICHAEL WIESE PRODUCTIONS
11288 Ventura Blvd., Suite 821
Studio City, CA 91604
1-818-379-8799

BOOKS:

_____
_____
_____
_____

CREDIT CARD
ORDERS

CALL
1-800-833-5738

or FAX
818-986-3408

OR E-MAIL
mwpsales@earthlink.net

Subtotal $ _____
Shipping $ _____
8.25% Sales Tax (Ca Only) $ _____

TOTAL ENCLOSED _____

Please make check or money order payable to
Michael Wiese Productions

(Check one) ____ Master Card ____ Visa ____ Amex

Company PO# _____

Credit Card Number _____
Expiration Date _____
Cardholder's Name _____
Cardholder's Signature _____

SHIP TO:

SHIPPING

UPS GROUND
One Book - $5.00
Two Books - $7.00
For each additional
book, add $2.00.

AIRBORNE EXPRESS
2nd Day Delivery
Add an additional
$11.00 per order.

OVERSEAS
Surface - $10.00 ea.
book
Airmail - $20.00 ea. book

Name _____
Address _____
City _____ State _____ Zip _____
Country _____ Telephone _____
Ask about our free catalog

VISIT OUR HOME PAGE http://websites.earthlink.net/~mwp

Please allow 2–3 weeks for delivery.
All prices subject to change without notice.